MANUEL ALVARADO

JOHN STEWART

MADE FOR TELEVISION
Euston Films Limited

THAMES
METHUEN

BFI Publishing

First published in 1985 by the British Film Institute
127 Charing Cross Road
London WC2H OEA
in association with Thames Television International Ltd.
149 Tottenham Court Road
London W1P 9LL
and distributed worldwide by Methuen London Ltd.
11 New Fetter Lane
London EC4P 4EE

British Library Cataloguing in Publication Data

Alvarado, Manuel
   Made for television: Euston Films Ltd.
   1. Euston Films Ltd — History
   I. Title   II. Stewart, John   III. British Film Institute
   384′.8   PN1992.8.F5

ISBN 0 423 01310 6

Cover: John Gibbs
Illustrations by kind permission of Euston Films and Thames Television
Printed by Tudor Press, Perivale, Middlesex.

Contents

Contributors

Manuel Alvarado has taught in secondary, further and higher education and worked for the Society for Education in Film and Television as well as editing its journal *Screen Education*. He has co-authored books on the television fictions *Hazell* and *Doctor Who*. He is currently Research Fellow at the Broadcasting Research Unit.

John Stewart is Television Access Officer at the British Film Institute. He has contributed articles to *Screen Education* and to the BFI Television Monograph *Coronation Street*.

Jim Cook is Adult Education Officer at the British Film Institute. He has published articles on television and the media generally in journals such as *Screen Education* and in books, most recently in *National Fictions*, published by the BFI.

James Donald is a lecturer in the School of Education at the Open University and a member of the editorial board of *Formations*. Previously he taught for five years in a London comprehensive school and was then editor of *Screen Education*.

Lucy Douch is Assistant TV Projects and Access Officer at the British Film Institute.

Gillian Skirrow is a lecturer in Film and Television Studies at the University of Strathclyde, has directed many educational films and was previously a Schools Producer at Thames Television.

Michael Winterbottom read English at Balliol College, Oxford before taking a postgraduate Diploma in radio, film and television at Bristol University. He works as an assistant film editor for Thames Television and is currently writing a dissertation on *Minder* for an MA in Film Studies at the Polytechnic of Central London.

Tana Wollen was born in Nairobi, Kenya, in 1957. She came to England in 1969 and studied at Churchill College, Cambridge and the Institute of Education, London University. She now teaches at North Westminster Community School, London.

Acknowledgments

First of all we would like to thank Muir Sutherland for allowing us to research the history of Euston Films. We would also like to thank Johnny Goodman, who had little to gain from our presence and yet was always good-humoured and supportive towards our regular requests for help and advice. We are also especially indebted to Trevor Preston; this book might not always be to his taste, but he encouraged us and gave unstintingly of his time and personal files. We would also particularly like to thank: Linda Agran, Roy Ward Baker, Barry Breckon, Jack Breckon, Chris Burt, Rosanne Chapman, Ted Childs, George Cole, Sally Croft, Alexa Dalby, Paula Eatough, Jane Gerson, Jim Goddard, Terry Green, Chris Griffiths, Tina Halvorsen, Tony Hoare, Jeremy Isaacs, Renée Kramer, Ian Kennedy-Martin, Verity Lambert, Lynda La Plante, Bill Launder, Val Lee, Roy Lockett, Dinah Marmery, John Paul, Mike Phillips, Roy Pointer, Lloyd Shirley, Ian Scott, George Taylor, Brian Tesler, Howard Thomas, Ian Toynton, John Walton, Dennis Waterman. There were others we should have liked to talk to, but the pressures of a tight schedule made it impossible. Finally, we would like to thank our editor, Edward Buscombe, for his encouragement, forebearance and assistance in clarifying our ideas and presentation.

The provision of entertainment has never been a subject of great interest either to economists or to economic historians – at least in their working hours. Yet in 20th century conditions it is proper to talk of a highly organised entertainment industry, to distinguish within it between production and distribution, to examine forces making for competition, integration, concentration and control and to relate such study to the statistics of national income and output, the development of advertising, international economic relations and – not least – to the central economic concept of the market which, in the 20th century, is as much concerned with leisure as it is with work . . . massive market interests have come to dominate an area of life which, until recently, was dominated by individuals themselves.

ASA BRIGGS

Introduction

Euston Films is not, we suspect, a name well known to most television viewers, yet the drama which the company has produced over the last decade has included some of the most popular programmes on British television. *The Sweeney, Out, Minder, Widows* and *Reilly – Ace of Spies* have all achieved high ratings *and* critical acclaim both in Britain and overseas.

The object of this book is primarily to recover the history of a company producing highly successful programmes for Thames Television, for the British commercial television network and for overseas television services via Thames Television International. In offering an account of that history we shall be looking at Euston Films in economic, institutional, social and cultural terms. We shall be looking at these programmes – one-off television films, drama serials and series – as *commodities*, that is, as artefacts which, like others outside the sphere of television, are produced, distributed and consumed. We shall also look at them as *texts*, available for, and requiring, reading and analysis in terms of their relationship to the social world they and their audiences inhabit.

Our initial impetus on this project derived from our enjoyment of Euston productions and from a more general commitment to a critical engagement with popular television. We had a sense of Euston Films as a company with a distinctive house style and we were interested in discovering what factors combined to shape this identity. As our research got under way we began to identify a number of questions surrounding the position of Euston within the film and television industries, questions which presented themselves as paradoxes. Why for example should the biggest and most profitable of British commercial television companies with a large investment in electronic television equipment and itself owned by two companies with major interests in the electronics industry set up a company to produce television programmes on film? How has a company with very little infrastructure and a bare minimum of permanent staff managed to build up such a distinctive profile and recognised body of work? Why should a company whose productions are of such a decidedly British character enjoy such a high level of overseas sales? And why, given the success of Euston Films, have other television companies not rushed to follow Thames' example and establish their own film production arms? In the pages which follow we have tried to explain these problems and paradoxes.

RESEARCHING THE HISTORY

This book began as a commission by the British Film Institute to edit a dossier of materials already published about Euston. It soon became clear that there was very little in existence apart from a small number of published interviews with Euston personnel and short, rarely illuminating journalistic pieces. Despite the popularity of its programmes, the company was virtually invisible outside of the enclosed world of the television industry. Even its name was vaguely anonymous, taken from the railway station situated in the same road as the headquarters of Thames Television, the parent company. The annually published IBA Yearbook has only once mentioned Euston in the twelve years since it began operating.

Clearly some primary research was required. Both Thames Television and Euston Films were extremely helpful when approached; past and present employees of each organisation proved, without exception, encouraging and friendly. But there were difficulties. The somewhat informal nature of a company which, by its nature, mostly employs freelancers means that written records are not extensive. Files are kept, of course, but once a production is finished they go into the vaults and the company moves on to the next commission. We did investigate some of these files, but they consisted largely of invoices and receipts.

As a result the book relies greatly on people's memories gathered in the course of interviews conducted by us between December 1983 and May 1984. In the nature of things these memories are imperfect and sometimes contradict each other. Nevertheless, we hope that a reasonably coherent account emerges from what we have pieced together out of what we were told, backed up with as much information as we could glean from other sources.

EUSTON FILMS IN CONTEXT

The history of Euston Films proper, however, needs to be understood in relation to its place within the wider television industry. The book therefore begins with a brief account of the organisation and operation of commercial television within Britain and some description of the structure of ownership and control of Euston and Thames, the company of which it is a subsidiary. At this point it is worth calling attention to the work published by the Open University in support of its 'Mass Communications and Society' course. In it Graham Murdock distinguishes two levels of control in the operations of business, namely the *allocative* and the *operational*, which display the following characteristics:

Allocative control	*Operational control*
1. Formulation of overall policy and strategy.	1. Implementation of policy and strategic decisions.
2. Decisions on whether and where to expand and when and how to cut back.	2. Decisions about effective use of resources already allocated.
3. Development of basic financial policy.	3. Implementation of financial policy.
4. Control over the distribution of profits.	4. Not involved.

Clearly, while it is tempting initially to understand Euston Films as an autonomous and independent production house – implied by its status as a limited liability company making its own returns to Companies House – it really needs, as this book shows, to be viewed more as a subsidiary of Thames Television, a subsidiary, moreover, whose production policies can never be divorced from the activities of the Thames Drama Department and from Thames' needs when offering a portfolio of drama to the ITV network. As such, Euston's relationship to Thames accords more with the concept of Operational Control as outlined above. Furthermore, it is no secret that the Independent Broadcasting Authority, fulfilling its role of regulating the commercial television industry, has in the past been concerned about the extent to which Thames itself was functioning in an 'operational' role *vis-à-vis* BET and Thorn-EMI, the two companies who own it; though recent financial changes at Thames have allayed these fears. Despite this, it is still the case that decisions about financial resources are not the only ones of consequence, and that Euston Films continues to have a firm sense of its own identity.

CONDITIONS OF PRODUCTION

Our interest in production encompasses all the elements which play a part in determining the finished programme: aesthetic, technological, economic, institutional and social. But one aspect is particularly worth highlighting, since it appears to call into question some assumptions often made about the nature of the work process within television. Mention has already been made of the apparent paradox whereby in a period of rapid advance in the field of electronic camera and recorder technology a company can be successful through an exclusive concentration on the older technology of 16mm film. Now one reason for setting up a *film* company, as this book reveals, is the degree of flexibility in working practices which it makes possible. The question of labour costs is an ever-present one within the industry, since labour represents such a high proportion of the expense in making programmes while at the same time television production can never, for obvious reasons, become a fully automated process. Euston is also almost entirely reliant on freelance labour; the relative absence of full-time employees provides another means of limiting costs.

Historically, the unions in the film and television industries have taken the view that casualisation is a threat to the interests of their members – for very good reasons. However, as the experience of Euston shows, freelance working *can* produce a change in the social relations of production. Instead of the often alienated workforce of those permanently employed in the television studios, who are unlikely to work consistently through a long-running drama series, Euston Films employees have the chance of a closer involvement with a programme as a whole. Crew members are, for example, rarely unwilling to work overtime, since they are more actively a part of the production, and the system is more democratic in that there are greater chances of promotion 'through the ranks', as the credits of Euston productions show. The recent rush of highly qualified people out the BBC and the ITV 'majors' into small companies producing independently for Channel 4, though undoubtedly in part motivated by the prospects of higher earnings, also appears to point in the same direction.

CIRCULATION OF PROGRAMMES

One further aspect to which we would like to draw particular attention at the outset is the question of programme sales. The international circulation of television drama is a little-researched subject. This contrasts strikingly with the growing body of work on the international flow of news, the work of the international news agencies and the 'new information order'. This is a serious omission; the ideological significance of drama is surely no less than that of news and information. For this reason we have tried to open up this question with some preliminary investigation of the sale of Euston Films productions overseas. Sales abroad have now become central to the economics of British television. Over the past two decades ATV pursued the most aggressively international policy with its Light Entertainment spectaculars and, through its subsidiary ITC, a range of 'mid-Atlantic' drama series such as *The Persuaders*, all clearly produced with an eye to the American market. Another area of particular success for British television has been the export of costume drama, often set in a royal or upper-class milieu.

Thames, through its subsidiary Thames Television International, has now become the most successful ITV company in foreign markets, based partly on its sitcom and Light Entertainment productions (for example, *Benny Hill*) and on its period dramas such as *Edward and Mrs Simpson*. But Thames has never made a 'mid-Atlantic' action adventure series and it does not seem as if Euston, the unit best equipped to do so, has ever been

x

asked to provide one. To its credit Euston has not trod the easier path to foreign sales; the very 'Britishness' of a programme such as *Minder* makes it impossible to sell in America, though doubtless the company enjoys the irony of the fact that it is this very 'Britishness' which probably makes it so popular in Australia. Unfortunately it is American, rather than Australian, dollars which really count. Whether it can pursue its production policies in the light of such facts is one of the most important questions about Euston's future.

CONSUMPTION OF PROGRAMMES

The second section of the book moves us into the area of programme analysis. As an appendix we publish some detailed information on the viewing figures for Euston productions. The interpretation of this data we have left to the reader (though one line of enquiry which might repay the effort is the question of how far these figures confirm the stereotype of commercial television as entirely dictated by ratings; the first series of *Minder*, Euston's most successful programme ever in terms of the number of episodes made, never got into the Top Twenty). But we felt that this book would not be complete without some analysis of notable Euston programmes. Accordingly we commissioned five people to write on six separate productions.

Each has done so from a particular point of view. James Donald's contribution draws on work originally done for the Open University's Popular Culture course. He argues that *The Sweeney* needs to be seen in the context of the changes in policing in Britain signalled by the arrival of Robert Mark at Scotland Yard; the narratives of *The Sweeney* then explore through Regan's 'individualistic anti-authoritarianism' the resulting tensions. This conjunctural reading thus opens up some possible explanations for the success of the programme.

Jim Cook in his essay on *Out* and *Fox* confronts directly the problem of why, despite the fact that both productions were, in terms of writing and directing, entirely the work of a unified team (Trevor Preston and Jim Goddard being therefore available for critical canonisation as auteurs), the critical response to these major pieces of television fiction was so dismally uncomprehending.

Minder is interesting not only because of its continuing success but also because of the ways in which it deftly sidesteps the police series which is its closest point of reference and which, in the shape of *The Sweeney*, had given Euston its biggest success up to that point. Michael Winterbottom both provides valuable information about the process of production and sets that information within the framework of an understanding of how *Minder* plays with the constraints of the police series genre.

That Euston productions are usually male-orientated has been often remarked. Equally, the protagonists have been almost invariably white, with the exception of *The Sailor's Return*. The arrival at Euston of Verity Lambert and Linda Agran meant that changes began to take place. The setting and subject matter of *The Flame Trees of Thika* marks a striking departure for Euston, from London working-class life to the world of a child in colonial Africa. But clearly the programme has a contemporary resonance, and Tana Wollen explores its relevance to the Britain of the 1980s.

Finally, *Widows* demands to be read as a deliberate attempt to contest the male-dominated world of the crime series by creating a narrative based on four female characters. Gillian Skirrow assesses the extent to which *Widows* can be seen as a genuine breakthrough, and whether not only its female protagonists but its serial (as opposed to episodic) structure subvert and transform the genre.

After concluding with an indication of the future projects of Euston Films – both actual and possible – we present a final section of the book which consists of four appendices. In addition to the detailed information on viewing figures compiled by Lucy Douch to which we have already referred, this includes credits for all Euston's productions; a note on overseas sales; and a reprint of a two-part article which appeared in *Televisual* at the turn of the year, written by financial journalist William Phillips.

The constraints of a relatively short book and the brief time available for its completion have meant that we have been able to do no more than touch upon the many theoretical considerations raised by the production processes of popular television. Nevertheless, we hope that this book can make a contribution to our knowledge of an area which, given its importance in the lives of most of us, is still too little explored.

PART I
EUSTON FILMS LTD

1 Contexts

The story of how and why Euston Films was founded and the description of its working methods and achievements begins properly in the next part of this book. But an understanding of the distinctive and slightly paradoxical nature of the company (why, for example, the newer technology of television should still be apparently so reliant on the older one, film) requires a brief detour through some of the particularities of British television.

Fig. 1 explains well enough the general structure of commercial, or 'Independent', television, that part of the total system which is financed by the sale of advertising time. As can be seen, Thames is one of the so-called 'network' companies, the five biggest who between them produce almost all of the programmes which ITV makes for itself and which are networked, i.e. shown in all fifteen ITV regions. Employing 2,370 people, Thames is in fact the largest and wealthiest of the companies (by contrast the smallest, Channel TV, employs just 75). The area of London and its environs which Thames shares with London Weekend Television (Thames broadcasts from Monday morning till 5.15pm on Fridays) contains 19.9% of all the homes in the country capable of receiving ITV.

Thames Television is a private limited company owned jointly by Thorn–EMI and British Electric Traction (BET). Thorn–EMI is one of the twenty largest manufacturing companies in Britain, with over 1000 subsidiaries and interests in domestic electrical appliances, consumer electronics, telecommunications, military technology, television set manufacturing, record companies, cable TV, film studios and cinemas, film production and TV rental services. BET is involved in electronics, printing and publishing, transport and construction, and various leisure and service industries.

Though in relation to the total turn-over of the two parent companies Thames is a relatively small operation (currently Thames' turn-over is about £160 million, whereas BET's is in excess of £1 billion and Thorn–EMI's nearer £3 billion), nevertheless it has over the years been a reliable profit-earner and is strategically placed *vis-à-vis* the companies' other

3

FIG. 1: THE ORGANISATION OF INDEPENDENT BROADCASTING IN BRITAIN, 1983 ONWARDS

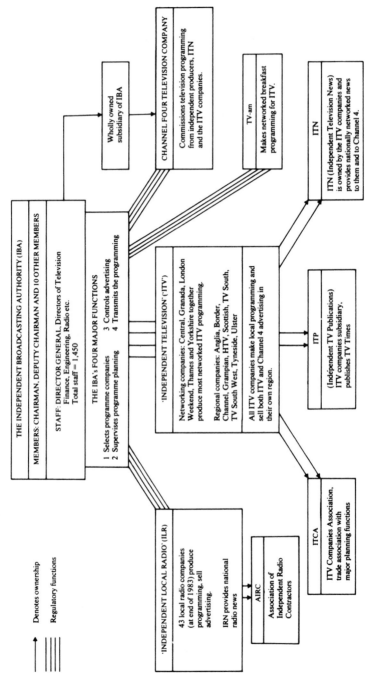

→ Denotes ownership

⫴ Regulatory functions

THE INDEPENDENT BROADCASTING AUTHORITY (IBA)

MEMBERS: CHAIRMAN, DEPUTY CHAIRMAN AND 10 OTHER MEMBERS

STAFF: DIRECTOR GENERAL, Directors of Television Finance, Engineering, Radio etc.
Total staff = 1,450

THE IBA's FOUR MAJOR FUNCTIONS

1 Selects programme companies
2 Supervises programme planning
3 Controls advertising
4 Transmits the programming

Wholly owned subsidiary of IBA

CHANNEL FOUR TELEVISION COMPANY

Commissions television programming from independent producers, ITN and the ITV companies.

'INDEPENDENT TELEVISION' ('ITV')

Networking companies: Central, Granada, London Weekend, Thames and Yorkshire together produce most networked ITV programming.

Regional companies: Anglia, Border, Channel, Grampian, HTV, Scottish, TV South, TV South West, Tyneside, Ulster

All ITV companies make local programming and sell both ITV and Channel 4 advertising in their own region.

TV-am

Makes networked breakfast programming for ITV.

ITN

ITN (Independent Television News) is owned by the ITV companies and provides nationally networked news to them and to Channel 4.

ITP

(Independent TV Publications) ITV companies subsidiary, publishes TV Times

'INDEPENDENT LOCAL RADIO' (ILR)

43 local radio companies (at end of 1983) produce programming, sell advertising.

IRN provides national radio news

AIRC

Association of Independent Radio Contractors

ITCA

ITV Companies Association, trade association with major planning functions

Reprinted from *The Media in Britain* by Jeremy Tunstall (Constable, 1983)

activities, many of which are in the general area of leisure provision and/ or electronics. In particular, Thames will be an increasingly valuable asset as Thorn–EMI and BET pursue their plans to become involved in new ways of distributing television. *Screen International* recently reported that a new company, Thames Cable and Satellite Services, has been set up, owned jointly by Thames Television, Thorn–EMI and AR-TV Plc, the subsidiary through which BET holds its shares in Thames.

Thames will normally broadcast for around 3,600 hours during the course of the year, and of this about 940 hours will consist of programmes which the company has made itself, the rest being provided by other companies within the ITV system and outside it. Of these 940 hours some 700 will be first-time transmissions and the rest repeats. The total annual budget for these Thames-originated programmes is currently £28.5 million, meaning that the company allots approximately £30,000 an hour for programme costs on average. However, this figure represents only the direct, above the line costs. True costs, including overheads such as a charge for equipment and facilities or the salaries of permanently employed staff, would be at least twice as much. Note also that the costs of different kinds of programming vary widely. Drama productions, for example, are among the most expensive at around £100,000 an hour for direct costs and as much again below the line.

The costs of the nearly 2,700 hours programming a year which originate outside the company are much less; about £11.5 million in all. This relative cheapness is due to the low prices of bought-in films and (mostly American) series and to the exchange system operated by the network, details of which are given below. The accompanying diagrams (Figs. 2, 3 and 4) show how the staff allocation and turn-over of the company as a whole breaks down, and how programme costs are assigned to the different categories of production.

Plays, drama series and made-for-TV films comprise about 20% of the total output of the ITV companies and within the system Thames has a high reputation for quality drama. This drama output, however, has over the years had more and more to adapt to the constraints imposed by the structure of the ITV schedule. *News At Ten*, which all stations are obliged to show by the Independent Broadcasting Authority, the central regulatory body, has for a long time occupied a virtually immovable spot at 10.00pm. The IBA also pursues what is called a Family Viewing Policy, which means in effect that material considered unsuitable for children cannot be shown before 9.00pm. Since Euston Films have historically specialised in prime-time adult drama this has meant in practice that almost everything they have made has had to be adapted to the one hour (in fact 52 minutes, allowing for commercial breaks) format which will fit between 9 and 10.00pm. This has now come to seem so much the standard length for drama, especially within the ITV network, as to appear the natural and inevitable one. But it's worth noting

5

FIG 2: PERSONNEL SUMMARY 1983-4

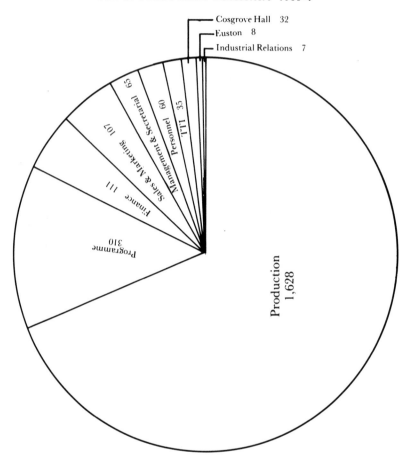

Cosgrove Hall 32
Euston 8
Industrial Relations 7

ITT 35
Personnel 60
Management & Secretarial 65
Sales & Marketing 107
Finance 111
Programme 310
Production 1,628

that several of the very first Euston productions were of one-off 'plays' running longer than this.

One further aspect of the ITV system is of particular relevance to Euston Films. Because each ITV company relies on the others to provide programmes for its transmission schedule, no company being able to produce all the programmes it shows, there must be a system of exchange. The essence of the system is that each company is charged on its share of the total income of the system (technically its NARAL, or net advertising revenue after levy, the levy being an excess profits tax). In other words, a company pays according to its means, and companies which produce programmes for the network are compensated in accor-

6

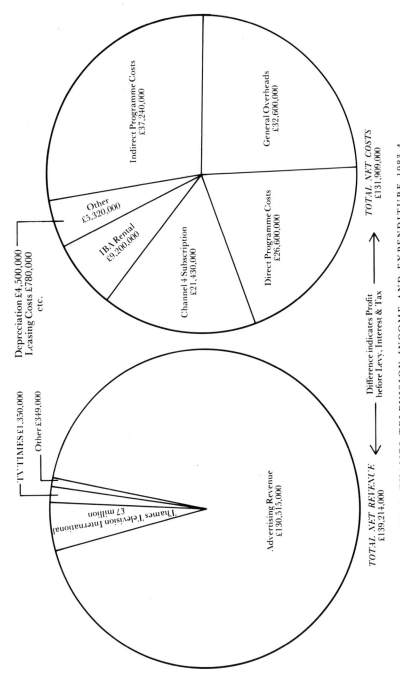

Indirect Programme Costs
£37,240,000

General Overheads
£32,600,000

Other
£5,320,000

IBA Rental
£9,200,000

Channel 4 Subscription
£21,430,000

Direct Programme Costs
£26,600,000

Depreciation £4,500,000
Leasing Costs £780,000
etc.

TOTAL NET COSTS
£131,909,000

Difference indicates Profit
before Levy, Interest & Tax

TV TIMES £1,350,000

Other £349,000

Thames Television International
£7 million

Advertising Revenue
£130,515,000

TOTAL NET REVENUE
£139,214,000

FIG 3: THAMES TELEVISION INCOME AND EXPENDITURE 1983-4

7

FIG. 4: THAMES TELEVISION: DIRECT PROGRAMME COSTS 1983-4

Hours
produced

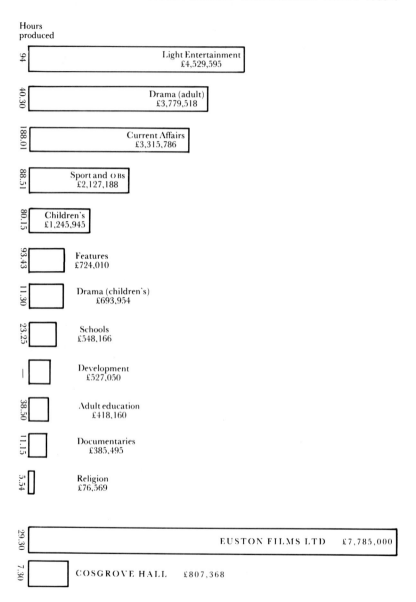

94	Light Entertainment £4,529,595
40.30	Drama (adult) £3,779,518
188.01	Current Affairs £3,315,786
88.51	Sport and o Bs £2,127,188
80.15	Children's £1,245,945
93.43	Features £724,010
11.30	Drama (children's) £693,954
23.25	Schools £548,166
—	Development £527,050
38.50	Adult education £418,160
11.15	Documentaries £385,495
5.54	Religion £76,569
29.30	EUSTON FILMS LTD £7,785,000
7.30	COSGROVE HALL £807,368

Note that the figures for Euston and Cosgrove Hall are *total* costs, above and below the line. The only excluded costs for Euston are the £355,000 spent on administration, half of which goes on salaries of permanent staff.

8

dance with a tarrif, a scale of the relative values of each kind of programme. Companies therefore do not receive payments according to the success of a programme in attracting high ratings, nor according to the programme's true costs, but simply according to a pre-arranged rate. Of course a popular programme will eventually have an effect on the price that can be charged for advertising time. But the only direct financial profit will come if the programme can subsequently be sold abroad. For this reason and others, foreign sales are becoming increasingly important, and because Euston Films productions, for reasons which will become clear, lend themselves readily for exploitation in foreign markets they have come to assume a key place within Thames' total output. Because of this it's worth going into a little more detail on this aspect of the company's activities.

OVERSEAS SALES

British commercial television companies are required by IBA regulations to produce a complete range of programmes for the ITV system – that is the basis on which a company is awarded a franchise. Thames Television, as this book has already indicated, is highly successful and profitable as a company trading purely in the British Isles. However, in common with all other commercial companies and the BBC, Thames has been developing its overseas sales (Department of Trade figures for all the companies for 1982 showed a net overseas earning of £78 million) through Thames Television International Ltd which, like Euston Films, is a wholly owned subsidiary.

The attitude of the IBA to this development of overseas sales can to some extent be assessed from the Authority's treatment of the subject in its annual reports. Under the sub-heading 'Programme Exports' the first reference to overseas sales appears in the annual report 1962-3:

> During the year ended 31st March 1963, Independent Television made over 14,000 programme sales overseas. These British produced programmes were exported to sixty countries for use by their television organisations. . . . More than 200 different titles were exported, either as series or individual programmes. They represented every category of television production. Drama series and light entertainment programmes accounted for many of the sales; half the titles, however, were of a more serious character and altogether more than 1,850 sales were made of serious programmes, covering science and natural history, religion, educational material and current affairs.

The Authority's concern that programme contractors' first responsibility would be to a domestic audience presumably made overseas sales, particularly the activities of the Midlands programme contractor ATV,

9

a sensitive issue. The policy of ATV, and its subsidiary ITC, was to produce for a world market and the Authority had been criticised for allowing ITV companies to produce programmes primarily for the American market knowing that they have a guaranteed British outlet. The Authority's annual report for 1963-4 notes that programme sales overseas were 50 per cent higher than the previous year; no mention is made of programme categories. For the 1968-9 annual report the section on programme exports was expanded but no sales figures are included. Instead there is a rather chauvinist account of ITV's contribution to the world-recognised 'excellence' of British television. It is interesting to note from the beginning of the section both the suggestion that it is the quality of essentially British programmes which makes them attractive commodities and how the nettle of ATV is firmly grasped:

> Whether or not television is going to create the 'global village' which has been prophesied it is true that many of the best British television programmes find ready buyers overseas. This is important simply in terms of international trade in a highly competitive field; but it is important, too, that British television should be seen to compare favourably with the best that is shown to viewers anywhere in the world.
>
> ATV and its film-making subsidiary ITC were first in the field. Of all the countries in the world which have television services only two – Red China and Albania – do not show ATV programmes. More series from ATV were purchased by USA networks for screening in 'prime time' during summer 1969 than from any single native American producing company except MCA/Universal. *The Avengers* from Thames was given a peak-hour autumn showing in the USA; and it was seen altogether in over ninety countries.

After a lengthy paragraph listing examples of programmes sold and the image of British TV they carry overseas ('We are known as skilled storytellers, with series like *The Saint, The Prisoner, The Champions* . . .') the section concludes with the following statement in which, significantly, the argument that foreign sales are necessary to recover production costs is accepted:

> Television programmes of every kind are sold abroad and almost every company plays some part, though not all can hope to have the elaborate overseas sales organisations of some of the larger companies. Thames Television for instance is developing plans for a major effort in Japan to coincide with the Tokyo Expo 70. Even this incomplete list, however, demonstrates a number of things. It is beyond doubt true that the major television series is now so expensive that its cost can only be recouped by international sales. On the other hand it is clear that even relatively modest programmes from the

10

smallest companies can, given the will, make their contribution to the nation's balance of trade. And the evidence is equally clear that programmes made by ITV companies have been able to compete very successfully in a world market with those of any other television service.

The increasing importance to the ITV companies of overseas sales is registered in the 1970-1 annual report as follows:

The year saw a more concerted effort by companies to exploit the overseas market. It was not surprising that ATV was honoured for the third time in six years by the Queen's Award for Exports, but the past year also saw Thames setting up a full-scale international sales organisation, a Television Fair held in Glasgow by Scottish Television, HTV and Anglia, and wider participation in the world television market in Cannes.

Although there is a long way to go before television systems are technically compatible across the world, the market is without doubt an expanding one, particularly for British companies who produce a greater number and range of television programmes than any other group apart from the USA networks.

There is, however, a concern about the effects of this interest in other markets upon programming. The Authority is keen to stress that many of the programmes sold abroad 'are made first and foremost for the home market', making the point in relation to situation comedy 'which might be thought virtually unexportable because of the nuances of language and social behaviour on which it largely depends' but with which 'companies have discovered that they have a very favourable position indeed in world markets'. It is also noted, however, that 'ATV's rather different approach . . . provided sales in 88 countries and a foreign turnover of £15 million in the past year.' At the end of the section the anxieties and criticisms relating to production for overseas sales are acknowledged directly and the Authority's position is made clear:

In a technical sense, programmes on film remain easier to handle for foreign stations, though Thames is placing faith in its facility to provide separate music and effects tracks with videotape recordings which will improve the export potential of electronically produced programmes.

Adventure and action series are almost always more successful on film; at the same time film costs roughly four times as much as videotape. The probability is therefore that major series in the same category as ATV's forthcoming *Persuaders* with Roger Moore and Tony Curtis will continue to be made either as co-productions with an over-

11

seas company or as a product aimed from the start at more than the home market. The success, in domestic terms, of previous series such as *The Avengers* or *The Saint*, not to mention the international character of both production and marketing in the film industry, should not therefore give rise to undue fears of a pallid mid-Atlantic flavour in such programmes. In fact, the great majority of exports are programmes produced originally for United Kingdom viewers. Such programme exports not only earn valuable revenue for the companies but present, from many individual and sometimes idiosyncratic points of view, a picture of British life and British attitudes to the world beyond the United Kingdom.

Thames Television International

By the end of the 1970s overseas sales had become big business, with all the ITV companies involved. Thames Television International is just over ten years old and the success of the company is such that on 22 April 1984 it was announced that TTI had won the Queen's Award for Export Achievements 1984 – the company having declared a turnover of £17,798,000 for the year ending 31 March 1983. For the same period the BBC had announced record gross sales of £26.1 million (£3 million more than the previous year) through its wholly owned subsidiary, BBC Enterprises Ltd, but its operation is much older and larger and the Corporation has more than twice the number of programmes for sale.

As we shall see Euston Films has played an important part in the success of TTI but then the reverse is also true: the international success of programmes like *Minder* and *Reilly – Ace of Spies*, indeed the fact that *Reilly* was produced at all, has been due to the efforts of TTI. Thames Television International consists of a staff of 35 with approximately 20 independent agents based in other countries. The company sells to 127 countries around the world and since its inception turnover on programme sales has increased by more than 3,000%. From a turnover in 1983 of nearly £18 million, profits were just over £6 million, a far better ratio than for either the parent company Thames or its holding companies BET and Thorn–EMI.

The business arrangements of Thames Television International were originally established by Muir Sutherland (now Director of Programmes for Thames TV) and the overseas agents – who work on a commission basis – are expected to work on behalf of TTI in two complementary directions, offering the foreign market an extensive knowledge of Thames' programming on a regular basis (with plenty of follow-up) and at the same time providing Thames with a constant feedback of market conditions.

Thames Television International earns revenue from most countries with a television service. In 1982-3 the top ten markets were: 1) USA, 2) Australia, 3) English-speaking Canada, 4) Italy, 5) UK (TTI also op-

12

erates as British agent for some overseas producers), 6) West Germany, 7) French-speaking Canada, 8) France, 9) New Zealand, 10) Spain.

TTI sells programmes to Eastern Europe but hardly at all to the USSR. There is no trade with China and very little with Japan (which only imports approximately 5% of what is shown – a mixture of American shows and BBC natural history programmes). However, what distinguishes Thames Television from the other British commercial TV companies is the high level of American business the company conducts.

The American market is by far the most difficult (and most competitive) in which to trade and Thames' success stems from its being the only UK company to trade in all sectors of this market. This is not to say that Thames manages to compete with British programmes against US-produced major prime time network programming, but it does mean that TTI has succeeded in pioneering new areas of trade.

The richest area of American television but also the hardest for British companies to crack is that part controlled by the three networks: NBC, CBS and ABC. Though the networks make hardly any of their own programmes, buying them in from independent producers, it is still very difficult for British companies to break into this market. Thames has made some inroads through selling formats, i.e. selling not the finished programme but its original conception. For example, the Thames sitcom *Man About The House* became the highly successful *Three's Company*, which has seldom been out of the top ten shows for the ABC network over the last six years. TTI is the international distributor of the show and gross sales had topped $100 million by summer 1983.

Thames have so far never sold a finished programme to the American networks, only formats. Mike Phillips, managing director of TTI, explains that except in cases such as the recent series on the Kennedys produced by Central Television, where the subject matter was already American, the dangers of having to adapt to American requirements would be too great. He gave three particular reasons why the networks were resistant to British shows. First was the oft-quoted problem of unintelligible accents, and the second was the difference in the sense of humour (despite the fact that resistance has finally been broken down in the case of *The Benny Hill Show*). Lastly, it seems that Americans are too predisposed to see British shows as 'cultural' and hence non-commercial.

For this reason the most important market in the US for both BBC and ITV programmes is PBS, the Public Broadcasting System. PBS is a national network operating through a group of privately- and sometimes publicly-owned stations. Its finance comes partly from the Federal Government, partly from local donations and subscriptions and partly from commercial sponsorship, most notably from the American oil companies Mobil and Exxon (Esso). These two companies have consistently sponsored series under umbrella titles such as *Masterpiece Theatre*

13

(Mobil) and *Great Performances* (Exxon), series which have used a great deal of British programming, thus going far to justify the joke that PBS stands for Primarily British Series.

Mobil Oil, which works through the Boston station WGBH, has been Thames' most consistent sponsor and has presented a number of Euston productions in the US: *The Flame Trees of Thika, Reilly – Ace of Spies* and *Danger UXB. Reilly* is a particularly interesting programme in this context because it is the only Euston programme thus far to be sold at script stage (and not just to the USA but also to Australia, French Canada and Holland), necessary since it was recognised from the beginning as being a very expensive project. The problem of going for money 'up front' is the (very real) fear of interference. However, as Mike Phillips told us, this isn't a problem when approaching Mobil and PBS:

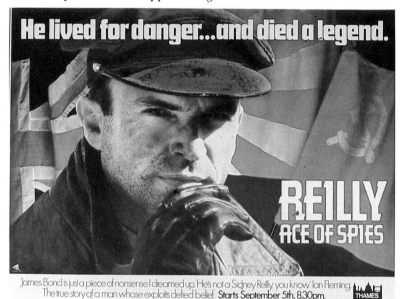

'James Bond is just a piece of nonsense I dreamed up. He's not a Sidney Reilly, you know.' Ian Fleming. The true story of a man whose exploits defied belief. **Starts September 5th, 8.30pm.**

Poster for *Reilly – Ace of Spies*.

With *Reilly* we actually went to Mobil, who've bought a lot of material from us in the past – they're very sophisticated as far as the British market is concerned and very knowledgeable about British talent. They've been buying in this market for ten years or more; they have a number of people who spend most of their time dealing with Britain and they're a very good partner for British companies because they will commit up front whilst their requirements, in terms of creative input, are really minimal. For example, when it came to casting we certainly kept them informed and we took on board their opinions.

14

As a matter of fact they were rather keen on an English actor (for the part of Reilly) but Verity [Lambert] saw a lot of people before deciding on Sam Neill. The nature of Mobil's involvement in television is not particularly commercial – they're really in the public relations business. They're an oil company saying, 'We're presenting the best of British programming' and therefore it's not in their interests particularly to have inappropriate American casting.

Besides the networks and PBS, there are the independent stations. The number of Independents in a market depends on the population and wealth of the area. Thus major conurbations like New York, Chicago and Los Angeles can support about four Independents as well as the three local network affiliates and PBS. Some companies own groups of stations and some own a mixture of network affiliates and Independents. The largest station group – Metromedia Inc. – can rival the networks in power and profitability.

The Independents produce their own news and, sometimes, talk programmes, but most of their schedules are made up of network show repeats (e.g. *I Love Lucy* – an area that Channel 4 would seem to have entered for some of its programming) and movies.

Selling to these individual stations is known as syndication and can be highly profitable if one has an appropriate series. In response to the power and wealth of the networks and the fact that they are constantly launching new and massively promoted shows the Independents have developed a scheduling strategy known as stripping in which the same series or serial is played in the same slot five or six times a week. This has proved to be a successful strategy in terms of encouraging channel loyalty at a regular and particular time but it does require shows which achieve high ratings and also are available in large numbers, e.g. at least 80 episodes. This, of course, rules out most British programmes from the start.

Thames Television International entered the syndication market in 1974 with *The World At War*. This was followed by success with *The Benny Hill Show* which was re-packaged as 75 half-hour shows licensed for up to 20 transmissions in the key markets of Los Angeles and New York. TTI's latest venture into syndication has been to launch a package of 125 half-hours of 'Britcoms' comprising *Man About The House, George and Mildred* and *Robin's Nest* under the title of *The Thames Originals* on station WNEW New York. Their success has been such that they have now been sold to 17 other stations including Los Angeles and Chicago. But this is not an area in which Euston's product has been sold because it requires a high number of episodes. The only Euston programmes with a reasonably high number of episodes are *The Sweeney* (53 episodes) and *Minder* (65 episodes), both rather low for stripping. And they are considered to have the language problems mentioned earlier in this chapter.

15

Publicity posters. The poster for *The Flame Trees of Thika* is for the American transmission, sponsored by Mobil. The poster for *Widows* is to advertise its release by Thames Video.

As Mike Phillips said to us: '*Minder* is considered to be a foreign language programme in America.'

This is not to say that the Americans are uninterested in *Minder*, but their interest is in the format and not in the syndication of the original. Mike Phillips:

16

We've had a lot of interest in *Minder*. Mainly from American producers wanting to take it to networks. Indeed, we've presented it to networks who, I think without exception, have liked the show but feel that it's a very special kind of chemistry there (the casting) and say 'come back to us with ideas of American casting and maybe we'll talk.' We haven't been able to resolve that problem.

Overall, however, Euston programmes like *The Sweeney*, *Minder* and *Fox* are seen very much as purely domestic shows and the success of *Minder* in Australia is icing on the cake.

Finally, there is cable. By the mid-1960s there were over a thousand cable systems in the USA but the business began to expand dramatically in 1975 when Home Box Office (a subsidiary of Time Inc.) launched a highly commercial satellite-fed service of recent movies for which they charged a monthly subscription fee. By 1982 HBO was more profitable than *Time* magazine, with more than 12 million subscribers and a stranglehold on the cable business. Two other movie services – *Showtime* and *The Movie Channel* – have merged in an attempt to establish an equally successful rival operation but so far with only limited success, and many other companies have attempted to set up a new non-movie channel. All these alternative attempts have so far failed.

This is an area that TTI has yet to exploit but the general feeling is that the non-movie cable channels are a risky prospect. In 1982, for example, two American and one Canadian cable channels went 'belly up', as the Americans describe it, though TTI have sold some shows – most notably *The Benny Hill Show* (in original form before being re-cut for syndication) – to Home Box Office. Nothing from Euston has yet been sold to a cable company although there might be possibilities of co-production deals (as with Goldcrest's *The Far Pavilions* or LWT's *Marlowe: Private Eye*). The only possibility so far has been Home Box Office's interest in *Widows*, as Mike Phillips explained to us:

In fact Home Box Office were very keen on *Widows* and it went through a lot of screenings over there but, at the end of the day, they said, 'No, it's just too English.' They would probably have shown it as three 2 hours if they had bought it, but they finally decided against. We could perhaps sell it to stations but again there would be problems – I think they would probably re-dub some of it. So there was strong interest right from day one – both from some movie producers and from one of the American Pay TV services who were interested in our making an American movie version of *Widows*. We are weighing up various possibilities and it's still under discussion.

After America, Australia is the most significant market, but it represents a very different situation for British television companies. Both the

17

language and the close colonial links between the two countries mean that the country possesses cultural affinities to Britain. The BBC and Thames sell a wide range of product to Australia (unlike America, which is only interested in commercial shows) and the BBC has even engaged in a number of co-production deals with Australian companies, for example *Bergerac*. It is this ability to sell a diversity of programmes, not just drama and light entertainment but also education, documentaries, sport, children's programmes, etc, that makes Australia such an attractive and important market despite the comparatively smaller revenue earned from a population of only 16 million.

In operation in Australia on 30 June 1982 there were 50 commercial, 86 national and 2 Special Broadcasting television stations. However, this proliferation of stations doesn't hide the fact that the ownership and control of the Australian commercial media are among the most highly concentrated in the world. The four groups of companies which dominate all branches of the Australian commercial media – Murdoch's News Corporation; Packer's Consolidated Press; John Fairfax Ltd and The Herald and Weekly Times Ltd – own all six commercial television stations in the two largest markets, Sydney and Melbourne. Furthermore, to take just one example, The Herald and Weekly Times has an interest in Adelaide's Channel 7 and, through its subsidiaries, in Channels 7 in Brisbane and Perth, 6 in Hobart and 10 in Adelaide.

The result of this high concentration of ownership amongst the 'Big Four' is that they are in a very strong position to influence television programming in other cities and the regions. They are highly competitive, financially successful and not only buy a large number of a whole range of American shows, but present them in an American style with frequent advertising breaks.

The ABC on the other hand, which is state-funded, has had a difficult time. It has to work with small budgets, it wasn't given a second channel, it was severely criticised by a government review in 1980 and regularly loses successful programmes to the commercial channels. However, not only the BBC but also Thames have a special relationship with the ABC which generally (not always – as in the case of *Widows*) has first option on their programmes. And then, if a programme is very successful on the ABC, there is a high probability that one of the commercial channels will bid for it and repeat it.

The ABC has a very small share of the audience – about 10% – and they are up against three highly competitive networks playing a large amount of American material (one of the reasons why it's not easy for British companies to gain a first run on Channels 7, 9 or 10). But TTI have found that if their programmes get good ratings on the ABC, and get talked about then they can usually be sold for a higher price to one of the commercial channels. Thus, for example, *Minder* episodes will continue to be shown on the ABC as long as Euston is making them and

18

then once the ABC's rights on the show have expired, the whole package will be sold to a commercial network.

Widows represents an interesting deviation from this practice. TTI does try for initial sales with the 7 and 10 Networks and scored a noteable success with *Widows*, which it sold for a record price at Cannes. Channel 7 also has an option, at the same rate, if a second series is made (as we now know it will be). Mike Phillips explains the situation:

> When we made the deal for Australia we actually sold *Widows* direct to a commercial network because they were just very, very keen to have it and it was a good deal. We knew that there was a strong possibility at that time that we would make another six so we did a deal with them that they would take another series as well, if and when it was made. The rate was fixed at that time and of course who benefits out of that depends on how successful the first six are. If the first six die in Australia then we've done very well because otherwise they wouldn't have bought it – if it goes through the roof then maybe we could have got more for the second series.

It's worth noting that whereas the prices obtained in America from PBS for British programmes will be far below the prices paid for network shows (perhaps $30,000 an hour compared to $800,000 an hour), in Australia a programme like *Minder* will sell for a price comparable to an American series such as *Hill Street Blues*.

One point about overseas sales of particular relevance to Euston is that programmes made on film are much easier to sell than those on videotape; not least because of the fact that there are three different television systems in the world (NTSC, PAL and SECAM). Each is incompatible with the other two, and as a consequence programmes made in video on one system have to be electronically transferred to another if they are to be shown. With programmes on film, of course, there are no such difficulties.

Besides selling programmes for transmission on the television systems of other countries, Thames are increasingly involved in exploiting their programmes in the field of non-broadcast television, i.e. video.

Thames Video
Established in March 1981 as a small unit within Thames Television International, Thames Video made Thames the first British television company to venture into the video market with the release of *The Naked Civil Servant* for home video use. A year later the spring 1982 issue of *Studio,* the Thames TV magazine, contained a supplement which reported on Thames Video's first year of operation. By this time Thames Video had a catalogue of twenty-six titles and Marketing Manager Ken Maliphant answered questions on, among other things, Thames Video's

markets and most successful titles:

We're developing important overseas markets. We've just completed a deal in the United States for distribution. In Scandinavia we're working with various distributors. We're now beginning to look at Germany, France and Spain, and we've begun doing business in Australia with excellent results so far. There's also a possible deal imminent with New Zealand either for the whole catalogue or for individual titles. We're looking at each territory individually, examining the profile of the market and just who is best in that market place, and then moving accordingly. It's a genuine international operation. . . . Two of our most successful titles, apart from *The Royal Wedding* which is a special case, are *The Kenny Everett Video Show* and *The Benny Hill Show*. So at the moment we are planning new releases for both. We're actually quite pleased about the possibility of releasing *The Flame Trees of Thika*, which will be edited onto one cassette and will run at feature-film length. I think it will make an excellent tape because it was such an excellent programme. We'll be continuing to release *The World At War* series until the end of this year and we're marketing the series as a part work. It's proved very popular.

By May 1984, we were told by Product Manager Chris Griffiths, Thames Video was the biggest TV video company in the UK and distributes through Thorn-EMI's video operation to the home video market in twenty-four countries around the world. Top of the league in terms of units sold is the United States, followed by the UK, then Australia and Scandinavia. The current UK catalogue consists of some fifty titles and includes Thames productions of Alan Ayckbourn's *The Norman Conquests*, John Mortimer's *A Voyage Round My Father*, as well as the series *Edward and Mrs Simpson*, *Botanic Man* and *The Best of George and Mildred*. Important contributors to the Thames Video catalogue are Thames' two subsidiary film companies, Euston Films and the animation company Cosgrove Hall. *Danger Mouse*, the Cosgrove Hall production, was a big hit for Thames Video and *The Wind in the Willows* is due to be released as part of Thames Video's pitch for the children's market. Euston Films is more important still; the video release of *Widows* did well and is to be followed by *Reilly – Ace of Spies* in August 1984 and two episodes of *Minder* in early 1985.

Thames Video has been able to release these Euston productions in the UK because the BFTPA agreement under which they are produced allows for such exploitation, whereas the separate ITCA agreement under which Thames' other drama productions are made did not until recently provide for any simple means whereby a programme can be released on video.

To explain the difference between these two agreements requires
20

some understanding of the whole question of unions within ITV. If the complexities involved are sometimes daunting, they are nevertheless inescapable, since the whole history of Euston Films has been very much bound up with the situation of the unions, particularly the ACTT, within the television industry.

LABOUR RELATIONS

The subject of labour relations within the television industry is a controversial one. While everyone we asked was willing to discuss questions relating to the organisation of labour within television (occasionally 'off the record'), whatever their perspective they were all at pains to stress the sensitivity of the issue, and there was a common anxiety that an ill-considered account of industrial relations could jeopardise either existing working arrangements or negotiations to change them. Although we acknowledge the basis of these anxieties and recognise the difficulty of producing a neutral account of the issues involved, an examination of the organisation of labour within the television industry is crucial to an understanding of the determinations on its products, and as we shall see these matters have had important consequences for Euston Films.

There is a high degree of division of labour in television and, in common with most areas of British industry today, labour is organised into trades unions. Within Independent Television those unions are: the Association of Cinematograph, Television and Allied Technicians (ACTT), which organises what are known as production staff such as directors, floor managers, designers, production assistants and location managers, as well as technicians such as camera and sound crews, editors and engineers; the National Association of Theatrical, Television and Kine Employees (NATTKE), whose members are make-up and wardrobe, props, scene shifters, certain secretarial posts and others; the National Union of Journalists (NUJ), which involves reporters on current affairs and news programmes; and the Electrical, Electronic, Telecommunication and Plumbing Union (EEPTU), for electricians and plumbers involved in television production. There are also the performers' (or what are often referred to as the 'talent') unions: British Actors Equity Association, the Film Artistes Association, for extras on film work, The Musicians Union and the Writers Guild of Great Britain (ACTT also organises writers).

The factors governing industrial relations in television are much the same as in other British industries. Two particularly important aspects, though by no means exclusive to the television industry, are the existence of a pool of unemployed unionised labour and the introduction of new technology. Casualisation has been endemic among film technicians since the late 1940s and is the characteristic way of life for workers organised by the performers' unions. Television companies wishing to

21

increase productivity and keep abreast of their competitors technically must introduce new equipment which, even when it is not specifically designed to reduce labour costs by cutting down on the number of workers required, involves the acquisition of new skills and the establishment of new working practices. Unions must protect the jobs of their members and negotiate provision for adequate retraining and where necessary compensation. They must also seek the extension of work prospects for their members and an equitable distribution of available work by attempting to reconcile the needs of freelance members with those in permanent employment.

The general position within ITV is outlined in *Action – 50 Years in the Life of a Union*, published by the ACTT in 1983:

> Commercial television is a closed shop. In other words a person who is not a member of ACTT, or another appropriate union, may not be employed in jobs the scope of which is covered by agreements between the unions involved and the employers. This situation, which is in many respects analogous to the relations between members of liberal professions – doctors, lawyers, chartered accountants – and their professional associations, without whose approval they may not practise their trade, is a legacy of the early days of commercial television.
>
> Until the 1950s, the BBC, a non-profit-making enterprise, was the only broadcasting institution in the country. Commercial television was instituted by a Conservative government in response to pressure from a powerful political lobby whose members were interested in using television as a vehicle for profit-making. Such entrepreneurs saw nothing threatening in a closed shop. On the contrary, the orderliness of recruitment, and the stability of employment that a closed shop implied, had an attraction for them. . . .
>
> . . . In April 1955 ACT made its debut in commercial television with a strike for recognition as the official union of the technicians working in the new branch of the industry. Within a year the second 'T' was added to the Union's title and for the first time, just over a year later, in August 1957, the programme contractors put their signatures to the first agreement on behalf of the technicians employed in commercial television.

In a formal sense, agreements are made between the unions and each of the separate Independent Television companies, since they are the employers, but negotiations on terms and conditions of employment are carried out at a national level where appropriate through the Independent Television Companies Association (ITCA). In addition to the national agreements there are, however, local agreements reached between individual ITV companies and their union shops. Also important

22

is the principle of 'custom and practice' where no formal agreement covers a particular operation, for example crewing levels in a TV studio. In such instances any change in established procedures would involve consultation between unions and management. It is under the terms of these general agreements, known usually as the ITCA agreement or the Television agreement, that most Independent Television programmes are produced.

Since the inception of ITV, however, some television programmes have been produced under a different set of agreements, those between the British Film and Television Producers' Association (BFTPA) and the production and performers' unions. The British Film and Television Producers' Association Ltd (formerly the British Film Producers' Association Ltd – the word television was incorporated within the title in 1981) is an employers' association representing producers of films for the cinema and for television. Its members include major film production companies such as Paramount Pictures (UK) Ltd and Goldcrest Films and Television Ltd, as well as smaller production companies and a number of Independent Television company subsidiaries producing films and filmed series for television. The BFTPA owns a subsidiary company, Central Casting Ltd, an organisation for supplying crowd artistes to film and television production, and runs a joint industrial relations service with the Independent Programme Producers Association Ltd (IPPA), the producers body recognised by Channel 4 Television.

In the BFTPA annual report 1982-3 it was announced that:

It is important to register that in terms of industrial relations the BFTPA and IPPA are now unified in that all agreements, apart from the cinema films agreement with British Equity, are now in common and where they are not yet signed by IPPA this is a future formality.

Euston Films Ltd is a member of the BFTPA and all Euston productions are made under the terms of the BFTPA/IPPA agreements. In fact Euston Films' Executive Director of Production, Johnny Goodman, is a member of the Executive Committee of the BFTPA and serves on several of the Association's industrial relations and negotiating committees, which he sees as a significant part of his job:

I feel it's important that I should be there playing a key role in deciding conditions of work and all the detail of Union agreements, because after all that affects me very much in how I make pictures. So I play a large part in labour relations and keep the Board informed on how things are going on that front.

Although there are some significant differences between the ITCA and BFTPA agreements, which are examined below, in general terms they

23

cover the same areas, establishing working hours, rates of pay, general conditions of employment and procedures to be followed in the case of disputes. Each separate union agreement obviously covers matters relating to the specific work undertaken by its members; the agreements with ACTT stipulate minimum levels of crewing for filming and those with Equity have clauses concerning the nature of an artist's performance and the exploitation of performances in terms of repeat transmissions, foreign sales and so on. The agreements are amended at intervals by negotiation and at the time of writing a new agreement between the BFTPA and the Writers Guild was still under negotiation, the former agreement having expired in 1981.

Although the existence of two sets of agreements governing television production seems unusual, this situation can be explained at a simple level by the hybrid nature of television itself. Since the earliest days of television some programming has been originated on film, and some by electronic means, initially live transmissions or tele-recorded live shows, nowadays mostly videotape recordings. Because labour within the film industry was effectively organised long before the arrival of ITV, union agreements on film production were already firmly established. The production of films and film series made for ITV could be and was carried out under the terms of these agreements.

In his book *The Truth About Television*, Howard Thomas provides an informative account of the rationale for filmed TV series production in the early 1960s. The advantages of filmed series did not lie in their lower cost:

To film a programme is at least twice as costly as to produce it 'live'. Film stock, processing, cutting, sound dubbing and mixing are all additional costs to studio, script, sets and actors. When a television company budgets for its programmes, costs are generally at two levels, 'above the line' and 'below the line', meaning actual cash payments to writers and performers, plus 'below the line' the overheads of running a studio and staff. When films are commissioned the overhead costs of the film studio, equipment and technicians have to be paid in cash, so that a half-hour programme which might cost £3,000 'live' in a television studio (plus the inescapable overheads of maintaining television studios) is likely to cost £10,000 in its final form as a film.

After describing the economics and expansion of American filmed TV series production Thomas proceeds to describe the American penetration of the British market, the restrictions on American imports and the need for domestic production:

The volume of production [in the US] grew immense. Bursting point in the film vaults was relieved by the shipment of films overseas

24

to the new markets as television grew world wide. Salesmen hurried to Canada, Britain and Australia, to South America and to the Continent, seeking further distribution for the film series which had already paid their way in the home market.

American product was welcomed by new television stations, especially in the early days when it was difficult to fill programme hours. Furthermore, the American series were competent and professional, most acceptable to viewers as entertainment, and were offered for sale at reasonable prices related to the size of the audience. Stations with a monopoly were in a happy position because there was a surfeit of product and only a few hours to fill, in a single market, so the distributors had to sell at 'take it or leave it' prices.

In Britain the situation changed rapidly when ITV began. Prices much higher than the BBC's low rates were offered and the cream of America's filmed programmes were acquired by the ITV companies, as a key move in building up audiences.

This situation had been foreseen by legislators and the Act stipulated that the ITV programmes should be predominantly British. To restrict the amount of imported film shown in Britain the ITA decided to set a quota. As a result of meetings with the entertainment industry trade unions the Director-General of the Authority decreed that a maximum of 14 per cent of imported film would be permitted. Related to a 50-hour programme week this meant that little more than one hour a day of foreign film could be shown, a rule that has been strictly enforced ever since.

The BBC did not make an identical arrangement but decided to adopt the same practice. . . . therefore there arose urgent need for filmed programmes of British origin. Urged on by the British film unions it looked as though the British studios, too, would be following in Hollywood's wake. But the economics were very different. American television film makers might be able to get their money back with a sale to one network, but in Britain not more than a quarter of the production cost could be earned in the United Kingdom. (Howard Thomas, *The Truth About Television*, Weidenfeld and Nicolson, 1962)

So, the importation of American filmed series had whetted audience appetites for this style of entertainment; the imposition of quotas on foreign material stimulated the production of filmed series in the UK. By all accounts it was Lew Grade who first began to finance the production of TV film series under the then BFPA agreements, having convinced the unions that this would not affect the production of television programmes within ATV but would allow him to break into the American market, thus providing an additional source of employment.

He sold his first T V series to America back in 1965, having gone across specially to New York to let the big American networks see his A T V series *Danger Man*. . . . It was shown successfully although not networked. Six months later, Lew sold to N B C the first British-made T V series to be shown on the American network, *The Saint*, which had cost A T V £50,000 a show to make. It ran in the U S A for 117 episodes. (Hunter Davies, *The Grades: The First Family of British Entertainment*, Weidenfeld and Nicolson, 1981)

Howard Thomas switched the A B C series *The Avengers* from tape to film and scored a notable success, including an American network sale. For the production of these filmed series the television companies did not attempt to renegotiate the I T C A agreements to make them more amenable to economic in-house film production but looked instead to the film industry and its purpose-designed film production agreements. Underemployed studios and a large workforce of skilled and freelance technicians eager for work laid claim to T V film production as an offshoot of the film industry.

The B F T P A (formerly B F P A) agreements were designed to take account of the nature of film production and embody elements of flexibility perceived as necessary for that activity. An often quoted illustration of this flexibility is an openness to the re-scheduling of technicians' working hours at short notice. Such a facility is claimed to be essential nowadays when so much filming takes place on location. This is contrasted with the demand under the I T C A agreements that at least 96 hours' notice be given of changes to rostered working hours, the penalty for failure to give such notice being a significant increase in labour costs as 'any hours worked outside the hours originally published shall rank for payment as overtime hours'. As Lloyd Shirley, Thames T V Controller of Drama and one of the founders of Euston Films, explained:

If work is all to take place in a studio those sanctions aren't particularly worrying because by its nature studio scheduling is fairly cut and dried. It can never be totally, but it's reasonably predictable. You know what you're dealing with. You've got your text, it's been worked on, you've got experienced backroom people and you can fix a schedule for recording a show three months from now and you will probably come in within minutes of what you had planned. That doesn't happen when you're filming.

The elements of flexibility built into the B F T P A agreements with the production unions were regarded as highly desirable, even essential, for television film production by most of the people we spoke to. Some films are made for television under the I T C A agreements, however, and parallel with Euston Films operations Thames Drama department pro-
26

duced such films as *The Naked Civil Servant* and more recently *Saigon: Year of the Cat*. But to do so is costly and difficult, as Jeremy Isaacs, former Director of Programmes for Thames TV, explained:

> You can make one film a year like *The Naked Civil Servant* under the ITCA agreement but doing so was horrendous. You have to go out on location and the national agreement provides that people can only be rostered for 38 hours per week and everything over that is on vast amounts of overtime, and I mean *vast* amounts of overtime. You pay for the hours it takes them to get from their base to where you are going to shoot and you have huge wage bills. The labour cost becomes a vast part of the cost of the production and this has a poisonous and demoralising effect on the rest of the company because people who happen to be rostered to work on that production start earning two or three times as much as their mates who are working on a studio show and there is great jealousy and bitterness. Managers find themselves managing an outfit which may work hard and efficiently but in which people doing less responsible jobs are earning two or three times what they are earning.

The reasons for producing filmed drama under the ITCA agreements are clearly, in the short term anyway, not economic ones.

Many people we spoke to believed that the nature of the ITCA agreements have remained basically unaltered since they were drawn up to cover the exigencies of studio based live television production. In Jeremy Isaacs' view:

> The ITCA agreement is designed for live television, not even video recorded television, for live television, in order to bring people together for 12 or 14 hours on two consecutive days in a studio out of which you are going to get one hour of live drama. That's when you need everybody in the studio for those last 12 hours. But when you are making a film and doing five minutes a day the 'live' agreement becomes penal in its cost implications. It simply was never meant for it.

Former Euston Films producer Ted Childs offered a different perspective:

> I think to be fair the ITCA agreement in essence is not quite as crippling and inefficient as it is often portrayed, certainly in its so-called 'Third Schedule' version. The difficulty is that it has become submerged under a welter of local custom and usage and local shop agreements. I think the managements of the television companies are really to blame for this for they have always bought off trouble in the

27

short run rather than lose advertising revenue. To concede on some quite small issue over which a union is making a fuss seems eminently good sense from a company director's point of view. But over the period of time that commercial television has been going, it has now built up, in production management terms, a mass of restrictive practices.

He was, however, quite clear about the benefits of the BFTPA agreements when producing *The Sweeney*:

You see we could be very flexible, which was a tremendous advantage; we could re-stage the schedule. We were in a strait jacket of really having to make one every ten days, of not wanting to go over budget, because I had a strong feeling that Euston Films could only survive while we remained economically viable and could make an effectively popular type of programme within the price parameters laid down by Thames. So we had very flexible arrangements, we would often get a writer in at the last minute to change something or change the schedule to keep within the ten day cycle of production. We could do this, but it would be very difficult to do in a studio with the strict rules about rostering and the use of equipment across a wide range of programme areas. We were a law unto ourselves so we had a much easier time in many ways than a producer trying to make a comparable show in a BBC or ITV studio structure.

The benefits of a television company continuing to use their permanently-employed studio staff and expensive studio facilities in making videotaped productions under the ITCA agreement, and at the same time employing, through subsidiary companies, freelance workers for film production under the BFTPA agreement, seem obvious enough. There are other benefits too. One consequence of the fact that the BFTPA and ITCA agreements were conceived in different eras and for different purposes is their varying attitude to the question of sales of programmes both abroad and through other media than broadcast television. As we have seen, such sales are already important and likely to become more so. Broadly speaking, the BFTPA television films agreement, in keeping with feature films agreements, is designed to facilitate the maximum exploitation of a production. For money up front the producer buys out most rights in the production. Contrary to this, the ITCA agreement is designed primarily to cover the production of programmes for domestic transmission, although it does contain some provision for further exploitation. These differences have had important effects on Thames' ability to exploit their past productions on video. As we have seen, several Euston productions have already been released because the agreement under which they were made (the BFTPA agreement) makes
28

provision for such exploitation, whereas Equity, the Musicians' Union and the Writers' Guild have permitted only a brief trial of releasing material made under the ITCA agreement. Following the expiry of this first home video agreement, eighteen months of negotiations resulted in a new agreement announced in July 1984. The agreement is a complex one and like its predecessor will require renegotiation after a limited period of time, in this case one year. This recent development should be of great benefit to Thames Video, but Euston Films productions made under the BFTPA agreement will continue to play an important part in their expanding operations.

One further advantage arising out of the BFTPA agreement should be mentioned. In addition to the normal corporation tax paid by ITV companies, an extra tax is imposed by the government in the form of a 66.7% levy on the advertising revenue the companies earn. Certain expenses, including programme costs, can be deducted from revenue before the levy, and two-thirds of a film or film series' production costs can be written off against levy. If the production is then sold abroad the resulting revenue is free from levy.

Given the advantages which accrue from running Euston as a separate operation exclusively devoted to the production of films and filmed series, and the evident success of the productions which have been made, one might wonder why all the major ITV companies have not followed suit, with equal success. But as the following pages will make clear, the advantages of Euston have come only at the cost of some very real difficulties, while the success of Euston's productions cannot be explained simply in terms of the effect of economics or institutional structures. As will, we hope, become clear, there are enough idiosyncracies, both personal and otherwise, in Euston's history for its success not to be capable of any easy or automatic imitation.

2 Production

Whilst working for ABC Television in 1965, Jim Goddard, Trevor Preston and Terry Green collaborated on a proposal for a small film production unit. Somewhat strikingly produced as a report, complete with graphics, programme ideas and script extracts, the proposal announced itself as a 'personal manifesto'. It suggested the formation, within ABC TV, of a small experimental production team whose members' roles were interchangeable but who consistently worked together developing television's use of 16mm film. Whether this particular proposal, entitled ABC/NUCLEUS, provided the initial idea for Euston Films is a matter of conjecture but its existence does indicate that the potential of 16mm film and the possibility of different working relations within television was under serious consideration in the mid-sixties.

Those most closely associated with the establishment of Euston Films Ltd, Lloyd Shirley, George Taylor and Brian Tesler, regard the genesis of the company as three individual film projects made during the early days of Thames Television, although their connections ran back into ABC Television. On the formation of Thames Television out of the IBA-enforced merger between ABC Television and Rediffusion Television in 1967, Brian Tesler was appointed Director of Programmes, Lloyd Shirley Controller of Drama and George Taylor Head of Film Facilities. All three had held the same or similarly important positions with ABC TV and consequently knew each other well; in fact Lloyd Shirley and George Taylor were old personal friends.

Lloyd Shirley described how at the beginning of Thames TV's operations George Taylor was able to identify a spare capacity in his department and suggested the possibility of producing some drama on film. As a result, Lloyd Shirley engaged Mike Hodges to direct a Trevor Preston-scripted children's series entitled *The Tyrant King*, which was shot on 16mm film. Significantly, Mike Hodges, Lloyd Shirley and George Taylor all had a background in factual television and experience of 16mm film location shooting. In fact it was Hodges' 'sense of improvisation and ability to shoot well on location' which led Lloyd Shirley to select him for the project.

Following the success of *The Tyrant King* experiment, Lloyd Shirley persuaded Mike Hodges to write and direct *Suspect* after convincing Brian Tesler that this filmed play could be produced for approximately the same cost as a tape show if shot on 16mm. They were so pleased with the result that another was commissioned, entitled *Rumour*. *Suspect* had the distinction of being Thames TV's first colour drama production and was transmitted on 17 November 1969 as part of Thames' first night of colour television. Curiously no one associated with Euston Films mentioned this fact to us although the programme was thought by some to have been the first all-16mm film drama production shown on ITV; hitherto filmed drama, even film inserts for taped shows, had been on 35mm. This claim proved difficult to verify and although it was not dismissed it was thought unlikely by the IBA engineering department responsible for technical standards. *Suspect* could, however, have been the first all location shot 16mm film drama production shown on ITV. Both *Rumour* and *Suspect* were transmitted in the Monday night ITV Playhouse slot and 'did very well'. Brian Tesler outlined the subsequent developments:

So a year or so after we began Thames, and we'd got over the teething troubles and we were planning the future of our drama output, it occurred to me that it would be marvellous if we could not only do more film drama but do as much or as little film drama as we wanted to without taking on an enormous staff and then finding ourselves committed to always doing a great deal in order to use that staff. So I discussed this with Lloyd Shirley and George Taylor and we talked about having a very small nucleus, literally one person running it creatively and one person running it organisationally, which could make as little or as much as we wanted, which was totally elastic. Not only that but it wouldn't occupy a studio, just an office and a telephone. So when we wanted to make something, that nucleus would engage freelance writers, directors and everybody else and the television studio staff would not be affected. I didn't realise at the time, naive of me perhaps, that it would create some union problems. It seemed to me that there was no reason why it should, because our studio drama was going ahead at full steam and all our television staff were fully occupied and it never occurred to me that it might be upsetting to the staff in the union shops if rather more exciting, glamorous work on location and on film was being done by others and not by themselves.

The idea of a subsidiary producing TV films and film series was not new. ITC had been doing so since 1955, but another ITC was not what was under discussion, as Lloyd Shirley explained:

Suspect and *Rumour* seemed to open up interesting possibilities and

31

George Taylor and I talked about how to take this forward into the more ambitious area of trying to do a series that way. At that time the only really all-film series being done in the UK were through Lew Grade's subsidiary company, ITC, and although this was perfectly honourable stuff, most of it was done in conjunction with the Americans and therefore had a kind of attitude of mind, a kind of mid-Atlantic feel about it, the best of it being *Danger Man* and *The Prisoner*. Well, we didn't want to do that particularly because it seemed to us that Grade and ITC would do it a heck of a lot better than we were ever likely to and, secondly, why should we try and duplicate the work of somebody else?

Where ITC's lead was to be followed was not so much in working methods and the nature of productions but rather in terms of the agreements under which they would be made. The question of union agreements has been discussed earlier but it is worth quoting George Taylor on the subject:

> It occurred to us that the agreements and the treaties we were working to [while shooting *Suspect* and *Rumour*] weren't particularly suitable for contemporary drama shot on location. So we looked into the BFPA treaty and quite sensibly it was more apt for this sort of work, in other words 'horses for courses'. . . . So we discussed it with Howard Thomas who was then Managing Director of Thames and we felt that it would be a good idea to start a film company but working to the BFPA treaty.

Brian Tesler takes up the story:

> It was very easy to persuade Howard Thomas to go ahead with it, because after all it wouldn't cost anything until we started making a show and the shows we made would be sold to the network and perhaps overseas, so in the end they wouldn't cost anything either. And we weren't taking on extra staff who, should we ever cease production, would be redundant or hanging around doing nothing.

With the support of Howard Thomas, Brian Tesler prepared a paper 'describing the plan and the arguments for it with the financial equations', which was submitted to the Thames Board.

STARTING UP: THE RELATION TO THAMES

This proposal was accepted by the Board. In Lloyd Shirley's words: 'They were happy to give us a button to see if we could sew a suit on it.' The company was registered as Euston Films Ltd on 9 March 1971.

32

Originally it was set up because Thames' profits, at that time, were pretty high and it was suggested that some of those profits should go back into making quality film material. Hence setting up Euston Films. That was one of the reasons. And indeed, it was a big reason for running *Armchair Cinema*. But, I don't know that you can actually quantify the profit, you see, because the show isn't actually sold on the network as such, it has a notional value. If it's successful, as most of these have been, then it kind of sells itself – the only profit that comes from it is normally overseas sales.

That was George Taylor talking. We have already quoted Brian Tesler suggesting also that Thames was prepared to experiment because Euston Films cost nothing to establish in terms of capital expenditure and permanent staff. It would seem, however, that whilst these are obviously good reasons there were additional factors that would need to be taken into account, as we shall see.

For the first few years, whilst George Taylor and Lloyd Shirley ran Euston, there was no separate administrative organisation; production and administration were combined and based in the building especially rented for a particular project.

This was part and parcel of Thames' intentions to organise film-making for television on a totally freelance, non-capital expenditure basis. We assume that this was possible as a short-term experiment as long as the initiators were running the operation and as long as the work didn't expand. Once productions began to overlap and run at the same time, administrative work was likely to change.

In fact Euston did prove to be viable and successful; Lloyd Shirley and George Taylor did decide to leave and there was an increasing commitment to commissioning programmes specifically for Euston to make (largely as a result of Verity Lambert's commissioning policies as Head of Drama at Thames), with the result that a more permanent and centralised office and staff became an essential requirement for the smooth running of the operation. Hence the renting of permanent office space at 365 Euston Road, almost directly opposite Thames Television's central London studios and Head Office.

The intention, however, was still to operate with the minimum of permanent administrative staff. Currently there are eight:

Johnny Goodman	– Executive Director of Production
Linda Agran	– Head of Scripts and Development
Bill Launder	– Administration Manager
Roy Baker	– Projectionist
Renée Kramer	– PA/Secretary to Johnny Goodman
Denise Pienaar	– PA/Secretary to Linda Agran
Angela Baker	– Receptionist

Euston Films staff April 1984. (Back row, l. to r.: Dominique Whittaker, Roy Baker, Denise Pienaar, Bill Launder, Renée Kramer, Veronica Ford; front row: Linda Agran, Johnny Goodman).

The annual cost for this central administrative operation is approximately £350,000, of which about half is spent on salaries. This sum is accounted for quite separately from each individual project, each of which is budgeted for on a total (i.e. above and below the line) basis and which is made on a cost recovery basis. To quote the annual report and accounts for Thames TV in 1976-7: 'The cost of own productions and film rights is wholly written off on first transmission.'

In addition to the regular office space in 365 there is a sizeable open plan office which is only periodically used. It is designed for pre-production planning by a team preparing to move into the rented accommodation which will provide the shooting, editing and general post-production base. These production bases have always thus far been large enough (an old school and an industrial office/warehouse block have been rented) to encompass a small number of permanent sets for wea-

34

ther cover (i.e. offering the possibility of filming indoor scenes in the advent of bad weather). In the case of *Minder,* for example, the base includes a set of the Winchester Club and of Arthur Daley's 'lock-up'.

Since its inception Euston Films has sought not to own but to hire equipment as and when required for each production. This continues to be a firm principle of the company, for a number of reasons explained by Johnny Goodman:

> I'm against having equipment for all the reasons you appreciate. First of all everything gets out of date so quickly, and if you try to accumulate it then you take on warehouses, insurance, heating, storekeepers and in the end it's better that every production has a budget that copes with your requirements for that particular show and then on the last day of production you have no commitments, nothing to sell off, nothing to maintain and that's the end of that. And you're always working with the most up-to-date equipment. What I do insist on, is that we don't favour any particular equipment company – my great war cry is that I don't care if it's a laboratory or equipment-hire people, they can all throw their hat into the ring and if their equipment is right and the price is right, and the particular producer or cameraman wants to go with them, then I'm open to listening to them. So we have the advantage of using the best we can get at the best price we can get. A certain company, that I wouldn't dream of mentioning, approached me once with the attitude that I wasn't doing my job right – if I went to them they could do me a deal on everything, consequently I'd get the best. And I'm against it on two counts. One is that I genuinely believe that in this industry, to make it survive, everybody should have a little piece of the action because to keep a few healthy companies is good news frankly. Secondly, once you get into a situation of using one company only, and they've got you tied up in a deal, your muscle is limited, if things go wrong or you get messed about you're stuck. Whereas if you're dealing with one company at a time, they know that they might not get another picture unless they really service you jolly well on that one.

The original directors of Euston Films were Howard Thomas, Ray Dicks, Clive G. D. May, Brian Tesler and Colin S. Wills, with Ben E. Marr being the first (and to date, the only) Secretary of the Company. The Directors who served throughout the year up to 31 March 1983 were: Bryan Cowgill, Johnny Goodman, Verity Lambert, Ian Scott, Muir Sutherland, Colin S. Wills, The Lord Brabourne (John Ulick Knatchbull). Nigel Ryan resigned on 4 June 1982 and Mike Phillips joined the board on 5 January 1983.

Howard Thomas described the low-key approach to the setting up of the company:

35

When I named the company Euston, I purposely chose what was admittedly a dull name. [The name derives simply from the fact that Thames' headquarters are in Euston Road. The company's logo, reproduced on the cover of this book, is a train because Euston Station is nearby.] If I had called it 'International Productions' or something grand it would have attracted the attention of many people, including the ACTT. So I thought, as the whole thing is very modest, let's call it something plain and ordinary, even as dull as Euston Films. With this unglamorous name, quietly, without any publicity or press releases, we started up.

But things didn't proceed quite as smoothly as anticipated. Brian Tesler:

> We thought it was going to go sailing ahead, but suddenly found ourselves up against the problem of the in-house staff, supported by television branch [of the ACTT] not wanting the essentially freelance activity that Euston Films would represent. This is certainly the problem that other companies, including LWT, have faced subsequently.

This situation seems to have delayed the beginning of the company's operations by about 18 months, as Euston didn't commence production until September 1972. Clearly, discussions took place between Thames management and the union shops of Thames' drama department at Teddington Studios, but as Lloyd Shirley recalled:

> We didn't have much to do with that. Really the only assurance they wanted was that Euston's activity wouldn't mean a diminution of their work. If what Euston's product was doing was replacing what might be bought in from abroad, that was great, and by and large that has always been the case.

George Taylor, in his account of Euston's beginnings, stressed that:

> A very important point would be that it was an overflow situation from the studios. In other words, the studios had sufficient product; what Euston would do was produce over and above the normal product flow so there could be no question of problems occurring with Thames' staff.

Having received such assurances from Thames management, the union shops agreed to the operation of Euston Films, but an anxiety about the erosion of work and concern about the possible lack of exciting, creative opportunities for permanent staff must have lingered on, for they were to re-emerge at a later date, though not before Euston Films had encoun-

36

tered union problems from another quarter.

THE WIDER CONTEXT

Before examining these specific disputes and their contexts, it is worth describing the more general situation within the television and particularly the film industries which formed a backdrop to the establishment of Euston Films. The purpose of doing so is not to dwell unduly upon matters of industrial unrest but rather to highlight those aspects of the economic and social forces within the industries which, although held in uneasy equilibrium, manifest themselves in recurring problems.

Anthony Smith has given the following trenchant account of those factors which have determined the attitude, policies and strategies of the ACTT:

The whole experience of the ACT in the 1940s and 1950s was that employers could not be trusted. The vast majority of technicians worked in an utterly freelance, not to say, casualised, mode; they waited for American capital to arrive, to exploit them and then depart to some other part of Europe. They watched a number of wretched film deals in Wardour Street result in unfinished films, crews left unpaid or stranded in faraway locations, talented cameramen and recordists left without work for months. The kind of trades unionism which resulted was highly localised, flexible, tough; vindictiveness against unreliable and sometimes dishonest employers was a valuable technique. It was necessary to extract the highest possible rates of pay for the brief periods when work was available. It was necessary to protect members against fly-by-night companies. A great fear of casualisation was born and a great dislike of facilities firms, small production companies, inexperienced entrepreneurs.

Television provided the ACTT, as it became, with an opportunity for work which was regular and supervised from the public sector. Employers could be gentlemen. It was a profitable sector of the industry and it brought into existence a large number of subsidiary activities of great value to the membership. The labs were expanded. There were commercials to be made, and filmed drama series. There was now a career structure available which could take members from the studio floor into executive jobs. There was easier access to the management and to the regulatory authority, and even to the government which sat behind it all.

There continued, however, to be great insecurity, but of a different kind. In the early 1950s the membership of the ACTT was still little more than 1000. The numbers swelled as company after company opened up and the ABS was excluded from negotiation, but within a year or two calamity struck and several hundred members were laid

37

off. ITV was going to take a little longer to get off the ground. Only a decade later the franchises were recalled and new franchises given out; a period of dislocation and sudden unemployment started. There were times when advertising revenue fell. There was the era of the Heath administration's Industrial Relations Act which represented a threat to tough trades unionism and then again, under Wilson and Callaghan, an extended period of wage freeze and wage policies when the essential mechanism of ACTT bargaining – local deals – was rendered almost impossible. In the era of commercial television the ACTT developed a dualism between general national agreements and local arrangements over precise payments, fringe benefits and manning. During pay freezes, however, there was nothing left to argue about at local level, even though the profits of most of the companies went through one of their embarrassing periods of soaring into the sky.

The ACTT's vision of the world is of an unstable environment in which promises may be kept, but not for long, in which a multiplicity of employers, some of whom are grossly underinvested, are juxtaposed with immensely rich companies who can afford to pay very high wages. The problem has been to achieve some kind of harmony and equality. Franchise reallocations, dips in the advertising economy, technical change, undercutting through product importation, are the great fears and reinforce the historic dread of insecure employment. (Anthony Smith, 'Just Another British Industry', Edinburgh International Television Festival Programme, 1979)

In the early 1970s UK feature film production was at a low ebb, experiencing one of the cyclical slumps which had characterised the industry since it had come to rely predominantly upon American financing. There had been an accelerating decline in the number of operating British film studios from 25 in 1948 to only 14 in 1972. Some former film studios had become television studios; Ealing, Riverside and Shepherd's Bush had all been taken over by BBC TV, and Teddington by Thames Television; others had been put to less glamorous use as factories, warehouses and residential property. The ACTT Nationalisation Forum report stated that studio employment had dropped from 7,700 in 1948 to 4,400 in 1949 and was only approximately 1,700 by the end of 1972, but:

In spite of this sharp decline in permanent studio membership, the film production membership of ACT has increased since the war. In 1949 film production membership, which includes not only feature film production staff but also shorts and documentaries, was about 4,500. At the end of the third quarter of 1949, 1,528 technicians were employed in the studios. By 1960 it had dropped somewhat, partly as a result of film production members transferring to the television branch of the Union. In 1965 ACT film production membership topped the 1949 figure and by 1970 it had reached 6,000. Most of the 1,500 new members came into the Union during the production boom produced by massive American investment in 1967, 1968 and 1969.

The dramatic increase in membership combined with the casualisation of the studio-based labour force has resulted in the growth of the Union's Freelance Shop. More than 90 per cent of the total Union film production membership is now casualised and a little over 50 per cent of NATTKE's film production membership is in the same position. *(Nationalising the Film Industry, ACTT, 1973)*

American film production finance, attracted to the UK by low costs and subsidies intended to aid domestic production, had helped to create something of a boom during the late 1960s. The report went on to outline the factors which caused the Americans substantially to reduce their European production financing:

Their financial situation became shaky. Walt Disney apart, all the American majors registered large losses or very small post-tax profits in at least one of the years between 1969 and 1971. They had been spending too much on too many films and their US overheads were extraordinarily high. The state of the American economy was also a factor which seriously affected the film companies and the conglomerate companies which control many of them. The shareholders were screaming, and the simplest solution was a drastic cut-back in production until the film companies could put their respective houses in order. . . . The majors and the major-minors made 110 films abroad in 1968. This total dropped each year until it reached 42 in 1971.

In the section on television's use of film technicians the Forum reported that:

Television in this country is dependent upon the casualised labour force of film technicians and craftsmen in a number of areas. The most definable of these areas is the production of television series which pre-dates the creation of independent television. Television series are made with full feature crews recruited from the casualised labour force. In recent years companies allied with ATV, London Weekend Television and Thames Television have been producing series for repeated transmission here and sale abroad. A sudden decline in the production of television film series in 1969-1970 coincided with and deepened the unemployment crisis created by the massive withdrawal of American investment in British feature films. The volume of British television film series production has proved as unstable

39

as feature production.

The response of the ACTT was a new resolve to fight casualisation and the replacement of the studios by 'four-walling'; the consequences for Euston were soon to become clear.

During this time, the late 1960s, there were, beside these acute problems within the film industry, a number of factors which combined to make these years difficult ones for ITV. 1968 saw a marked decline in ITV's audience share as recorded by the newly established JICTAR (Joint Industry Committee for Television Advertising Research). Presumably connected with the drop in audience ratings, which fell to 47% in October, was a sharp downturn in advertising revenue. The year also brought labour disputes resulting from the dislocation of workers brought about by the allocation of new contracts by the IBA. In 1969 the newly enfranchised companies had to bear the costs of colourisation, which involved a shift from the 405 line VHF system to the 625 UHF system. They had also to suffer an increase in the rate of the levy on advertising revenue. The 1969-70 annual report of the Independent Television Authority paints a fairly gloomy picture:

The start of colour television meant a substantial increase in costs, both in capital and revenue. There has been no compensating increase in income for Independent Television, because the amount of colour viewing is still below the level at which adjustments in advertising rates could be made for this reason. Indeed, far from an increase in income the summer and autumn of 1969 saw the start of a fall in the amount spent on television advertising which became even more acute as the winter drew on. On top of this the industry was feeling the impact of the increase in the rate of Levy announced in the Budget of 1969, which came into operation on 1st July 1969 and which was designed to increase the yield by an extra £3 million or so in a full year. The combination of these factors meant that for virtually the whole of the year under review there was great financial uncertainty in the system. Following representations by the Authority to the Minister of Posts and Telecommunications, the Minister announced on 16th March 1970 a reduction in the rate of the Levy, effective from 15th April 1970, estimated to reduce the yield in a full year by some £6 million. At the same time it was announced that the costs and revenues of the programme companies would be referred to the National Board for Prices and Incomes.

The reduction in the Levy provided relief at a time when it was urgently needed if a serious threat to programmes was to be avoided. This was action in the short term. With a continuing downward trend in income on the one hand and rising costs on the other, it was apparent that there was more than a short-term problem, and the reference to the Board was seen as providing for an independent and authoritative examination in the light of which consideration might by given to the further measures needed for long-term financial stability. Even with the reduction in Levy, the total surplus of all the companies for the year to the end of July 1970 was estimated to reach only about £4-5 million before tax, while the forecast position for the following year to July 1971 was that, without any further change in the Levy, the system as a whole might do little more than break even.

Howard Thomas, Thames TV's Managing Director at the time, related what this meant for his company financially:

In July 1969, within a year of the inauguration of the new chapter of ITV, the government levy on television advertising revenue was increased by the Labour Chancellor of the Exchequer, Roy Jenkins, scalping another £3 million out of the revenue. Once again Independent Television was in a struggle for survival. In its first year Thames could show a profit of only £759,000, a poor return on its £7 million capital employed on a six year contract. (Howard Thomas, *With an Independent Air*, Weidenfeld and Nicolson, 1977)

This situation did improve, however, and the annual report of the Independent Television Authority for 1970-1 indicates the degree of success of the lobby by the ITV companies and the Authority for recognition of ITV's serious financial position and a reduction in the levy:

The year began with a reduction, at an annual rate of some £6 million, in the amount of the Exchequer Levy payable on advertising revenue with effect from 15th April 1970. The end of the year saw a further reduction with effect from 26th February 1971, which at the level of advertising revenue then prevailing was at the rate of about £10 million a year.

The granting of the first of these reductions was accompanied by an announcement that the costs and revenues of the programme companies would be referred to the National Board of Prices and Incomes. The Board's report, presented in October 1970, confirmed the evidence presented to the Board by the Authority and the companies that the system's troubles were due to a combination of declining advertising and increasing costs. The report indicated that for the year to the end of July 1971 the net profits of the companies before tax, and at the rate of Levy then in force, would lie between £2.5 million and £4.5 million, dependent upon what assumptions were made about advertising revenue. It concluded that the rate of return on capital derived from the industry's forecasts over the period 1968-1974 was substantially lower than the level of return required to sup-

41

port a sound financial structure, on the assumption of an unchanged rate of Levy on advertising revenues.

Following the publication of the Board's report, the Authority strenuously urged that there should be a further and early reduction in the Levy. It based its representations primarily upon two factors, related to the two spheres of the Authority's responsibilities: the first was the need to leave an adequate income with the companies if programme standards were not to be prejudiced; the second was the Authority's own requirement for a substantial increase in rental from the companies if it was to be able to increase its rate of station construction so as to have broadly the same UHF coverage as the BBC by the mid-1970s.

The Authority warmly welcomed an announcement by the Minister of Posts and Telecommunications in February 1971 of the further reduction. It was also glad that the Minister stated that this reduction was a holding operation until mid-1972 and that the basis of charging the Levy would in the meantime be reviewed. It is the Authority's view that when money is short the Levy, which is a first charge on income, is in principle likely to work against the maintenance and improvement of programme standards.

By 1971 ITV's finances had begun to recover. Having fallen from £129 million in 1969 to £125 million in 1970, expenditure on TV advertising in 1971 was £143 million and by 1972 had increased to £176 million. As the rate of levy decreased, advertising revenue increased and more cash was available within the ITV companies.

Although both the ITV companies and the Independent Television Authority had urged that the levy be placed on net rather than gross income, their arguments were not initially accepted by the government. It was not until May 1974 that the procedure of assessing levy upon revenues less programme expenditure was enacted under the 1974 IBA Act. A PEP publication published in 1970 (C F Pratten, *The Economics of Television*, PEP Broadsheet, September 1970) provides some interesting information on programme expenditure. Pratten states that the costs of making programmes account for about 85% of the costs of television broadcasting in the UK, and the costs of transmitting programmes account for the remaining 15%. It also indicates that the television industry is extremely labour intensive, labour costs (wages, salaries and payments to artists, etc) forming a high proportion of programme costs – around 80%. On the question of the increase in costs for colour programme production he states that:

The extra current cost, excluding depreciation and interest on capital, of making programmes in colour instead of black and white averages about 19%. Artists' fees are not directly affected by a switch to

42

colour and much of the increase in costs relates to the extra cost of processing film and lighting. The increase in costs for colour varies from about 5% for some outside broadcasts to 40% for drama series with a substantial film content.

Clearly any effective attempt to reduce expenditure would need to be directed at labour costs without unduly antagonising the unionised workforce.

Another important factor affecting ITV during this period was the de-restriction of broadcasting hours. ITV had campaigned for the allocation of another television channel, the possibility of which had been under consideration since 1966. In December 1971 the Independent Television Authority published its proposals for a second ITV programme service. In January 1972 the Minister of Posts and Telecommunications postponed the decision on the allocation of a fourth TV service but announced that the hours of broadcasting would no longer be subject to Government restriction. In response to ITV pressure some expansion within the existing structure had been allowed and, as the Independent Broadcasting Authority annual report for 1972-3 noted, this de-restriction of broadcasting hours 'led to the introduction in October of a number of new serials screened on weekday afternoons'. These included ATV's *General Hospital,* Yorkshire Television's *Emmerdale Farm,* Granada TV's *Crown Court* and Thames TV's *Harriet's Back In Town.* It seems reasonable to speculate that this measure, which led to an increase in Thames' utilisation of studio staff and facilities on the production of network daytime drama, would have had an important bearing upon the establishment of Euston Films, in that spare capacity in the studios was now effectively used up.

THE EARLY YEARS – ESTABLISHING A STYLE AND SYSTEM

This then was the industrial and economic context within which the discussions preceding the establishment of Euston Films took place. Euston Films had a board of directors but was to be run by Lloyd Shirley and George Taylor even though they continued in their original jobs. From the beginning, Thames' Director of Programmes had an important role in determining Euston Films projects, commissioning from the company what was required for Thames' portfolio to be taken to the ITCA Programme Controllers Group. Lloyd Shirley described the company's beginnings as 'starting at the side of George's blotter and at the side of my blotter. The original brief was to do a 13-part one hour series and we opted for *Special Branch* plus some singles which would go out under the title of *Armchair Cinema.* A fairly obvious title but a logical one to the management of those days because of the long running *Armchair Theatre.*' Brian Tesler outlined his strategy as Director of Programmes:

Editing *Special Branch:* 'editors use Movieolas rather than the Steenbecks normal in television' (Janice Lanning and Chris Burt).

I wanted an action series from it to start with and I also wanted T V movies because I thought we could use the T V movies as pilots for subsequent series.

Thames had already produced two series of *Special Branch* as a tape show with film inserts and it was selected as a known quantity suitable for transfer to film. As Lloyd Shirley expressed it:

> We wanted to narrow our imponderables in the first Euston film exercise and it seemed to us a reasonable bet to take a tape series that had enjoyed decent public acceptance on to film, so at least we would know there was some sort of audience for it.

The series was recast and with George Sewell in the lead part 'Red Herring', the first episode and first Euston film, went into production in September 1972. George Taylor recalled the urgency as another factor in the choice of subject:

> It was virtually like firing a starting pistol. We actually had to launch a series within six weeks. Nobody would ever consider it now but we felt that it was a unique opportunity and it had to be done. So we used *Special Branch* which had been on tape as the format to put on film.

44

A short way into the series George Sewell was joined by Patrick Mower to take the whole narrative burden off one character which, though felt to be possible on tape, was proving too exhausting on film. What was to become a standard Euston procedure of taking short-term leases on premises and adapting them for production was established. Initially, there were two sets of premises, as George Taylor describes:

As well as having a production base and editing rooms in Redan Place, we had a shooting base at Colet Court, which is the old St Paul's Boys School down at Hammersmith. I think that *O Lucky Man* had just been made there and it was ideal for us because it had a front building which was administration and dormitory areas, then the rear building which was a series of multi-level classrooms around a huge hall. So we used the hall to build sets in and used the whole building extensively: police station, offices, etc. We took it for a month and we were there for five years. Extraordinary!

Although there was a base at Colet Court, a first principle was to shoot on location using the sets at base mainly for weather cover. Shooting 'on the streets' in this way not only saved money but also added an authenticity and distinctiveness to the films. Lloyd Shirley and George Taylor detected a processed quality in many film series which they were anxious to avoid. Their feeling was that this resulted from a particular pattern of working which had evolved for reasons of efficiency and cost effectiveness. In Lloyd Shirley's view:

This was at its worst in much of the American product, which was completely run from the cutting rooms. Because of the necessary cost consciousness, the supervising editor and production manager wielded great power. We wanted to avoid this at all costs because it seemed to me that you just don't get the best you can for the viewer by engaging a talented director then putting such strictures round the way they work. So we worked on a technique where the director would come in, do his recce, do his shoot, then do his own cut. ITC kind of accepted directors without exactly encouraging them; the Americans went even further than that, making it clear that the director's cut was of little interest to them.

In order to get the best out of directors but remain cost efficient, the practice of doubling up on lighting cameramen and assistant directors was instituted. This allowed the production manager, lighting cameraman, assistant director and director to undertake quite elaborate recces during which potential problems could be discussed and solutions found rather than confronting them during shooting. This system saved valuable time during filming and also promoted a co-operative team spirit

45

Special Branch: Detective Chief Inspector Craven (George Sewell) and Inspector Tom Haggerty (Patrick Mower).

amongst the unit, particularly useful given the tight shooting schedule of 10 days per 52 minute episode.

Although everyone was engaged on a freelance basis, a number of people who worked on the first Euston series of *Special Branch* have become Euston regulars. Series writers included Roger Marshall and Trevor Preston and directors included William Brayne, Douglas Camfield, Mike Vardy and David Wickes.

When we talked to George Taylor he was producing the fourth series of *Minder* and he commented upon the continuity of technicians:

It's interesting that Tony Dawe, for instance, the sound mixer, worked on the very first show, he's on the floor today, eleven years later. Dusty Miller, the lighting cameraman on the floor today, lit the very first show. John Maskall, the camera operator, he was the camera operator on *Special Branch* and he's on the floor today. It's amazing actually. You see the relationship is such that, because it became such a hard professional outfit, the bonds and loyalties are extremely strong. It's tough shooting in ten days and everyone has to have total confidence in everybody else so you tend to harden your little group and you don't want to change it.

Working on the post production of *Special Branch* were two of Euston's first employees, Chris Burt and Ian Toynton. Engaged as supervising editor and dubbing editor respectively, both were former feature film assistant editors who, though working freelance on each production, have pursued a career with Euston Films. Chris Burt was later to produce Euston's most ambitious and expensive project to date, *Reilly – Ace of Spies*, and Ian Toynton was to direct the highly successful *Widows*. Chris Burt was attracted by the concept of Euston Films, especially the production methods adopted to allow maximum involvement of directors:

> The directors actually felt they were making something worthwhile. Consequently, you could attract good directors, and once you could attract good directors you could attract good writers because it became *their* project and I think that has been the great success of Euston Films. When people are hired by Euston Films they know they are going to make something worthwhile and they will have control. They will have a benign producer above them because things are made on a very tight budget, but they will have an artistic control over their project. That was totally different from the other forms of making series at that time. All the other series were made almost on a factory basis where the director had very little power and very little say in what was done: he shot the schedule and that was that.

Chris Burt also noted that Euston directors usually came from television rather than feature films and that:

> By using television-oriented people we got more realism and they were much quicker and much more used to cutting corners.

After the first Euston series of *Special Branch*, with a production method established and working, with adjustments made to casting and format and with the beginnings of a 'stable' of writers, directors and technicians, the decision was taken to produce another thirteen episodes. As the producer of the first series, Geoffrey Gilbert, was working elsewhere, a new producer was needed and Lloyd Shirley recruited Ted Childs:

> I had worked with Lloyd Shirley and I knew George Taylor. In fact Lloyd Shirley had hired me at ABC Television and I worked in his department called Features, which in those days in ITV really meant factual programming – everything from current affairs to God. I was a researcher really and then I became a trainee director and then I

47

winged off into current affairs and documentaries and I was working for Thames as a documentary film maker, working in fact for Jeremy Isaacs on *World at War*. Lloyd had asked me on a number of occasions if I would be interested in getting involved in drama because I'd written a couple of scripts. But anyway, out of the blue really, Lloyd asked me if I would consider producing and I'm one of those people who when a chance comes up take it.

It was felt during the first series of *Special Branch* that the separation of production office and shooting base wasn't really working so the decision was taken to move out of Redan Place and locate everything in the old school at Colet Court. Ted Childs again:

> I moved in there as producer with a team I had sorted out with Lloyd and George and, although I felt that *Special Branch* as a television film format left something to be desired, I learnt a great deal. I brought in directors I'd worked with, some with a documentary background, and really what we tried to do was incorporate the 'wobbly-scope' techniques of 16mm documentary film-making into a drama situation. This is what Mike Hodges had previously done, coming as he did from *World in Action*.

Accompanying the attempted documentary look of *Special Branch* were efforts to produce a realist soundtrack by shooting with direct sound and mixing each episode soundtrack from the actual sounds recorded on location. Chris Burt:

> On *Special Branch* and all those things I think we did less than 1% post synch. Post synch was anathema. We might do it if we didn't like a performance but that happened very, very rarely.

Although episodes were dubbed in only two and a half days, Chris Burt considered the dialogue tracks to be of remarkable quality, which he attributed to developments in sound recording technology such as radio microphones as well as the skills of the sound mixer Tony Dawe, the boom operator Mike Silverlock and Ian Toynton the dubbing editor. The reason for departing from the procedure of using the recorded 'wild' track as a guide then post-synchronising the dialogue re-recorded by the cast was according to Chris Burt principally aesthetic: 'We were trying to get a really live sound to show the audience that these really were the streets we moved in.' There were of course distinct economic advantages in adopting this style: the post-production schedule was shorter and there was no need to re-engage or retain the cast for dubbing. Shooting in this way with portable lightweight 16mm equipment, utilising television documentary techniques, gave both the required look and sound

48

as well as the speed and flexibility needed to average five minutes of finished programme per day.

Towards the end of the second series of *Special Branch* production began on a series of individual films under the title *Armchair Cinema*. George Taylor:

> The idea was to get back to the single play. If it stood up in its own right, that was fine and quite exciting because after the original *Armchair Theatre* concept there just wasn't an envelope to put single plays in. And also it served the purpose of trying out pilots, which was marvellous.

In a profile of Lloyd Shirley in *Writers News*, Thames announced that: 'It was embarking on a new, exciting project called *Armchair Cinema* which would make thirteen 90-minute films for television.' When we spoke to Brian Tesler, he remembered planning an original slate of six, and in fact only six *Armchair Cinemas* were made. One of them struck gold: *Regan*, by Ian Kennedy-Martin, which spun into the very successful series *The Sweeney*. The first *Armchair Cinema* to be transmitted was *The Prison*, which was very successful as a single film, coming top of the ratings. It was adapted from a Georges Simenon novel by Geoffrey Gilbert who also produced the film and it was directed on location in London and Paris by David Wickes. George Taylor described other *Armchair Cinemas*:

> *Sea Song* was a one-off play and Peter Hammond directed that with Tom Bell and Kika Markham. It was about a round-the-world single-handed yacht race and she stowed away aboard his yacht . . . and the love affair between the two of them. We shot that down in Fowey in Cornwall. It was a splendid production but strictly a one-off. . . . We did a show called *When Day is Done* with Edward Woodward and that I believe we regarded as a one-off. It was about an out of work musician and directed by Reginald Collin. We also did one which we felt had series potential and I think it still has but it was never taken up. It was called *In Sickness and in Health* and it was about the plight of a doctor who had a social conscience and felt a responsibility to his National Health patients which conflicted with his family lifestyle. Our principal artist was Patrick Mower, Reginald Collin directed and John Kershaw wrote it. [John Kershaw also scripted *When Day is Done*.]

The final *Armchair Cinema* was *Tully*, about an Australian insurance investigator, intended as a pilot for a potential series. Shot on location in Australia, it was produced and directed by James Gatward. Although Euston was to return to the making of single films for television at a later

49

date, the decision was taken to discontinue the production of *Armchair Cinema* and to concentrate on the development of series.

Before examining the reasons for this decision and the development of *The Sweeney* we need to go back to the question of union relations and investigate a labour problem which interrupted the production of *Special Branch* and *The Prison*. Although it was resolved quite speedily in terms of Euston's activities, the issue involved was of major significance and its resolution had serious repercussions within the ACTT. The situation as regards film production in Britain and the official attitude and policy of the ACTT at this time has already been outlined. *Nationalising the Film Industry*, the report of the ACTT Nationalisation Forum, was published in August 1973 and since early that year the ACTT had been fighting the closure of Shepperton Studios. In late September EMI announced the impending closure of Elstree Studios. In October ACTT Head Office informed Euston of the Executive Committee's decision that their current productions had been blacked because of the allegedly unsafe and unhygienic conditions at Colet Court and at their Salvation Army Citadel location and that the productions should be made at EMI's Elstree Studios. What was in effect a dispute over 'four-waller' productions, part of the ACTT's attempt to combat casualisation, brought the growing dissent within the Film Production Branch to a head. Ted Childs gave us his account:

There was a strong feeling among the leadership of the Film Production Branch at ACTT – and I mean this was the elected leadership of course – that they should do all they could to prevent the final collapse of the old studio system in the UK. I can't remember what exactly had happened by then but I think that EMI had, or was in the process of, going four-wall, and that had left only Pinewood as the last mainstream studio with a mass of skilled and permanently employed labour. At the same time the Television Branch of the Union saw Euston Films, in their terms quite rightly, as the thin end of the wedge – it was Euston Films which worked on the basis of utilising the market for freelance labour and competitive rates for equipment hire. At the same time, from my point of view, and for all the people who were working for Euston, there we were left to our own devices, given a sum of money, and told right, go on, hire the cameras, hire the actors, write the scripts, go and make the movies. It was like something you dreamt about. There we were getting legless every night and having a marvellous time and thinking we were all wonderful, but out of that came a lot of group feeling. . . . What happened then was that – the union certainly didn't handle it very well – and

50

I'm not completely anti-union – but what happened was that we got a 'phone call on the switchboard at Colet Court saying you're blacked, and all the boys went bananas about this. So we got Les Wiles down, one of the Union organisers, and poor old Les was crucified. We brought the beer from the pub and we had a big conference in one of the rooms at Colet Court and then we led a deputation who fought their way into the Union Executive Committee meeting. Then there was a demonstration outside ACTT in Soho Square on the following Sunday, when the General Council were in session, where a lot of the actors and people who were involved with the show carried printed placards and so on. But what happened really was that it served as a catalyst, because then the whole movement started which was to change the nature of the leadership of the Film Production Branch of ACTT. . . .

I think what had happened was that a group of people had found their working environment was very exciting and interesting, and suddenly out of nowhere came this arbitrary decision to shut them down. Now the working conditions at Colet Court weren't marvellous compared with television but I mean they weren't that bad and, all right, there were a limited number of loos and they didn't always work but there was a pub over the road and we all got on very well, we enjoyed ourselves and we were left to our own devices and I think for a lot of people this more than off-set the fact that the conditions were not comparable with those in 206 Euston Road. To sum it up, I think the feeling was the union, ACTT, was supposed to preserve our employment prospects, not destroy them, as it seemed determined to do. But it became a political football, and out of that came the new order in the Film Production Branch – Robert Bolt became the chairman and so on. . . .

Ted Childs' recollection is substantially correct. The ACTT journal reported the Soho Square demonstration as taking place outside a General Council meeting at Head Office on 28 October. Three representatives of the Euston shop were allowed to put their case to the General Council and a resolution was carried allowing *Special Branch* to finish its schedule under Head Office surveillance of working conditions. Arising out of this opposition to the Union's position on 'four-waller' production, an Action Committee organised a special general meeting of the Film Production Branch and set vigorously about encouraging attendance. The meeting took place in Central Hall Westminster on 12 November and according to *Broadcast* was attended by 'nearly 2,000 members of the rank and file of ACTT's Film Branch, many of whom had never been to a union meeting in their lives before'. The ACTT journal reported the attendance as 'more than one thousand'. By all accounts the meeting was a stormy affair at which many of the Union's

51

film production policies were heavily criticised. Prominent in the moving and seconding of resolutions passed were Euston employees Chris Burt, Ian Toynton, Eamonn Duffy, John Maskall and Mike Silverlock. In fact it was Mike Silverlock and Stuart Freeman's motion that 'In the light of recent events which have caused considerable disquiet within the Freelance Shop, this meeting calls upon the Film Production Branch Committee to convene immediately a special meeting of the Freelance Shop under rule 21A to discuss the status of its chairman and committee' which when passed as a resolution took the revolt within the Union to its next stage. *Broadcast*'s coverage of the meeting (compiled from accounts by Union members – the press were not admitted) concluded:

> So: depoliticisation; no confidence in Branch representatives; a restriction on the ability of the Union to act without consulting its members; postal referenda and ballots; an implied rejection of the nationalisation policy; the end of the four-waller policy; a reaffirmation of the belief that film production is the primary objective of the film production industry; an instruction to the Union not to prevent production within the present agreements; and, perhaps the most important of all, a growing realisation on the part of previously inactive members that they can have a major influence on the way in which their Union operates. Not everything that the meeting wants to happen will happen, of course: that's the way of such things. But if the people who have now discovered their power over events maintain their enthusiasm and channel it into follow-up work, further meetings and work inside the Union structures, we can expect very real changes and new directions in the way the ACTT acts.
>
> Alan Sapper told *Broadcast* after the meeting that 'It was mainly an internal debate that emerged.' Not so. It was a debate which affected the whole future of both the film production and the television industries. (*Broadcast*, 16 November 1973)

In the ACTT journal General Secretary Alan Sapper performed a skilful balancing act, describing the conditions underlying the problem and the Union's pragmatic stance:

> When the anger and the shouting subside, most of the film production members at the Westminster Hall meeting will, I am sure, acknowledge two important facts. Firstly, that the problems in film production have emerged as a direct result of a very low level of membership participation in the decision-making structure of the union, and secondly, that a series of linked developments over the past three years have brought to a head the crisis in mainstream feature production.
>
> This time last year there were nineteen features in production: nine

studio-based and ten on location. This year there are only eight features being made. That's how much the situation has deteriorated in twelve short months. Look at the situation over a longer period and the position is even worse. Investment in features in the first six months of this year was £12.75 million, almost 45 per cent below the 1971 figure for the same period. Our studio resources, described by Robert Bolt at the Westminster Hall meeting as 'irreplaceable national assets', are poised on a knife edge. The NFFC, underfinanced and emasculated, has ceased to play any important part in providing capital for independent British production.

But television has continued to grow. In three years colour set sales have quintupled. The total number of sets in existence, thought to have reached saturation point in 1968, has grown by more than a million to 17.25 million in the past three years. Television is expansionary. Television is not starved of resources. Meeting the demands of extended hours has already placed a strain on existing TV studio resources. More and more film-makers are working in, or for, television.

We are now experiencing a deep historical shift in the nature, production and marketing of film material. Inevitably, that shift is creating great difficulties for our union. Our policies, our Agreements and our structure – and our employment and incomes – depend on the transition being carried through rationally and under union control. We cannot and should not discard the interests of studio-based technicians. Our proposed agreement on Shepperton shows what can be done to protect them. At the same time we must not, and should not, create irrational obstacles to film production, simply because it takes place outside the three major studios. Technological and aesthetic development has led to a massive increase in location filming. It is a vital part of our industry and we have *never* opposed it. (*Film and Television Technician*, November 1973)

The meeting to discuss the status of the Film Production Branch Chairman and Committee took place on 13 December at Camden Town Hall. This meeting was even rowdier than the previous one; Yvonne Richards was deposed as chair, to be replaced by Robert Bolt; some other new Committee members were elected but amidst fights and uproar further elections were postponed to a later meeting. Those elections took place at a meeting of the Freelance Shop on 3 January 1974 and elected to the new Committee were Euston regulars Chris Burt, Eamonn Duffy, Mike Silverlock and Douglas Camfield. The meeting also selected resolutions for the Union's Annual Conference including one lifting the ban on work in totalitarian or racist countries and another accepting 'four-waller' productions. Both resolutions were carried at the Annual Conference where Chris Burt was the mover of the resolution that:

53

The Conference accepts that the 'four-waller' type of production has proved itself to be a necessary and logical means of providing employment, maintaining and expanding British film production, also that the quality and quantity of future film productions, along with the interests of the majority of ACTT members, would be very seriously threatened if existing or potential producers were to be restricted in their choice of facilities. This Annual Conference believes that film production should be encouraged whenever and wherever possible, provided that current agreements and policies relating to pay and all working conditions are honoured.

He was also elected to the Executive Committee of the ACTT, on which he served for five years.

We asked ACTT Deputy General Secretary Roy Lockett about this upheaval within the Union and were told that at that time the very large Freelance Shop of the Union had become dominated by an inner core of Trotskyist activists broadly committed to the WRP. This they achieved by always attending meetings, always arguing and cultivating a nucleus of support. Though in many respects hard-working trades unionists, the political analysis of this group led them to care little about splits within the Union, for they felt that the labour movement could always be rebuilt from a principled nucleus. This attitude did not incline them to find ways of engaging the vast majority of freelance members, whose whole ethic was very 'laissez-faire' and individualistic, in union struggles and the making of policy:

What they were attempting to do was to graft a whole series of ideological objectives onto a union which couldn't even by and large get the freelancers to identify with the most basic union issues. So it was an enormous leap that caused a series of antagonisms. There was the policy on South Africa, there was the nationalisation policy, there were whole sets of issues on which the alienation got stronger and stronger. The Euston black crystallised it all and the backlash came.

Considering these events, Ted Childs felt that:

What that did in terms of Euston Films was weld us all very close together. The team working with me at the time were all freelance. There was no obligation to stay around, but it did bring us very close together and I think that was one of the factors which led – certainly during my involvement with them in the early days – to the kind of uniqueness and, within all its limitations, the quality of the product.

The year 1974 saw not only the changes within the Film Production Branch of ACTT described above but also important changes within the top management of Thames. Howard Thomas moved from his position of Managing Director to become Chairman of the Company and was replaced by George Cooper. Brian Tesler resigned from his position as Director of Programmes to take up the position of Deputy Chief Executive at London Weekend Television. The new Director of Programmes, Jeremy Isaacs, was not a former ABC Television executive but came instead from the Associated Rediffusion side of Thames with a background in factual television. These changes had important consequences for Euston Films. Jeremy Isaacs appointed Verity Lambert Controller of Drama and Lloyd Shirley became Head of Euston Films. Accompanied by George Taylor, Lloyd Shirley moved into Colet Court and from there they were able to devote all their energies to the running of their project. Both Lloyd Shirley and George Taylor were keen to pioneer the TV movie and had high hopes for the *Armchair Cinema* series which must have been bolstered by the ratings success of *The Prison*. By June 1974, however, with only four *Armchair Cinemas* completed and two transmitted, an article in *Cinema and TV Today* (22 June 1974) indicated that the future of this aspect of Euston's operation was in question. At a cost of around £85,000 each the films were expensive programme material and required a UK prime time slot and foreign sales to justify this expenditure. The films were not made primarily for an international market, however, and in terms of British television there was a scheduling problem. *News at Ten* was in a fixed slot and the IBA imposed a 9.00 pm 'watershed' between family and adult viewing. Unfortunately the films were in the latter category and usually ran for about ninety minutes. Brian Tesler had initially wanted action series *and* single films from Euston. The new Programme Controller Jeremy Isaacs just wanted a hit series:

> It was obvious that in the crime area if we could find the right people and the right sort of format that was perhaps the most useful thing Euston could do. . . . In other words, produce something on film by Euston that would have the same impact for Thames' ratings that *Callan* and *Public Eye* achieved and with that kind of integrity.

He got what he wanted with *The Sweeney*.

'THE SWEENEY'

When Euston Films produced *Regan* as an *Armchair Cinema* it was generally thought to have series potential but we doubt whether anyone could have predicted the success of its spin-off, *The Sweeney*. Thought by Jeremy Isaacs to have been 'one of the most successful series ever done

The Sweeney: John Thaw and Dennis Waterman.

for British television', *The Sweeney* ran through four series (fifty-three episodes in all) and generated two feature films. It provided Thames with a 'banker', a surefire ratings success which could in a sense buy the right to take chances with other productions. Verity Lambert joined Thames as Controller of Drama shortly before the transmission of the first series of *The Sweeney*:

> Which was, I have to say, an extremely good thing for me because it was so successful and so popular it did allow me the freedom to make things like *Rock Follies* and *Bill Brand* which were somewhat more chancy. So that was always a terrific back up.

Ted Childs produced *Regan* and all the series of *The Sweeney*; he told us:

> Lloyd had a property which Ian Kennedy-Martin had written as a tape show. It came with John Thaw and was basically about a maverick policeman. I think it was called *The Outcasts*. That was the time Robert Mark was coming into the Metropolitan Police – I don't know if he'd actually arrived but he was certainly on his way – and the idea was, as actually happened, that a new order was being established in the management of the London Police and a lot of coppers didn't like it. It was an interesting area to talk about.

George Taylor:

I think Ian came to us with an idea about the 'Sweeney' and Regan, this particular classic copper, old type cop, a loner who bends the rules, and so we commissioned the ninety-minute script and that was *Regan*. . . . When it was transmitted it was certainly in the top ten, if not number one, and we knew immediately that we had got potential. The casting was right – John Thaw and Dennis Waterman as a duo seemed to work very well – so we said right we'll have a go and we'll try thirteen.

Ted Childs and Ian Kennedy-Martin began work on developing the series but found they held conflicting views on the direction it should take. Finally, it was Ted Childs' concept which prevailed and Ian Kennedy-Martin left the series. Ted Childs:

We had lots of fights about how it should be done, there is no denying that. I felt very strongly that we ought to pioneer a film technique rather than a tape studio production technique. So what we really had to do was evolve a format where we exploited our advantages and obviated our disadvantages. I mean, given that we had to make these films in ten working days normally, and shoot five minutes a day, there were things we were very good at in comparison with a tape production in the TV studio – they were action and two-handed dialogue on the run. What we weren't good at were courtroom scenes and massive dinner parties because we had no rehearsal time. . . . I more or less got my own way and I wasn't alone in seeking it. I certainly had the support of people like Chris Burt, Ian Toynton, Tom Clegg (who directed *Regan*) and Terry Green. It was then that I sensed that *The Sweeney* was something over which I was going to have control, so I began to look for writers who would do what we felt as a group we wanted to do. I think Troy [Kennedy-Martin] was the definitive *Sweeney* writer because it was a logical development from the things he and John McGrath were doing on *Z Cars* before. He and Trevor [Preston] established how it would go in terms of script but there were other people who made a valid contribution to the look. Roger Marshall and, latterly, Tony Hoare were also important writers.

During the time spent on preparation for production of *The Sweeney*, Euston acquired the services of a retired police officer as an official adviser. Suggested by a nervous Scotland Yard, the idea of an adviser was resisted at first but finally accepted when Ted Childs and Ian Kennedy-Martin were able to nominate someone of their choosing. A format for the series was written by Ted Childs principally as a briefing document for writers. Its function was to familiarise writers with the parameters

57

of the series and establish characters so as to ensure that scripts were kept as simple as possible in production management terms. The format, which is reproduced in full below, provides insights into the ways in which the conditions of production determine the programmes produced.

This is a series of one-hour films featuring two detectives who work in the Flying Squad, the elite crime investigation unit of the Metropolitan Police.

The title *The Sweeney* is derived from Cockney rhyming slang 'The Sweeney Todd' i.e. The Flying Squad. It is a vernacular term used by both criminals and police.

The Flying Squad came into being during the 20s when criminals began to use motor cars. Then, as now, the majority of all crime detection within the Metropolitan Police district was handled by C I D units at divisional level. The Flying Squad was formed to transcend divisional boundaries in the effective pursuit of mobile criminals. At present the Flying Squad consists of some 150 detectives, headed by a Senior Officer of Commander rank. The operation element of the Squad consists of 4 units each commanded by a Detective Chief Inspector. Within each unit there are two Detective Inspectors each commanding two Detective Sergeants and a varying number of Detective Constables. A small number of women detectives work within the Squad.

The Squad's main task is to prevent major crime by establishing very thorough networks of intelligence within the criminal fraternity. The Flying Squad hope that if they cannot prevent a crime their specialist knowledge will enable them to arrest the people who perpetrated it fairly quickly. The Squad itself relates with the other senior crime detection units which have subsequently been formed within Scotland Yard, e.g. Serious Crime Squad, the Regional Crime Squad, the Robbery Squad, the Fraud Squad, the Drug Squad and latterly, the Bomb Squad.

The candidates for the Flying Squad are normally selected from C I D personnel at Divisional level who have shown particular prowess. Of course, it is possible for a detective to be selected from a Division, to serve in the Flying Squad, to return to a Divisional appointment upon promotion and subsequently to rejoin the Flying Squad at a later date.

The term Flying Squad derived from the fact that the unit was originally equipped with a fleet of sports cars co-ordinated by wireless telegraphy. This was one of the first attempts in Britain to apply radio control techniques to police work. High mobility is still a feature of Flying Squad operations. The Squad is still equipped with high performance cars, normally within the 2½ to 3 litre range.

One interesting feature of the Squad's operations is that its detectives do not normally drive themselves. Each car is driven by a 'driver'. These drivers are not detectives but expert Traffic Division constables. They are seconded to the Flying Squad to work in plain clothes. Drivers do not undertake detective work *per se* although as police constables they may well assist with arrests, etc.

The overall episode screen time (ex. titles) is 48.40. We expect the final draft script to read at about 53 minutes. Each film will open with a teaser of up to

3 minutes duration, which is followed by the opening titles. The story is played across three acts, each of which must be no more than 19 and not less than 8 minutes in length.

The two running characters are Detective Inspector Jack Regan and Detective Sergeant Carter. Regan will appear in every episode, Carter will appear in approximately 10 out of 13 episodes. In addition to these running characters, each script should be built around three major speaking parts with up to ten minor speaking parts.

Experience indicates that within this film format, it is better to provide a small number of major parts which attract leading actors and actresses rather than a cycle of cameos which are difficult to cast. Few players of ability are interested in a one-page scene.

Each film is shot over ten days. We must, therefore, shoot an average of five minutes edited screentime a day. This means we have to impose restrictions on the number of locations we use. Normally ten locations, i.e. one per shooting day, is enough. By location we mean an area in which a number of scenes can be shot. For example, a school or college (during holidays) affords us a variety of interesting locations – chapels, classrooms, laboratories as well as extensive grounds and does not necessitate the uneconomic use of the film unit's time. The more time we spend loading and unloading vehicles and driving around London, the less time, within the ten days, we have to actually make a film.

There is one standing composite set at Colet Court, which provides our weather cover option. This is a representation of the Flying Squad offices at Scotland Yard. It consists of a large open plan office, part of which is referred to as the Squad office and contains the desks at which the detective inspectors sit, and another section called the Reserve Room, in which detective sergeants and below congregate when not on outside duty. The set also contains the switchboard and radio transmitter which serves the particular needs of the Flying Squad. In addition, there are two other smaller offices which can serve as offices for more senior officers, as interview rooms, etc. There is also a corridor area adjoining this set with lifts, staircase, entrances, etc. (see accompanying plan).

We normally schedule two days in the ten week shooting cycle in the office composite set. This means we anticipate ten minutes of any film being set within these Scotland Yard offices.

Since we are shooting through the summer months, exterior night shooting is very expensive for us to undertake and we cannot normally anticipate more than three minutes exterior night material in any script. Interior night scenes are not normally difficult to contrive.

The series is set in London and we do not propose to take our unit on journeys of more than one hour's driving time from our base in Hammersmith.

We would point out that some locations that appear to offer attractive possibilities can present difficulties. For example, London Transport, although prepared to allow us to hire buses, will not normally let us film any material which relates to fictitious criminal events on its property or its railway trains. British Rail is more obliging although one is usually restricted to off-peak time in the Greater London area.

Although we can obtain film facilities from airports such as Heathrow and Luton, the authorities insist that operational requirements take priority. This means they can cancel a location booking at the last moment and cause us con-

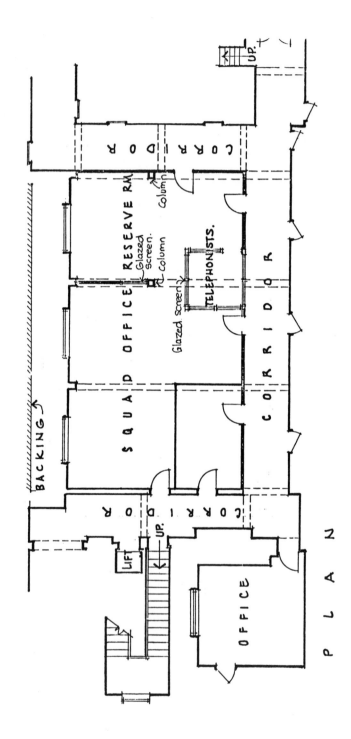

FLYING SQUAD OFFICE COMPOSITE

PLAN

60

siderable embarrassment. We do not, therefore, usually entertain such locations.

Nor can we obtain facilities from the Metropolitan Police. Under certain circumstances they will allow us to film people and cars leaving and entering police stations and Scotland Yard. However, we must give them considerable notice of any such intention.

Similarly, it is not possible to film interiors of H.M. prisons or any other Home Office properties which relate to the police service or the law courts. The police will not normally allow us to stage crime in public thoroughfares. It is best if we plan shootings, hold-ups, etc. for staging on private property.

In general writers should not be too specific when delimiting locations. Where names are vital to the plot it is wise to use totally fictitious names which can be quickly approved by our legal representatives before we proceed with filming. A quick glance at the Yellow Pages will often indicate whether a business or trade is being practised under the name a writer intends to use.

This series is based on the use of a film unit which moves very quickly across a number of locations. The nature of our film operation itself very much determines the style of our films. In general terms, we can cope with action more readily than we can with multi-handed dialogue. Unlike television, where extensive rehearsal facilities and the use of several cameras for any given scene enable fairly complicated sequences involving several actors to be staged quite easily, we have to light every shot individually for one camera. Also we cannot enjoy the luxury of extensive rehearsal. This makes complicated dialogue comparatively difficult for us.

On the other hand, the mobility of our equipment and the sophistication of our editing and dubbing techniques allow us to produce action sequences which can attain a considerable degree of pace and excitement. This is not to say that we do not need good dialogue in our scripts. Clearly an investigatory police thriller does depend, to no small extent, on good dialogue but in general terms it is better to write uncomplicated story lines which deal straightforwardly with crime and criminals where dialogue scenes are short and sharp rather than intriguing. [. . . .]

However, when talking of action, it must be made clear that we are not in the 'Bondiana' league. We can cope with a limited number of fight scenes, car chases, shoot-outs, etc. We cannot blow up 'Jablite' representations of St. Paul's nor bring the whole of Oxford Street to a grinding halt in order to wreck three police cars inside Selfridges' front window!

Major crime is very often violent and one does not wish to flinch from the reality of this. Nonetheless, the series is being produced for transmission in both afternoon and evening family viewing hours. Accordingly, we must respect the rules laid down by the IBA in respect of language and the detailed description of pathological forms of behaviour. Four-letter words are not permissible, nor can we indulge in 'souped up' horror, e.g. represent, in slow motion, a security guard having his head blown off by a shotgun.

Action, within our brief, does not mean continual violence. With the techniques at our disposal, it is possible to show characters in a variety of interesting real situations, where movement and action serve to underline the pace and style of cinematic story telling based on short dialogue scenes. This is the particular style we are trying to set.

The Sweeney: 'we can cope with action . . . '

The main character in 'The Sweeney' is Detective Inspector Jack Regan (36), a tough, resourceful detective who is to be played by John Thaw. Regan has been a policeman since he came to London from Manchester when he was 22. He served the statutory 2 years as a probationary police constable then applied to join the CID. He served as a temporary detective constable and following this was made up to substantive detective constable and served within a division as a CID officer until he was promoted Sergeant and transferred to the Flying Squad. Following his promotion to Detective Inspector, he worked within a divisional unit once again before returning to Flying Squad where he has been for the past four years.

Regan is the 'total professional', a 24-hours-a-day cop. His commitment to his career led to the break-up of his marriage. He is divorced but visits his eight year old daughter fairly regularly. His ex-wife is now preparing to re-marry. Regan finds it difficult to develop lasting emotional relationships with people. With women he is prone to casualness, although not promiscuity. He is proud of the Flying Squad and its reputation. Like most Squad officers, he enjoys the considerable freedom the work pattern affords. This is one reason why he has not actively pursued promotion since this would probably result in his transfer. Regan is contemptuous of the formality and bureaucracy which characterises much of the police service. His casual style of dressing is one of his methods of articulating this resentment.

His basic philosophy is 'Don't bother me with forms and procedures, let me get out there and nick villains'. He fears the current developments taking place within the Metropolitan Police Criminal Investigation Department. Attempts are being made to rationalise the work of the department. A number of specialist crime fighting units have been formed at Scotland Yard in recent years – the Serious Crimes Squad and the Robbery Squad. With the freedom of action that top detective work demands, it has been difficult to prevent a measure of 'empire building' and it is often alleged that the different squads are inefficient – and ineffectively covering the same ground and wasting too much time in conflicts engendered by in-house politics.

For story purposes, we are assuming that an amalgamation of the various 'top squads' is being enacted. With some justification Regan fears his wings are about to be clipped. The new top detective is likely to be much more an 'organisation man' working through committee and much more heavily dependent on specialist forensic and other services.

Regan has been a successful detective. He has made his name by being very much 'his own man'. Intuitive, with a keen understanding of human nature, he can appear an emotive, mercurial man. He will sometimes pursue criminals with a degree of ruthlessness which can shock people used to seeing him as a cynically humorous but compassionate human being.

Regan, then, is a good detective but a man approaching middle age whose fears for his own emotional stability and long-term job security sometimes float to the surface.

It is against the background of the life and times of a particular policeman dealing day to day with major crime in a modern city that the series is to be set.

Regan works regularly with a subordinate with whom he enjoys a very good relationship. Detective Sergeant George Carter (26) is a tough, sharp Cockney who hails from Notting Hill. A working-class lad on the make. Were it not for the fact that a concerned school teacher had instilled in him notions of public service, he might have ended up 'on the other side'. Several of his school friends have. A keen sportsman, a former amateur boxing champion, he maximised use of the extensive sporting facilities which are available to young policemen. By chance he found he had a natural detective skill and was eventually offered an appointment within the Flying Squad. He admires Regan very much and enjoys working with him, although they often argue over detailed methods of approach and styles of working.

Carter is now in the Flying Squad for the second time. He returned to the more staid life of a Divisional detective after he married. His wife – a secondary school teacher with ambitions – realised that promotion and a stable marriage are unlikely to come the way of a young Flying Squad detective, particularly one who has fallen under Regan's charismatic influence. Mrs Carter believes her husband should endeavour to climb on to the promotional 'gravy train' the CID amalgamation has engendered instead of hanging round pubs and clubs with informants. She feels her husband would be better employed studying for promotion examinations and indulging in that measure of sycophantic behaviour necessary for advancement in any highly structured organisation.

Carter argues that his return to the Flying Squad will offer him the most likely chance of appointment to a higher rank. His wife remains unconvinced and Carter does run into trouble from time to time. His standing excuse is that if he comes home that particular night he might miss the big break which will lead to his promotion. The argument is wearing thin.

There is to be one more running character, Chief Detective Inspector Thomas Laker. Laker is Regan's immediate boss. At 32, Laker is young for the middle management of the Flying Squad. He is very much the 'bright young man' on the way up, the epitome of the new, technocratic, computerised Scotland Yard detective. A determined careerist who sees the changing situation within the CID affording an ideal opportunity for accelerated advancement.

Laker is from a lower middle-class, London suburban background. Grammar school (with two 'A' levels); he joined the Metropolitan Police after he failed to gain entry to Sandhurst. After quick transfer to CID he was selected for the 'Special' (High Flyers) Course at the National Police College. He then made a name for himself in the Serious Crimes Squad, was promoted to CID and re-assigned to the Flying Squad as part of the new amalgamation.

Laker is the antithesis of Regan. Cold and detached, he has none of Regan's intuitive understanding of crime and criminals. He believes in the firm application of logic and method. Given enough time to check and analyse the available data, most crimes can be solved, claims Laker. Unfortunately, for Regan, Laker's method will often work. It may be more expensive and less exciting than Regan's way, but it does maximise the use of mediocre police talent and has enormous PR value for the public and, not least of all, the criminal fraternity.

Nonetheless, Laker knows that, in being placed over Regan, he is being tested for the next rung of the promotion ladder. To make Superintendent, Laker has to show he can handle the awkward but necessary mavericks of the Force. Regan knows the rules. He cannot openly defy Laker in matters of discipline, but he persistently avoids following in the detective methods Laker advocates. Regan has an almost ideological commitment to his hunchy, intuitive method of work. Win, lose or draw, Regan is not going to concede to Laker on that.

Laker is determined to avoid abrasive confrontations. In consequence, the conflict is conducted on a variety of levels, often quite subtly.

Laker is tall, well-dressed, austere. Regan is short, scruffy, outspoken and extrovert. Laker is articulate with intellectual pretensions. Regan is idiomatic, at times coarse. Although Regan is a man of warmth and humanity, his private life is in ruins. Laker is cold and opportunistic but has all the appurtenances of a happy home life; a wife (he married well: the horse-faced daughter of a wealthy chartered accountant who is a Tory county councillor), two plain daughters and a modern detached house in Pinner.

Laker attempts to turn Carter from Regan (yet another fighting for Carter's soul). Laker offers the carrot of easy advancement for 'safe' men and the stick of professional failure for those who aid and abet Regan. Carter is conscious of the validity of Laker's exhortations but cannot bring himself to be disloyal to Regan.

The detectives of the Flying Squad are in the business of preventing major crime. For much of their information about developments in the underworld they depend on informants and being around locales where suitable intelligence can be culled. From time to time they are formed into larger units to deal with particular crimes but normally their brief is to be out around town finding out what is going on.

Their main concern is major crime, usually forms of robbery, including any-

64

thing from hold-ups to hijacks. To an increasing extent they are becoming involved with 'organised' crime, where the proceeds of one crime are used to finance other crimes in addition to apparently legitimate enterprises.

EUSTON GETS INTO ITS STRIDE

Trevor Preston scripted 'Ringer', the first *Sweeney* episode to be transmitted, and recalled that it was written and produced in great haste. The departure of Ian Kennedy-Martin at a relatively advanced stage of pre-production meant that the commissioning of scripts had to be done rather swiftly in order to keep to the planned production schedule, itself determined by the transmission slot allocated to the series.

As producer of the series, Ted Childs was particularly involved with the scripting of *Sweeney* episodes:

> . . . really, not letting writers overreach themselves, which is why I did that bible [the format] very early on. I mean, my philosophy was, let us do what we can do within the economic and time constraints as well as we can.

Trevor Preston was sympathetic to this perspective and enjoyed working on the series:

> Ted gave me the *Sweeney* format, the do's and don'ts, and briefed me, because you have to be objective about writing, you mustn't go beyond the parameters they give you because they are budgeting on those parameters. . . . You got a month to write a script on contract but it was a tacit understanding that you got it in as quickly as you could. The quickest time I wrote a *Sweeney* in was three days; on average you could write a *Sweeney* in seven to ten days. Ted used to make suggestions about areas not yet covered but he didn't do that often. He never cramped you as a writer. You used to sit with him for an hour or two and sort it all out. . . . Ted tried to use a lot of writers and introduce a lot of new writers but after a while the machine was going at such a lick that if you came in on it as a new writer it belted you sideways. You couldn't on *The Sweeney* go to third and fourth drafts, no way, it was on the street already. Second drafts were a bit frowned on. . . . Ted and I got on very well. He had this marvellous thing of trying to pair up writers with directors, not all the time, but I did a couple with Terry Green. If you knew the director well you knew his strengths and his weaknesses and you could actually write for the director. I really must say that as a writer I've never looked forward so much to going to work as I did on *The Sweeney*.

The eight and a half week production schedule for each *Sweeney*

65

episode was essentially the same as that established for *Special Branch*, i.e. two weeks pre-production (principally casting and finding locations), two weeks shooting, four weeks picture editing (the first two weeks of which overlap with the shoot), two weeks sound editing and two and a half days dubbing. Once the scripts were in, Ted Childs explained, much of his time was spent 'just making the schedule work. I had some good production managers and George Taylor was always there and production and post-production were his forte.' In fact, Ted Childs also wrote and directed some episodes.

In terms of style there was a continuation of the *vérité* documentary techniques of *Special Branch* but there was some hostility from the IBA about the technical quality in the early days. For this reason, and the technical reason of not having lenses fast enough to shoot in low light levels, *The Sweeney* was felt not to be gritty or grainy enough by the production team. Ted Childs:

> We weren't using zooms enough, we were using fixed lenses. They didn't have the super speed lenses then, so we were constrained and I think a lot of it looks much prettier than it should but that was because the quality control people at the IBA insisted that 16mm wouldn't work in drama.

The first series of *The Sweeney* firmly established that a distinctive 'parochial police show' could be efficiently produced on film and enjoy very high audience ratings. For Jeremy Isaacs, Euston Films had found its metier. Whereas further series of *The Sweeney* would be produced, the policy of producing 90-minute *Armchair Cinemas* was suspended. Jeremy Isaacs recalled that it was a unanimous decision of the Euston Board, of which he was a member, not to proceed further with the 90-minute films:

> Howard Thomas had got it into his head that *Armchair Cinema* was a winning title and that was it. It wasn't thought through much beyond that. Now had the first three or four films been marvellous, then that would have stuck but since none of them was frightfully good and one or two of them were only pilots for series it seemed like the honest thing to do was to make series.

A second series of *The Sweeney* was rapidly put into production and proved even more successful than the first. Following on production of series two of *The Sweeney*, the decision was taken to produce a Sweeney film for cinema release. This was produced by Euston Films in partnership with EMI and thus guaranteed a UK release through the EMI-owned ABC cinema chain. Ted Childs was the film's producer and Lloyd Shirley and George Taylor the executive producers. Ted Childs:

Well, Nat Cohen's [of EMI] view of this was, 'Well, you boys do a very good job, you get them round the telly on a Monday night, but what are you going to do that will get people to put their raincoats on and go out on a wet night to spend a pound or so to see the film?' We had no answer for that, but we had a feeling that it might work. There were lots of misgivings about the first script because we were under strong pressure to try to make the Sweeney film different. Now, the purists will argue that the first Sweeney film was very unreal because it was not within the genre that had become established, and that was true because we were under pressure to make a film that people would pay to see not only in the UK but elsewhere. But it worked well. It was the same crew. We had 35mm cameras this time. This was the only difference, and it was in the main all the technicians who had always worked on the TV series.

The feature film, *Sweeney!*, was shot on location in London over five weeks during the spring of 1976. The film's director, David Wickes, in an article in *Screen International*, also stressed the attempts to distinguish the film from the TV series:

What we are hoping to produce is something which will inevitably be compared with *The French Connection*, inevitably compared with the best cinematic cop thriller films.

The same article reported that:

Sweeney! – for which Thames is putting up the majority of the £1.4 million budget, in partnership with EMI – marks Euston's feature debut. And in the event of independent television involving itself heavily in feature production – in line with the Working Party's proposals on the matter – it could prove a significant one.

The observation about the recommendations of the Working Party on the British Film Industry is an interesting one and could partly explain why Thames' diversification into feature film production in partnership with a branch of one of its parent companies was not frowned upon by the IBA. The film was successfully released in the UK immediately following the second series of *The Sweeney*. Perhaps it was felt that if the film was successful abroad, especially in the United States, it could pave the way for sales of the TV series.

Sweeney! the feature film was followed by a third TV series, then finally a fourth series, another feature film *Sweeney II* and a Sweeney 'special' with guest stars Eric Morecambe and Ernie Wise. George Taylor explained the basis for the 'special':

The Sweeney had become so popular they [Morecambe and Wise] invited John and Dennis onto one of their programmes for one of their
skits and of course it was a natural for us to invite them. It was fun.
I don't know if it actually worked or was in keeping with what *The
Sweeney* was expected to be, but it was fun to do and very successful.

During production of all *The Sweeney* series and the two feature films
there was a large degree of continuity in terms of technicians, writers
and directors. The existence of a Sweeney team was something a number
of people commented upon. Ted Childs:

> You get a group of people together who are good at their job and keen
> to do well and you get very good relationships. For the four years that
> I was involved with *The Sweeney* on and off, it wasn't with the same
> people *all* the time but the majority of the technicians who worked
> on the show were the same people and of course we all became very
> close and very friendly, like the crew of a small ship. This is unlike
> a television company, where people come and go because they are
> working to a certain schedule – you know, it's his day off today and
> so on – and you don't necessarily get the people you want because
> they have got forty sound recordists, or whatever it is, and you can't
> have the one you want on the day you want him.

Trevor Preston also mentioned the feeling of co-operation and esprit
amongst the members of the unit:

> In all those years we worked on *The Sweeney*, Roger [Marshall], Troy
> [Kennedy-Martin] and I, it's all we ever did, we didn't need to do
> anything else, it was well paid and it gave us security. The writers
> all used to talk to each other and we were influenced by Dennis
> [Waterman] and John [Thaw]. They had an influence on the script
> and the other actors. One of the reasons it was such a happy crew
> was down to them – they were really fantastic.

It was stressed to us on numerous occasions that the continuity of employment over a whole series or even a number of series led to a co-operative team spirit within the unit. The informality of relations and the arduous conditions of production helped to compound a sense of involvement and commitment in crews who, although freelance, identified
strongly with the company and its productions.

This aspect of freelance working is rather contradictory in that, although there is little or no job security, employees feel a strong sense of
involvement in productions and less alienation in the selling of their
labour. It was also suggested to us that freelance technicians choose to
be freelance, which means permanently casualised, for advantages in re-
68

lation to tax liabilities and for the freedom of being able to choose which productions they worked on. Jeremy Isaacs:

> They want the tax advantages of being freelance, they want the choice advantages of being freelance – I will do this, I won't do that – they want the kind of excitement and camaraderie of the work style of coming together to make a production feeling that they have made a huge and wonderful contribution because they made it, they made all of it. And when it's over they have a drink and a couple of weeks off and then they go off and do something else.

From the point of view of the employer, both sides of the contradictory position of freelance workers are advantageous. Jeremy Isaacs again:

> The crew are working on a production they feel a commitment to and secondly they want to work on the next series, and since they don't know where the next job is coming from they are keen to work hard and well.

THE 'VAN DER VALK' AFFAIR

These issues of job satisfaction and job security, or the lack of it, were to surface in a labour dispute over *Van der Valk*, Euston's next production. Nicholas Freeling's Dutch detective, Van der Valk, had already been developed as a television series by Thames' drama department with Barry Foster as the eponymous hero. In fact, there had been two series produced in the Thames studios at Teddington with filmed inserts shot on location in Amsterdam. In some respects it seemed a natural choice for Euston: like *Special Branch* before it, *Van der Valk* had demonstrated itself to be viable and, because of the exotic potential of Amsterdam locations, was a suitable subject for an all-film production.

Chris Burt, formerly Euston's supervising editor, was associate producer on *Van der Valk*:

> The problem with *Van der Valk* was that it went off at half cock because it was going very smoothly then there was a major hiccup which set it back and all the energies of the production team and everybody else went into just ensuring that it would be done. Then we suddenly had the go ahead and we had to go *then* and the scripts got behind and everything else got behind so it didn't have the sort of smooth run up it should have had or the real sort of location finding it needed.

The 'major hiccup' over *Van der Valk* was, like the problem over *Special Branch,* an intra-union row. This time the objection to Euston's activities came not from the Film Production Branch of ACTT but from ACTT

Television Branch members and EEPTU members from the Thames union shops.

Although the *Van der Valk* dispute was underplayed by some of those we spoke to, it was a particular manifestation of fundamental problems within the industry and therefore rather serious. The issues involved may have been settled in such a way as to allow the series to proceed but the factors producing those issues continue to generate disputes elsewhere. A fairly detailed account of the *Van der Valk* affair appeared in *Broadcast* magazine:

Thames Television has had to write off up to £150,000 in pre-production investment – and yet another split between the casualised members of Film Branch and their permanently employed fellow-members in Television Branch of the ACTT is looming large following the cancellation last week of Thames' order to its subsidiary Euston Films for a series of 13 hours of the *Van der Valk* action/adventure series planned for autumn production.

Prime cause of the cancellation was the insistence of members of the Electrical, Electronic and Plumbing Trades Union (EEPTU) employed by Thames under the ITCA agreement that they should work on the series, which was to have been made by Euston Films under the FPA film production agreement.

But an action committee elected by ACTT and NATTKE members employed at Euston Films itself has accused Television Branch shops of those and other unions of 'maintaining strong pressure on their respective union leaders in an endeavour to make film technicians redundant in order that they may have their jobs for themselves.' An action committee statement issued on Wednesday last week said that 'in an illogical drive to protect their already secure jobs, television technicians seem bent on preventing film productions when their studios already have more work than they can handle', suggesting that ACTT and NATTKE staff shops had attempted to prevent the transfer of the *Van der Valk* property from production within the ITCA agreement at Teddington, as in the first series, to Euston Films and the FPA agreement.

So the statement, drafted by Euston staffer David Wickes as elected spokesman, seems set to inflame once again the hostility between the casualised workers in Film Branch and permanent staff, to put union solidarity further to the test and to make ITV managements think very hard before investing further in the needy film production industry.

It is, in fact, true that the ACTT shop at Thames Euston had raised objections to the transfer of *Van der Valk* from Thames and the ITCA agreement to Euston Films and FPA production. But shop members there point out that this was by no means motivated by a desire to

70

Van der Valk: Barry Foster as the Dutch detective. Note the blimped camera: 'post-synch was anathema'.

deny work to film branch members. The reason why the question came up – it in fact reached Stage 2 dispute level – was because the Euston shop felt that management had not consulted in the usual way with the union over its intention to alter the status quo over *Van der Valk.* Assurances were sought from management – and given – that full consultation would be undertaken on further issues of this kind, management noted that staff members did not want all the creative, interesting and prestigious production to move outside of the company's walls, and so the objections to F P A production of the series were withdrawn.

Only the E E P T U remained adamant that its members should work on the show under I T C A conditions and payments; and Thames took the view that mixed crewing was an unacceptable method of working as well as a complex and possibly dangerous precedent. So on Friday the company issued provisional notice that it would cancel the series anyway. This, the company admits frankly, was a piece of brinkmanship. It was not unaware that A C T T general secretary Alan Sapper was due back from his holiday the following Monday, and knowing his views on the need to stimulate work in the Film Branch area, it

71

hoped that internal union activity as well as Sapper's representations to the EEPTU at Federation of Broadcasting Unions level would result in a backdown by the EEPTU. The ploy did not work; electricians' leader Frank Chapple declined to instruct his members to change their position, and in fact on Tuesday night the Thames EEPTU shop 'withdrew all concessions' it had already made on the *Van der Valk* issue.

On Wednesday night, therefore, Thames issued a formal statement to staff and Press that it had cancelled *Van der Valk*. The implications of the decision were made clear. Over 50 FPA jobs, many of them lasting a year, would not now be available. 200 work opportunities for Equity actors would be lost. Up to 2,000 FAA (walk-on) parts would be lost (this somewhat high figure is suggested by the Euston Films union action group) and the support industries, notably the British labs, would lose a bunch of work. In *Broadcast's* estimate, an investment of £700,000 in film production would be lost, and Thames would have to write off between £120,000 and £150,000 in production money on the series. (*Broadcast*, 30 August 1976)

Finally, after protests, petitions to the Prime Minister and negotiations between the unions, the EEPTU members withdrew their demands and the dispute was settled. *Van der Valk* went into production 3½ weeks behind schedule. Jeremy Isaacs:

Van der Valk was a mistake really, in the sense that it should either have been done on film from the word go through Euston or it should have been kept in the studio at Teddington with film inserts. . . . The freelance shop demonstrated, I think very importantly, for the right to be allowed to continue to work on the series for an ITV company. But when I became Director of Programmes an absolutely crucial thing that I had to do – I thought it was a sensible policy thing to do – was to be able to assure Teddington and all the people there who wanted to work on high quality drama that they would not suffer by the existence of Euston Films. I was lucky enough to be able to say there will be a certain amount of work which we are going to do through Euston, and you have to reconcile yourselves to that, but the quality of drama that is done at Teddington will be as high a quality as I can make it. To their very great credit it was quality and ambition that they were interested in. They wanted to know that in different ways and in different parts of the company we were going to do quality work. . . . One had to be able to say to Teddington not only will the quality of work done on video in the studios extend your abilities but also there will be some work done on film and wholly on film from Teddington, and so *The Naked Civil Servant* for example was done not through Euston Films but as a Teddington drama production.

We were told that the *Van der Valk* dispute was settled amiably enough with a commitment from Thames management to consult the Thames union shops about future Euston Films productions, thus allaying fears about the film subsidiary hiving off work, and also a commitment from Thames management to the production of prestigious and demanding work, some of it on film under the ITCA agreement, by the Thames drama department. Nevertheless, fears and suspicion continued. A sardonic item in the November 1976 issue of the ACTT journal offering a 'steward's eye view of television' reported on the resolution of the *Van der Valk* issue in terms that left no doubt of the strong feelings, amounting on the part of some to bitterness, that the solution of the immediate problem had not dissolved.

The difficulty of the ACTT's position and the contradictory demands made upon the Union in disputes like the one over *Van der Valk* were described by Roy Lockett:

> The interface between permanent employed and freelancing is never in equilibrium; it's always very dynamic because to enhance the permanent employment of people inevitably means inhibiting opportunities for employment for freelance people. And to extend the opportunities for freelance people means to threaten permanent employment. So there is no permanent equilibrium there and it's a very serious issue. It's not something that can be explained by people being silly; it's a fundamental problem. . . . These are real issues; they are not simple; they are about the economics of the industry and about profoundly different attitudes towards work and employment on the part of permanently employed people and freelance people. Our job is to maximise the opportunities and the security and earning capacity of both sides while attempting to keep some sort of equilibrium and it's very hard indeed.

Despite the initial union problems and a complicated production schedule, work on *Van der Valk* progressed efficiently during the twenty-six week shoot. Episodes were shot two at a time, alternating two weeks in England and two weeks in Amsterdam. On transmission the series was popular with audiences but to the disappointment of fans and Barry Foster (the star) no further series were produced.

In addition to being at the centre of a union dispute *Van der Valk* also marked a change in the management of Euston Films. The series was the first to be produced for Euston Films by Lloyd Shirley and George Taylor in a freelance capacity, both having resigned from the Company and vacated their seats on the Board. They explained to us their reasons for doing so. Lloyd Shirley:

> In setting up Euston, Tesler and Thomas said that if it worked then

73

they could make product not only for Thames but for anybody else, here or abroad. And the carrot was that if it worked we would all get a share of the action and that seemed to us kind of interesting and a challenge. After two or three years Thomas went from being Managing Director to Chairman of the Company and George Cooper came in, Brian resigned and went to LWT and Jeremy Isaacs came in as Director of Programmes. Now Isaacs and Cooper didn't see Euston quite in the way that Tesler and Thomas saw it. So instead of it being a company which could expand in any way we could make it, bearing in mind that the first responsibility would be to Thames as its owner, they said no, it's got to be tied strictly to Thames. So after a few months George and I approached them and said, 'look would you mind if under these conditions, without any bad will, we resign? Because this isn't what we wanted to do. We understand your position but hopefully you will understand ours and we don't want to be restricted in that way.' They were a bit upset by that and it went back and forth a bit but finally they said 'well, all right, but on condition that you accept a rolling contract from us to make stuff', which was quite practicable and at that time translated into being freelance producers contracted to Euston for specific projects but no longer with an executive function and no longer executive directors which we were originally.

George Taylor:

It was intended to run it as a company within its own right, producing its own profit but when Brian Tesler left and George Cooper came in I think they felt it should go in a slightly different direction, as a feeder to Thames. I think a number of things came into that, including the possible union situation so that if it was a true feeder, in the sense of an over-supply, then it would be better if it wasn't profit-making but just fed the material back through Thames' input. So Lloyd and I continued with them but we felt that as we had both held positions within Thames – Lloyd as Head of Drama and myself as Head of Film – and we had left those positions to work full time for Euston and join the Board and as the original objectives had changed, we felt that we ought to change our direction. So we then resigned from Euston and both went freelance, but amicably agreed with the board to complete a three-year contract to keep things running. During those three years they then built up an administrative apparatus to look after Euston and that was when Johnny Goodman and Verity Lambert were invited to take over.

With the second Sweeney feature film *Sweeney II* written by Troy Kennedy-Martin and directed by Tom Clegg and the fourth and final series of *The Sweeney* plus the Morecambe and Wise 'special', the first phase of Euston Films came to an end. Lloyd Shirley and George Taylor formed their own company, Seacastle Productions, and were contracted to produce a series of single films for L W T with Canadian co-production finance under the title *Where Danger Lives*. Unfortunately the Canadian money never materialised so only one film was made.

THE NEXT PHASE

In 1977 Johnny Goodman joined Euston Films as Executive in Charge of Production. He was responsible on the one hand for running the Euston main office administratively and financially and on the other hand for taking (at a distance) control of *how* the films were made once the creative and administrative decisions had been taken to put them into production. This latter aspect of his job means that he will take overall responsibility for crewing up, personnel and expenditure and will generally keep a watching brief on each production. It is difficult to illustrate the specific contribution of Johnny Goodman to each separate Euston production but, assisted by Bill Launder – an experienced production accountant – his role is crucial to the economic viability of all productions and therefore of the company as a whole. Each production has its own accountant and regular progress reports are made to Johnny Goodman's office in order that swift remedial action can be taken in the event of any falling behind schedule or straying over budget.

Given Euston's small infrastructure the task of ensuring that each freelance producer conformed to the systems and requirements of Euston Films and Thames T V was rather burdensome. To alleviate this problem Johnny Goodman collaborated with producer Christopher Neame to produce a guide for new producers which codified all the necessary information. The result was *The Euston Films Producers' Memorandum*, referred to affectionately as 'Johnny's Bible', a 55 page document containing samples of various forms and contracts currently in use by Euston Films as well as information on technical requirements, accountancy requirements, equipment rental, copyright and legal vetting and so on. The first new project that Johnny Goodman was fully involved with was *Out*.

Before that project was commissioned by Verity Lambert, however, she accepted her first film for Euston Films: *The Sailor's Return*, a project with a long and dispiriting history of not being made. Sue Summers has outlined the history:

> The rights to David Garnett's 1920s novel, about the relationship between an 18th-century African princess and her sailor husband, and its destruction by the hostility of the rural English community to

75

The Sailor's Return: Captain William Targett (Tom Bell) arriving home with his bride Tulip (Shope Shodeinde).

which they return, were bought by William Wyler in 1953, the year of *Roman Holiday*. In 1971, Otto Plaschkes, the producer of *Georgy Girl*, bought the rights from Wyler, with financial backing from the NFFC [National Film Finance Corporation]. Apart from the difficulties of finding appropriate stars. . . . 'We tried to set it up at the very point when English films came under a cloud,' says Plaschkes. 'The Americans had virtually withdrawn from the UK and everyone was running for the international gold.'

Otto Plaschkes had worked with the director Jack Gold on *The Bofors Gun* and, having made *The Naked Civil Servant* for Thames, Jack Gold signed a three-picture contract with Thames in early 1977. One of the projects he proffered Jeremy Isaacs and Verity Lambert was *The Sailor's Return*.

Verity Lambert liked the project but thought that it was a TV movie, which was the basis on which it was initially accepted. However, it was soon clear that the original budget of £92,000 was going to be woefully

76

inadequate and they were therefore going to have to seek outside finance. Otto Plaschkes saw this as an ideal opportunity to approach the NFFC again to put up half the revised budget of £400,000, to which they agreed. If he had approached a conventional film company it is almost certain that (American) star names would have been required, instead of Nigerian-born Shope Shodeinde, who had just left university, and Tom Bell.

So Euston Films found itself in 1977 making its third feature film for the cinema for which, however, unlike the two *Sweeney* movies, it couldn't obtain theatrical release. Verity Lambert still thinks it was a very good film (and one that was made at a reasonable price) which, had it been made six years later, would have worked in a cinema when placed in the context of films like *The Ploughman's Lunch*. The time just wasn't right in 1977 and so it ended up being transmitted first on television, despite not having been commissioned by the network, and then not until December 1980.

'OUT'

Out occupies an interesting position in the history of Euston Films because it marks a transition point in the careers of a number of people who worked around Euston at that time. It was the first production commissioned (as opposed to accepted, as in the case of *The Sailor's Return*) by Verity Lambert for Euston whilst she was still Controller of Drama at Thames in late 1977. *Out* also marks the point at which Linda Agran joined Euston as Script Executive and it gave the writer Trevor Preston a new motivation for work:

> It was always strange because although I'd had a lot of fun writing *The Sweeney*, I got very tired because I did write an awful lot. And I was very close to giving up writing completely – I was discussing going into a boat-building business.

It was his agent Stephen Durbridge who encouraged him to write down his idea and to send it to Verity. She liked it:

> She was extraordinary. I've never seen anybody make a decision so quickly as Verity. And I was writing it within three weeks – it was breathtaking. It renewed my energy because all of the things I have never been able to do on *The Sweeney*, and indeed on the other series work, which is a lengthy and complex look at character and relationships, I was able to do in *Out*. And so it gave me an impetus.

For Jeremy Isaacs too (then Director of Programmes at Thames), whilst it didn't mark a change in his career, the programme was impor-

77

tant – it was significant in relation to Euston's output and had a small effect on his own life:

> *The Sweeney* could go two ways: you could take the characters and try to put them in a milder, pleasanter, jollier, less violent situation – I think that idea led to the search for *Minder*; and the other way was through people like Trevor Preston and Jim Goddard who had worked on *The Sweeney* – Trevor came up with *Out*. And I remember that when Cowgill took over as Managing Director and was sitting very heavily on my back as Director of Programmes, the one thing I was delighted that knocked him out was *Out*. Actually, I thought that was another peak of achievement.

Out also marked the first time that Trevor Preston and Jim Goddard worked together – something that was to be repeated with *Fox*. In fact this was quite surprising because they had been close friends for many years and, with Terry Green, they had suggested setting up a Euston Films-type operation to ABC as early as 1965. Verity Lambert commissioned *Out* because she felt that it was so complete and took Trevor out of the mode of his *Sweeney* episodes. 'It just seemed to be a wonderful entertainment apart from anything else – which is why I choose most things.'

TREATMENT FOR 'OUT' – TREVOR PRESTON

'Frank Ross? He's a thief . . . a . . . I've spent my life trying to put filth like him away.'
'Frank Ross? When my Davey was killed he gave me a thousand. Didn't have to . . . just did . . . he's like that.'
'Frank Ross? If he puts his face through that door I'm going to blow it off!'
'Frank Ross? He's nothin' . . . been away too long . . . gone soft.'
'Frank Ross? I heard he put some poor bastard on traction in the nick.'
'Frank Ross? He's going to get himself run over . . . several times.'
'Frank Ross? Yeah . . . heard he was about again . . . heard there's a few sweaty hands around too.'
'Frank Ross? . . . Out? . . . Christ!'

Eight years ago, Frank Ross and four others were cornered like rats down a hole, in a tunnel, eighteen inches from half a million in a bank vault. Eight years ago a sergeant from the Sweeney spat in his face and laughed as he clipped on the cuffs. Eight years ago Frank Ross searched the familar faces in court for any sign of the betrayal he was certain of. Eight years ago he stood stoically as the judge sentenced him.

For eight years Frank Ross has thought about it. Two thousand nine hundred and eighteen days and nights he has never let it fade from his mind. A psychiatrist might call it obsession, to Frank Ross it is simply a way of keeping alive among the walking dead of a maximum security wing.

Eight years was more than a sentence to Eve, Frank's wife, it was the beginning of the end. Frank knew when they had married that she suffered from depression. He sensed that if he ever was put away Eve would find it hard to cope, that's why he was so thorough in his preparation, so cautious in his choice of associates, so ruthless with any hint of a loose tongue. But for all that the big one had gone sour. Someone . . . someone close had betrayed them, and Eve has spent the past six years in a private nursing home with the doctors trying to coax her back into life.

Even in prison Frank Ross was marked. His four associates, all hard men, all in different nicks, have all been released with full remission after six years. But trouble seemed to find Frank, however hard he tried to avoid it, however much he tried to stay uninvolved, trouble came sniffing at his door like a lost dog. In his first month inside, the ace screw thought he'd put the hammer on Frank, just to let him know how things were. Frank had backed off until there was nowhere left to go – but into solitary for putting the pig in hospital.

When he was told about Eve's breakdown he applied for a compassionate visit. It was refused. A week later, Frank Ross was the other side of the wall, on the trot, half the police in the country had his face in their book. He was soon back inside, gave himself up, after he had seen Eve and made arrangements for his nine year old son to be properly taken care of.

Now, eight long years later he was out, a free man, his 'debt to society' paid with interest. The prison governor had given him the routine spiel about 'a new life', a 'second chance', an opportunity to 'contribute to society', but the one man who had grown to know Frank Ross, his cell mate Tony Garrett, knew exactly what was on Frank's mind when they shook hands that cold March morning. Tony Garrett knew that whoever fingered Frank eight years ago was living on borrowed time.

But in eight years things change, people change, friends tend to forget, enemies are easily reminded. The news of Frank Ross's release is not altogether celebrated by certain individuals.

Like Eddie Nash. He and Frank were close until Eddie got greedy and started teaming up on blags with hooligans who were too quick with a pick helve. Everyone said that Eddie was nothing without Frank, and Frank knew that deep down Eddie Nash hated him for this.

Then there was the Banker, outwardly a man of impeccable social standing, but whose true vocation is known only to a select few. Frank had approached the Banker for finance to mount the big one, but the percentage demands were out of proportion to the investment and Frank found other funding, much to the chagrin of Mr Money!

And Pinky the wire man. He'd come to Frank with a reputation. Frank was delighted to have him on the firm until he found out he was using downers to keep himself together. Not able to accept the risk, Frank had pensioned him off, but for a fraction of what he was expecting from the job. Pinky wasn't happy.

Any one of these three or a dozen others who knew about the job could have been the one who, for some reason, jealousy, hate, greed, fear, revenge, put the finger on Frank Ross, who stole eight years of his life, who sentenced his wife to the grey limbo of insanity, and who made a stranger of his son.

But how do you find an informer? Where do you start, eight years later? Who do you start with? The man who took the whisper? The cozzer who slammed the gate? Detective Inspector Christie Brice? He wouldn't give Frank Ross the time of day. He hates villains, particularly clever, successful villains. He told Frank Ross that one day . . . one day he would put him down . . . and he kept his promise, even though it took him eleven years.

Frank got a whisper in the nick that maybe Lew Wilson knew something. Lew has eyes and ears everywhere, and he owes Frank from way back, before he became the big man, when Frank pulled a pair of south London soldiers off him in a club. But Lew Wilson isn't the sort of face who likes to be reminded of a debt like that.

Cimmie Vincent . . . at the trial . . . every day that anxious white face in the public gallery. Cimmie was a high class tom, she shared a lot of beds, listened to a lot of talk. Cimmie knew something, Frank was sure of that, but soon after the trial she went missing, where is she eight years later?

Frank Ross knows there is nothing more lonely or dangerous than to be caught between the law and the street. But that's exactly where he is. What few friends he has left tell him . . . 'Forget it, Frank . . . you've done your bird . . . the sort of questions you're asking are going to land you in more bother.' The Old Bill are more explicit with their advice . . . 'You're rubbish Ross . . . and you know what we do with rubbish . . . we bury it!' And the four men who were sent down with him certainly don't share his passion for retribution.

'I done time because of you Ross! Not even a little pension to come out to. And you were suppose to be jack the lad!'

'Stay away from me and my family, Frank, I don't want nothing to do with your sort. I've got a good job . . . prospects . . . I moved out here to get away from all that shit . . . You stay away!'

'It was eight years ago, Frank. I've got other things on me mind . . . Listen son, you might be just what I'm looking for. It's nothing fancy, maybe ten or twelve grand, old fashioned peter, shouldn't give you much trouble . . . You probably need some readies . . . eh?'

'Listen . . . Frank . . . the filth have got their nose up you. Tony McGrath has got you down for the pig farm when he finds you, and you're here asking me things you know I don't know. If I knew who snouted on us I'd break about a yard of his back! We did six, Frank . . . you forget that!'

Then there are the personal problems for a man who has been inside for eight years. The nursing home fees have trebled. When Eve begs Frank to take her home, she doesn't realise that he's had to sell the house to keep her in private care. And the boy, he's sixteen. To the couple who have brought him up, he's their son. Frank knows that coming back into his life can only confuse him, maybe even harm him. And Anne, Frank's mistress, he made her promise not to write or try to come to see him inside, but he knew she would be waiting when he was released. Anne is married and Frank knows that's the sort of problem he can do without. But a man who has been locked away for so long needs some sort of comfort.

So Frank Ross moves slowly forward, like a man picking his way through a minefield. One scrap of information leading to another. One piece of the eight year old puzzle locking into the next. One question answered, leading him on to what . . . another answer . . . or to blank faces, shaking heads and tight lips? Frank Ross knows only too well the code of his class, he has lived his life by the law of the three monkeys – you're blind, deaf and dumb, unless there's good reason to be otherwise.

So Frank Ross is both hunter and hunted . . . marksman and quarry. The police watch his every move, they know he's trouble, they want him back inside and are not particular about how they do it. To the underworld he's become a threat, they don't like his questions or the methods he uses to get them answered. And to the person that betrayed him, Frank Ross is a nightmare, as slowly, irrevocably, they are drawn towards each other, in a dance macabre that must surely end in someone getting killed.

This is a brief introductory piece on an idea that would be developed into a six-part serial. Each part would move the protagonist Frank Ross another step towards an inevitable nemesis in the final episode.

A device that would be used throughout would be the punctuating of the main drama with flash-backs (maybe in monochrome) of the preparation, recruitment, planning, execution and final downfall of the bank vault job eight years previous, as Frank Ross remembers it.

What interested me in this sort of idea, is that within the structure of a fast moving thriller format (like *The Sweeney*) to be able to develop at length the very real and I think moving dilemma of a man like Frank Ross, a man who, given different circumstances, may well have become the prison governor instead of the prison problem.

Too often we only get the chance to observe tele-villains, broken-nosed heavies who prattle on in a sort of pseudo, slang dictionary language as they pull their stocking masks on. I think there is a great deal more to say about some articulate, intelligent and strangely moral men who find themselves in opposition to society. Frank Ross is such a man.

COLLABORATIONS

For his part Trevor Preston might have reached the stage where he felt like finishing with TV writing but he is a writer who is deeply committed to TV and to writing popular serials and series as opposed to single, more culturally prestigious plays. Furthermore, he felt that he'd earned the right to produce large-scale and complex works like *Out* and *Fox*:

As a writer of series and serials you have to earn your freedom – I mean I've written 114 hours of television in eleven years – and you have to do all that graft. But I earned the right to do something original. The thing is that I always wanted to do *Fox* – not *Out*. *Out* suddenly came to me and I know that *Out* is the thing that everybody likes – but *Fox* is the best piece of work I've ever done. In a way *Fox* is a sort of family saga soap opera - the *Forsythe Saga* in 13 episodes about somebody who lives in Clapham. *Out,* on the other hand, is a pure cliché – it's a revenge movie in which you could see Charles Bronson if you like. But if you actually look behind what is happening in *Out,* if you actually listen to what is said, it is a more complex story of police corruption than *Law and Order* because basically all *Law and Order* is, much as I love it, is a 'gimme a bit of that and a bit of that'.

81

What *Out* is actually about is the corruption of a man's mind – a policeman's mind – who blames other people for his own corruption. Which happens all the time in the police force.

So you take a popular form like a good kick bollock and scramble about a man who comes out of jail but you weave these other things in, you weave in what happens to a criminal's family. It destroys a family when he goes in prison, it's like a hand grenade, his family blows up. All these sort of things. So you've got to have a text to pull them in – what's going to happen to Frank Ross; and then you get a sub-text underneath (for those people who want to take it) which is saying something.

Trevor discussed the outline in great detail with Verity and then with Linda Agran, who by that time had come to Euston from Warner Brothers. Trevor was initially very apprehensive about the arrival of Linda because, like so many writers, he has a natural wariness of script editors. However, his fears were soon allayed for Linda soon made it clear that she does not believe in rewriting other people's work:

Out was my first project and Trevor was a little alarmed. And I get quite annoyed when people call me a script editor because I've never edited a script in my life and wouldn't want to – I think the way other companies treat their writers is just appalling. I mean nobody would think of taking a painting and say 'It needs a blue bit here or. . .'

Trevor was also worried by Verity's decision to appoint Barry Hanson as the producer of the serial. With hindsight he would seem to be a natural choice given his work on the BBC Birmingham TV serial *Gangsters* and given the fact that he seems to have a predilection for film. Apparently, however, this wasn't so obviously the case at the time and it was perhaps only Verity that viewed him as a 'sort of commercial producer manqué' who had somehow got into an area of 'high art' and so she encouraged him towards *Out*. His reluctance lasted until he read the treatment and scripts. Trevor's reluctance to work with this 'high art' producer lasted two hours.

The one person Trevor Preston was insistent about working with was Jim Goddard and in discussing the project with us he interestingly complemented Trevor's account of *Out*. Trevor constructed an empathetic view of the criminal as anti-hero – 'I thought it was an important thing to try and do, to show in fact that – not by any means saying that Frank Ross is a good lad – but saying that at least he's a human being, he's got children, he's got a wife, he's got bills to pay.' Jim opened out the wider ramifications of the production:

So then Trevor has an idea – he said, 'why are all the heroes on our screens either nice guys or policemen, why do we have to identify with these do-goody people all the time?' And he said 'I don't ever' – and nor do I. So he had this idea about writing a story about a guy coming out of prison and all the things that happen to him and how state intervention into a person's life alters it. Also we thought that the Countryman operation would be over. In a way *Out* was a parody of Countryman except dealing with only a few people. And what we were concerned with was the police thinking it would be possible to do deals with a lesser set of criminals – illegal deals – in order to catch a larger set of criminals. And of course the means justified the ends and it was considered morally right to do that. Well, of course, once you cross that line you're in trouble because then your secondary criminals become primary criminals and say, OK you put the finger on us and we'll put the finger on you. So the police had lost control of the situation.

And it was also about loyalty – working-class loyalty, working-class villain loyalty – and Verity thought that it was a wonderful idea, I thought it was a wonderful idea and she commissioned it. And it was an attempt by all of us to say, OK the single play may be dead but we now see the possibility of starting something, if you like, called the television novel. Because they are novelistic in their structure – *Fox* was a novel.

The original intention was to have two directors working on *Out* because of its length, as was the case with *Reilly – Ace of Spies* and Granada's *Jewel in the Crown*, but it was Johnny Goodman's idea that Jim Goddard should do all six episodes. Verity Lambert felt that this was a good example of a practical decision being made, by someone with a vast experience of the film industry, which turned out to be a very creative decision because it unified the whole serial.

'DANGER UXB' AND 'QUATERMASS'

Out began shooting soon after work began on the final series of *The Sweeney* and as soon as it was finished Euston went straight into production on *Danger UXB*. It too was commissioned whilst Verity Lambert was still at Thames and it is the only other *series* (apart from *The Sweeney* and *Minder*) to have been initiated by Euston and the only one not to become a 'banker'.

UXB traces the life of a bomb disposal squad during the war, from the beginning of the Blitz to the preparations for the Normandy landings. No-one had been prepared for the problem of unexploded bombs at the beginning of the war (it was assumed they would simply go off) and the first instruction sent out by the Home Office ordered the police and ARP wardens to collect up the unexploded bombs and stack them

83

Danger UXB: Brian Ash, played by Anthony Andrews.

at the end of the street for the army to deal with! Eventually this problem was handed over to the inexperienced and largely non-volunteer Royal Engineers who formed special bomb disposal companies.

Danger UXB was Euston's first foray into period drama and whilst Verity Lambert said that she wasn't consciously intending to branch out she was looking to add to what was by then already a very solid base. She also felt that nobody had ever covered that side of the war before and she liked the idea that it was very much the antithesis of *The Sweeney* in being rather middle-class and about defusing situations!

Jeremy Isaacs had this to say about the series:

Then Thames tried to go more up market and be more adventurous as franchise time arrived and nobody was sure that things like *The Sweeney* were going to win you a franchise – particularly if people complained that they were a bit violent or portrayed the police in an unfortunate light. We deliberately ventured into other things. And I thought the great claim was always that it didn't matter if it was period, it doesn't matter if it's different – you can trust Euston to deliver it on budget. So one looked at the budget and we did a series

84

about World War II – *Danger UXB* – and I liked the idea of that because I thought that it would be marvellous – people just wouldn't know if a bomb was going to go off in this episode or not.

The genesis of the series was that John Hawkesworth – who had had a tremendous success with *Upstairs, Downstairs* and who was considered to be very good at mainstream drama – went to Verity with the idea, based on the book *Unexploded Bomb* by Major Bill Hartley, and she thought that it was interestingly different and original.

One important aspect of both *Out* and *Danger UXB* is that whilst Verity Lambert was still working at Thames (i.e. commissioning tape drama) she commissioned them for Euston in order that they be made on film: '*Danger UXB* could never have been done on tape – all those bombs and gardens and things.' This was part of her general policy to generate distinctive drama for the network which was anchored in a London setting and which 'got the feel' of London. Verity Lambert explained:

> That was a conscious decision. When I first went to Thames it seemed to me that the difficulty of doing drama in a London company was that people tend not to think of London and the South as a region, and it is a region. I felt that the companies that seemed to be the most successful at that time with drama – companies like Granada – had a very strong regional feel about their drama. So I decided to look upon London as a region – and a very rich region because it has so many different strata in it. I think people first saw all our drama as being cheap and that I didn't want people to travel, but really it wasn't to do with that, it was to try and give some identity to them.

At the same time it must be noted that in 1974 the IBA had criticised Thames for a general lack of regional programme making.

Twenty-five years after the television transmission of the original *Quatermass*, Euston embarked on its biggest project to date – a £1 million production of a new *Quatermass* story by Nigel Neale (the original creator), shot entirely in 35 mm Panavision. Verity Lambert:

> *Quatermass* came to us in the shape of four scripts which had been commissioned by the BBC and which had been turned down by them as being too expensive for them to make. It was very expensive – I think it was the most expensive thing we had attempted at Euston Films at that point. And we felt that the only way we could justify the expense was to make sure that we could re-edit it into a film which could possibly have theatrical release as well as have a four-parter. In fact the film hasn't been released yet.

85

On the *Quatermass* set: (l. to r.) Johnny Goodman, Lord Romsey (Norton Knatchbull), Ted Childs.

The Department of the Environment had refused to allow filming at Stonehenge and the BBC considered that a mock-up would be too expensive. This story is set in the future amidst urban decay and anarchy when an alien force draws strength from the gathering of young people who are 'harvested' from Earth. Professor Quatermass (played by Sir John Mills) fights back.

Because of the cost of the project, the crew spent a further week shooting 'bridging' shots so that the four-part series could be re-edited as a movie for commercial distribution. However, it has never been released as a movie in this country.

Quatermass was the first Euston Sci-Fi production and it somehow seems surprising to shoot such a movie 'on location'. Certainly Ted Childs saw it as rather a strange project for Euston to get involved with – his view of the reason for Euston doing it was that 'Verity and Linda wanted to put their own stamp upon things. I think they didn't want to come in and just do the same old routine – the kick bollock and scramble action adventure stuff that made the early name of the company.' He also identified what he thought were the reasons for its lack of success:

> I think there were high production values in it and I think that the performances were good but the primary problems with it were a) it was perhaps too depressing a story for a popular television audience and b) the punters were used to a fairly high standard of technical representation from American television – you know you had had *Star Trek* and then there had been movies like *Star Wars* and *Close Encounters of the Third Kind*. And we just couldn't afford that.

A NEW BANKER – 'MINDER'

> Originally I had written a film story, called *Minder*, a pretty nasty story – dark, gloomy, black and tough, though it also had a lot of humour in it. My agent read it and said 'You're never going to be able to sell it. Nobody's going to buy this sort of film in Britain.' So I didn't even think about it for a long time. Funnily enough it was my agent again who said 'You know, there are two characters in that *Minder* story who are just screaming to go beyond the big screen.' So I began to think about basing a TV series on those two characters, who were of course Arthur and Terry. (Leon Griffiths)

> We were looking for a series that would be popular and entertaining and which would hopefully attract a similar audience size to *The Sweeney*. We commissioned one or two treatments which didn't come up, and we received a format from Leon Griffiths and it clearly had all the seeds of originality in it. A tried and true thing but two very good, clearly delineated original characters who could interact with each other. Which is all you can hope for – I mean there are no new situations, it's only the way characters act and interact within those situations which makes something different. (Verity Lambert)

Two accounts of how *Minder* came into being, to which we could add others which would include certain stories and jokes that circulated around Euston Films about a 'minder' that was employed for a period on *The Sweeney*, and the lunch where Linda Agran and Leon Griffiths first discussed the possibility of such a project for Euston. What is important for our account here, however, is that Euston was looking for another 'banker' and Euston put their money on Leon Griffiths' format (reproduced below).

'MINDER' FORMAT – LEON GRIFFITHS

Minder is a new type of action/character television series featuring an independent bodyguard who often operates on the fringe of legality but always seems to end up on the side of the angels.

Do you remember the opening minutes of *Rocky* when the hero is collecting a debt for some heavies? He is tough but nice, mildly threatening but certainly not vicious. That incident could easily be a sixty-seconds pilot for this series.

The hero of *Minder* is 'The Magnificent Seven' minus six; a hero who takes on jobs outside the scope of the police and such organisations as Securicor.

It is a 'street' series relying heavily on the new 'exotica' of London. No more shots of Tower Bridge opening and closing - but a reasonable number of stories set among the Greeks of Camden Town; the Irish around Holloway and Kilburn; Indians in Southall; Bengalis in the East End; Italians who've moved from Clerkenwell to Stanmore (is Stanmore the Tuscany of the suburbs?); West Indians in Brixton and Cricklewood; Chinese in Gerrard Street; new towns full of old East-Enders; smart clubs where the new aristocracy of property dealers, BMW concessionaires and the wheeler-dealers of the pop industry congregate.

The series is predicated on several prejudices shared by most viewers and a lot of writers and directors:

a) They're getting sick of seeing cops chasing robbers through the streets of San Francisco and Belgravia.

b) The freelance do-gooder is only believable if you place him in the unreal world inhabited by the Saint and the Avengers.

c) The criminal as a hero is not acceptable as the protagonist of a long-running series.

d) One British private-eye is enough.

e) Heroes employed by strange unknown 'trouble-shooting' agencies are unbelievable and they'd rather have Starsky and Hutch anyway.

Yet there is a need for a hero who is on *our* side, who is rebellious, independent, tough and amusing and is not a villain. His name is Terry and he is the hero of *Minder*.

As I outline some of the stories the morality of such a series will become apparent. It will also become clear that there is no 'police' or 'private-eye' story that cannot be adapted to the format of *Minder*.

Violence is implicit in the character, but need not be explicit in the series. Terry is not a stunt-driver, so there won't be spectacular car chases that land everybody in the local Magistrates' Court the following morning. For Terry it is often enough to squeeze somebody's elbow and suggest that they stop being a 'silly feller' to avoid unrealistic shoot-outs and shattered balsa-wood bannisters.

Most successful series feature two running characters. *Minder* is no exception, but the relationship is more complex than in most series. It is not simply that one is older than the other, or jokier than the other.

Arthur is a 'face', a 'well-respected' man in certain parts of London. He fancies himself as a Godfather but often emerges from the stories like a well-dressed, dodgy employee of the Citizens' Advice Bureau. He is often to be found trying to shift 400 Draylon sofa covers while hiring Terry out to someone who needs a bit of looking after.

Arthur always takes the bigger share of the fee and is certainly not a man to depend on in a tight corner. Arthur lives in a world of favours bestowed and they'd better be returned.

Arthur is the fringe villain that all your rich friends know. Arthur is amusing

Shooting *Minder* (l. to r.) Sally Croft (unit publicist), Lloyd Shirley (executive producer), Leon Griffiths (series originator).

but a bit unscrupulous and he'd hire out Terry to protect someone from the armoured division of the Red Army if the price was right.

Terry is never going to reach the finals of *Mastermind* but he catches on quick in the world he knows and understands. He has a past and is desperately anxious to stay 'straight'. He knows he isn't much more than 'hired muscle', but at least he's good at it. He's got a reputation and is smart enough to know that there will always be another fast gun riding into town.

Do you doubt the existence of the Minder? Well, no pop star would be seen without one and ditto most international film stars. The euphemism is 'driver' or 'my man'. But we don't want it to be a series about show business. So who else would use a 'minder'? The man who owned the Spaghetti House chain for starters.

Our version of that story would probably run like this:

'Siege At The OK Corral'. Albert Delano is a second-generation Italian who owns six down-market restaurants trading under the name of OK Corral Steak Houses. Friday nights he collects the takings and he doesn't want two guys wearing funny crash helmets and uniforms accompanying him. He knows Arthur and has done so ever since 'the old days' and he regards Terry as a great deterrent to most of the known criminals who might be tempted to nick the takings.

The four black villains who attempt the robbery are amateurs. Terry saves the money but finds himself trapped with Albert, a couple of customers and the four villains in a downstairs storeroom.

Arthur hears about it on his car radio. He is soon on the spot hectoring and

89

hindering the Police. After all . . . that's his meal-ticket in there.

The police bring all the usual techniques into play . . . concealed microphones, video cameras on the drain holes, psychologists, sharpshooters, etc.

But it is Terry who eventually strikes up a rapport with the villains; it is Terry who unites villains and hostages in a common suspicion of the police methods; it is Terry who finally 'outfronts' the one really dangerous villain . . . and it is Terry, with his known police record, who is carted off to the local nick under suspicion of being party to the robbery in the first place.

Arthur and Mr Delano manage to establish his innocence and Arthur, naturally, gyps him on the fee. 'After all Terry, you got all the publicity. . . .'

What will become clear as the series progresses is that although Terry sometimes finds it hard to distinguish between legal right and wrong he is always certain about good and bad.

When he does get into a fight we will want him to win as fervently as we wanted Shane to win when confronting the bar-room bullies.

Inevitably many of the people who employ Terry have something to hide, answers to questions they'd rather not be asked.

We would not tackle a story like *Out* because Frank Ross wouldn't want Terry's help and Arthur would be unlikely to offer it. But we could well go into the area of 'George Somebody-or-other is innocent.'

In 'Innocent OK?' a journalist is writing a book on a man doing a life sentence. The journalist wants to meet people involved in the case . . . villains, suspects, coppers, wives, sweethearts, grasses . . . but his publisher is fearful for his safety. Terry will be his guide and protector.

But Terry finds that they are straying beyond the boundaries of his tribal territory. The journalist is being threatened as he upsets villains and coppers alike. Terry is 'on wages' which gains him a kind of immunity from some of the villains but also means that he must go all the way for the crusading journalist.

And all the way means forcing the real villain out into the open, seeing that justice is done without informing or transgressing his own simply constructed moral code.

Simple matters of protection soon develop into tough, complicated situations for Terry and Arthur. In 'The Bengal Tiger' Tariq, the local newsagent, seeks Arthur's help because he's having a hard time from some tearaways and realises that if he takes up arms or pick-axe handles to oppose them he'll be the one taken to the local nick accused of starting a race riot.

Arthur has long operated a nice take-away service at Tariq's expense - he takes away newspapers, magazines and a few Panatellas and puts them on a non-existent bill. For £300 he helps Tariq. 'Kids,' he tells Terry, 'bunch of yobboes. Sit in his shop for a week; there's a hundred and twenty in it for you.'

Tariq appears to have quite a few problems. His daughter, Shiva, is a pretty seventeen-year-old with an East-End accent, deeply opposed to the idea of a contracted marriage 'to some bleeding rice-picker from old Bengal.' Also the 'kids and yobboes' who are harassing Tariq turn out to be mature heavies from South of the river. Shiva disappears. Has she run away or been kidnapped? For now Terry has discovered that Tariq deals in more than the *Daily Mirror* and half ounces of Old Holborn . . . he's running a racket in forged entry permits to Mother England. In finding the girl Terry is obliged to break the racket.

[. . . .]

Terry is a boundlessly loyal person. Put him on the payroll and he'll die for you. He's the man you've seen on the newsreels flinging himself in front of the president; he's the good soldier who'll walk through mobs and gunfire because it's his job. He knows Arthur exploits him. But so what? He owes Arthur a favour once done . . . and it's so long ago he can't even remember what the favour was.

One episode might find him 'minding' a disco where they're having a spot of bother. Another will find him in an altogether bigger league.

'Arms - For The Love of Money': Mr Yunis is a Lebanese carpet dealer with a warehouse at the docks. He knows Arthur because once Arthur helped him shift 40 'genuine hand-woven Oriental carpets' (made in Belgium) to unsuspecting readers of the *Sunday Times* in a 'never-to-be-repeated' dockside sale.

Mr Yunis's cousin, Kamil, is coming to London. He's rich and needs someone to 'look after him'. He's working for his country's Government and will be visiting the annual armaments bazaar at Aldershot.

But Kamil is really working for a revolutionary party and is using phoney documents to buy arms. An Arab 'hit squad' is after him; the Israelis are keeping an eye on the Arabs and M15 is keeping an eye on all of them. Kamil is also out to get a salesman from a private armaments company who has double-crossed him in the past. It will be one of the few stories in which firearms are seen or used.

Terry is caught in the middle of political events and intrigue he can't even hope to understand. But a war in which both sides are supplied by the same arms dealers is something he *can* understand

When Kamil is killed it is Terry who tracks down the arms salesman and the hired killer responsible during a spectacular finale at the Aldershot 'war games'.

Minder will always seek to point out the ironies and contrasts of contemporary London life. If your £300,000 filly is entered in the Oaks then you hire Racecourse Security Services to protect her. If you're a Smithfield porter who's trained a greyhound in his spare time and the dog looks good for the fourth at Catford you might turn to Terry and Arthur to make sure nobody slips her a couple of pork pies an hour before the off.

Such a story could find Terry staying up all night to guard the dog. ('It's undignified, Arthur. . . . Like, I'm more of a cat man.') And maybe he'll have to go into action the following day to stop the heavies trying to rig the price on the Tote. (If enough heavies can prevent enough punters from placing their bets they can create a 'false favourite' for a race. It's an easy trick to work at afternoon dog meetings because of the sparse attendances; and the manhandled punters are scared to give evidence.)

The following episode would find Terry in an altogether different world. 'Bitches, Riches and Stitches' is about a beautiful titled woman who thinks her husband (a Lucan-type figure) is going to maim or disfigure her.

Lady Jane has had her fling on the fringes of the underworld and once had an affair with a 'Georgie Wright' character, now dead.

A jealous husband has been threatening her but there is no evidence to take to the police. She phones Arthur. (You can always phone Arthur . . . messages are left at half a dozen pubs and cafes.)

Arthur wouldn't mind protecting the beautiful Jane himself, but he thinks real danger threatens so he'll leave it to Terry. For a few days Terry is going to be her constant companion and chauffeur. He'll take Jane shopping, stay in the flat

91

On the 'Winchester' set in *Minder:* (back, l. to r.) Leon Griffiths, George Taylor, Frances Heasman, Ian Toynton, Tony Hoare, Andrew Payne, (front) Dennis Waterman, Verity Lambert, Johnny Goodman, George Cole.

at nights . . . put the frighteners on the husband if he shows up.

A kind of relationship develops. Jane wants to know about his job, how he recognises danger and deals with it. Terry explains:

> 'You walk into a pub or a club and you just glance round. You take it in very quickly, you get an eye for who could cause trouble, who could *hurt* you. There's big blokes who play rugby and've had too much to drink . . . pussy-cats. There's guys with cold blue eyes like you read about in the books . . . forget 'em; they're good in card games and shouting at the birds in the typing pool. There's guys with dark, smiling eyes, sort of confident-looking . . . make a note of them. They don't look confident for nothing. Then there's the fellers who do all the Karate stuff in the health club . . . nasty . . . but can they do the same in some smelly gents lav, or outside on the cobbles? Then there's the nutters . . . the worst of all. . . .'
>
> 'And what do they look like?'
>
> Terry grins. 'That's the hard bit of the job. They look like anybody.'

Jane will fall for him and Terry will realise why. He'll try and talk sense to the ex-husband but he can't act as a marriage guidance counsellor.

92

He's saved Lady Jane this time. But he knows the husband will be back. He knows the man will carry out his threat; he's seen it in his eyes.

There are aspects of the job that Terry detests. He hates snatching back a car for one of Arthur's dealer friends and sympathises with the punter who can't afford his 1976 Ford Cortina, but this would simply be an incident in a larger story.

Sometimes he is like the hired gun brought in to scare the homesteaders who ends up on their side. He'd never strike a man less physically capable than himself. Arthur would happily hire him out to a landlord who wanted to terrorise some squatters. If we did tackle such a story it would be heavily loaded . . . homeless mums rather than drop-out students. (Second thoughts: maybe the latter is more interesting.) But in a hard, tough series we have to be on guard against the soft centre. A leavening of humour is essential; and I hope some of that is conveyed in this outline.

If I must mention other series and films then I would suggest a touch of *The Rockford Files* rather than a dollop of *The Professionals;* a hint of the lead performance in *Baretta* rather than that awful do-gooding Italian/American lawyer whose name sounds like a bowl of soup; a nod in the direction of *Budgie* rather than Marker or Patrick Mower.

It is a London-based series, but not a London populated by chirpy Cockney 'sparrers' talking the kind of rhyming slang you need a Linguaphone course to understand. No 'Mister Bigs'. And no fights or chases in underground carparks. (How about a paper at next year's Edinburgh Festival on the significance of the underground carpark in the work of every second-rate TV writer and director?)

The Main Characters
Here are those biographies that usually include the passage . . . 'although basically a peaceful man Harry/Clint/Joe can use his fists with the best of them and is also a master of all martial arts. Unknown to most of his friends he took a PhD at Yale before becoming a longshoreman and part-time Marshal of Dodge City. . . .'

TERRY McCANN. Age 33. No education to speak of although he *did* play right back for the school football team and was good at sheet-metal work and geography.

Received a six-months sentence as a fifteen-year-old for 'screwing' the local TV rental shop. Dead-end jobs. A London Junior ABA semi-finalist at seventeen; a pro fighter at eighteen. Licence withdrawn after his eleventh fight. ('If you hadn't kept brushing the resin out of your hair when you was on the canvas we'd've been all right.')

Two short prison sentences for robbery and GBH. Vowed that he'd never go back inside. For that reason he turns down many an easy 'tickle' – but nobody could ever accuse him of going soft. He's been a bouncer at several dance-halls. He is excessively courteous to women. His girlfriends are always good-looking and one nearly got her picture on page three of the *Sun*. Mostly they tend to work as hostesses – drinking club hostesses, sauna bath hostesses. One day he hopes to pull a Pan-Am hostess.

Terry would never go on the dole. And when he first heard about National Insurance stamps he decided he wouldn't 'join'. He is not registered for purposes of VAT nor, for that matter, inland revenue purposes. He still works out at the

93

gym and is susceptible to 'crazes'. He's gone through macrobiotic foods and he tried that acupuncture 'after I done me hand in giving that feller from Putney a little smack.' Yoga is on the horizon ever since he read in *Reveille* that Muhammad Ali does a few relaxation exercises every day.

Terry still sees his Mum once a week and always leaves her a few quid. His Mum thinks he's a chauffeur and often that's all his job amounts to. He's tough and straight and a promise made is a promise kept.

Sometimes he wonders what he's going to do when he grows up. He votes Labour because his Dad was a docker and 'We've always been Labour.'

ARTHUR DALEY. Aged 50 and slightly worried about it. Arthur could have gone to Grammar School – but he happened to be in Borstal at the time. He's been nicked for robbery, receiving and assault. But he hasn't been inside a jail for twenty years except to visit friends.

Arthur is sharp. He knows who the Chancellor of the Exchequer is and could tell you every boxing world champion since the turn of the century. He's vain and fastidious and he dresses well. ('Little Cypriot feller off the Whitechapel Road . . . makes all the suits for Savile Row.')

He still runs the odd long-firm racket, does a bit of tax-free bet placing, and always has a couple of hundred in readies in his pocket. He's known and re-spected; a keen supporter of local charities; a friend of professional footballers. He loves to attend a function.

Arthur would be deeply offended if you accused him of running protection rac-kets, but he does look after one or two places in the area. He admires Sir Keith Joseph and always knows the real story behind what everybody else thinks is the real story. He hints at friends in high places and the Housing Convenor of the local council is 'a personal friend of mine'.

Arthur is married (just) and is inordinately proud of his two children's slightest achievements. He's flash but canny. The drinks are usually bought for him, but if he gets the round in it will be a big one and everybody will know about it. His word is his bond (nearly) and he'll let Terry fight to the death to prove it.

In Conclusion

I've no doubt that there are arguments against such a series as *Minder*. Anticipat-ing one I would simply say that it would have a deeper sense of morality than most contemporary series.

One of the most positive arguments in its favour is that the hero is truly at the centre of the action. The stories pivot around him and whoever he is looking after – unlike most police series where the hero enters from the sidelines. There is also the mildly worrying idea that it's never been done before. . . .

'MINDER' – A NICE LITTLE EARNER

One of the initial difficulties of *Minder* was that the other writers had to write sight unseen – all they had to go on was the format. Furthermore, in the early stages the series was uncast. Writers were informed that it was hoped that Dennis Waterman would play Terry McCann but George Cole was not cast as Arthur Daley until quite late on. Clearly, this didn't matter for Leon Griffiths himself, who was writing six of the scripts, but the other writers were working in the dark – they didn't even have a reference point like *Regan*, as the early *Sweeney* writers had.

It was Linda Agran's responsibility to brief the other writers on the basis of lengthy discussions with Leon Griffiths and both she and Verity Lambert felt that it was a mark of the strength of the original format that the first series worked out as well as it did. However, the first series was not a ratings success due, it would seem, to a number of factors.

For one thing *Minder*, like the later *Charlie Muffin*, was first shown the week after a three month strike in ITV when the screens had been dark and the whole pattern of domestic viewing had changed. There had been no pre-publicity and:

> We were giving the audience something unexpected, something we hadn't been able to build them up to because of the strike. They were coming back to ITV in the first week having all been watching BBC for the last three months (except for those people who had been watching the blank screen – some of which were recorded on the ratings) and I think it would have been a miracle if we had been successful.

Secondly, Dennis Waterman was not sure about doing *Minder* because it came so soon after *The Sweeney* and it was another series about London - the fear of typecasting clearly worried him. However, having read the format and the initial scripts he thought it was so funny and different that he would be stupid not to do it.

But Verity thought that the audience found it confusing to see Dennis Waterman in a different but 'similar' type of series to *The Sweeney*, a point that Leon Griffiths took up:

> I think for a lot of the time, a lot of the audience were confused, weren't quite sure what to do. Should they laugh? Because it's very unusual in this country to have a drama series where you can actually laugh aloud. You think 'Wait a minute, are we supposed to be laughing here? I am – but maybe I shouldn't be. . . .' I think it took about six weeks before the audience really thought 'yeah, this is pretty good'. Also we had the problem of the strike that was on at *TV Times*, and I'm sure that for weeks the audience had no idea what they were seeing. They probably thought it was *The Sweeney*, that at any minute they were going to see John Thaw come crashing in. . . . But the critics were well ahead of the audience. Right from the start we had critical acclaim, and the third series became a kind of cult – though I've no idea why; and I'm pretty sure nobody at Thames really knows either.

Given the seeming failure of the first series the decision had to be taken as to whether or not to embark on a second. Verity Lambert presented the wider problems indicated above to Bryan Cowgill, who by then was Managing Director of Thames, and it was his decision to risk a second series. Linda Agran:

The decision to go into a second series was taken by Bryan Cowgill, thank God, and he gave the green light at the end of the first series. In fact we had a double problem. One was that the series had not been a hit and the other was that Leon suffered a stroke and was lying in hospital – we thought unable to write ever again. And I, quite frankly, didn't know what to do. So Bryan said to me at a cocktail party where I was airing my misgivings, 'Look, you know it's good, and I know it's good – people will come to it in the end.' Which is exactly the right attitude and so we went rocking into the second series. And Leon picked up an award for the second series and he hadn't written one of them – he didn't like this but it started him writing again.

Since then, of course, the programme has become an enormous success both in Britain and overseas (particularly Australia) and Thames keep asking Euston if they can make just one more series. *Minder* was in production whilst this book was being written and it is planned to make a final six early in 1985. The people we spoke to all gave different and equally plausible reasons for the success of *Minder*. George Cole thought it was partly because it appeals to all classes; Dennis Waterman mentioned the limitless possibilities of scripts that weren't constrained by the 'goodies and baddies' of police series; and a number of people suggested that most of the population either thought they knew an Arthur Daley or would like to be like him and further, would like to have a 'minder'! The TV critic Chris Dunkley gave another reason in an article he wrote in the *Financial Times* entitled 'Fifty Golden Cheers for *Minder*':

The most important element of all in achieving this credibility, the essential feel of the series, is the practice of making it on film on location. Like Euston's other work, *The Sweeney, Fox* and *Out,* and like some of the best Ealing comedies of the forties and fifties, *Minder* exploits not the London beloved of Hollywood (Westminster, Chelsea, Hampstead) but the London only Londoners know: Plaistow, Hammersmith, Notting Hill Gate, Acton. You don't often glimpse Big Ben or the Bank of England in *Minder* but breakers' yards, railway arches and cul de sacs feature very large.
    This dedication to film clearly runs deep. The episode titles are almost invariably cinema parodies: the first ever was called 'Gunfight at the OK Launderette' and so far the current series has featured

'Rocky Eight and a Half' and 'Senior Citizen Caine' with 'High Drains Pilferer' coming along tonight.

Finally, Linda Agran:

I think the more our society is going the way it is, the more people are understanding and identifying with the little men trying to fiddle, or whatever, their own success and somehow get an edge. Actually I've got the feeling that under a Labour government *Minder* might have been completely different – under this government you have to show that you can survive.

TV MOVIES

Verity Lambert always wanted to make some one-off films on a regular basis at Euston – perhaps one or two a year. A start was made with *The Sailor's Return* and Euston proceeded with *Charlie Muffin* and *The Knowledge*, which were shot simultaneously although *Charlie Muffin* was initiated first. Thames were happy about the concept of making one-off films at first but the problem proved to be the cost and the difficulty of scheduling single productions.

Charlie Muffin is a comedy thriller adapted by Keith Waterhouse from a novel by Brian Freemantle and is the tale of an espionage deal involving defecting top agents between the Russians, the British and the Americans. Charlie Muffin is a down-at-heel special agent, played by David Hemmings, who manages to turn the tables on his superiors who have decided he is 'expendable', and ends up with the money intended for a defecting Russian.

The film was not a success due, Verity Lambert thought, to it being unfairly compared with *Tinker, Tailor, Soldier, Spy*, which had recently been transmitted. She felt that it wasn't recognised that the film was a send-up, that it attempted to be the very antithesis of the Le Carré adaptation. Ted Childs, who was co-producer on the project, felt that Thames were partly to blame for this confusion:

I felt that Thames presented it very badly – that their publicity people tried to pretend that it was a kind of ITV answer to *Tinker, Tailor*, which clearly it wasn't. It was a very lightweight spoof thing. I think it worked quite well at the level it was supposed to – any suggestion that it was the definitive Intelligence Thriller Genre piece was a bit over the top. But it was quite fun to do – we had the Berlin Wall in the West India Dock. . . . But I guess it was the same routine – trying to get a quart out of a pint pot.

The Knowledge was the last single film to be made by Euston (all of which

97

Using the Steadicam system to shoot *The Knowledge:* 'you're always working with the most-up-to-date equipment.'

have been shot on 35 mm) and is a light-hearted, semi-accurate account of the trials and tribulations faced by a young man seeking the coveted badge of a London black-cab driver. Learning and being tested on all the London routes is referred to as 'the knowledge' in the business. Verity Lambert saw this very much as a one-off project: 'Jack Rosenthal and Bob Brooks had this good idea – it was Bob's idea and Jack wrote it.' It was directed by Bob Brooks and produced by Christopher Neame.

'FOX': A SOUTH LONDON GODFATHER

Euston Films felt that they'd had a terrific success with *Out* and so they approached Trevor Preston and asked him to write something else for them. In fact he wrote up six ideas and submitted them all to Verity Lambert. The one she liked the best was *Fox*. As mentioned earlier, this was the serial Trevor had always wanted to make and he had always wanted to include musical interludes.

Fox tells the story of a South London family – Billy Fox, his second wife and their five adult sons, their girlfriends and families. It's about how the family disintegrates after Billy's death and is pulled together by one of the sons. In the original treatment Billy dies in the first episode

98

Fox: the family without the patriarch. Elizabeth Spriggs as Connie surrounded by her
sons: (crouching) Kenny (Ray Winstone), (standing, l. to r.) Ray (Derrick O'Connor),
Phil (Eamon Boland), Joey (Larry Lamb), Vin (Bernard Hill).

and it was Bryan Cowgill who suggested that he shouldn't die until half
way through the serial – he felt that it was a great pity that the audience
had no chance to see the family held together by this patriarch before
dying. Trevor Preston seems to have accepted this suggestion quite
readily and we publish the revised outline below. This is quite short –
the original was 14 pages long and included many outline stories which
were not used and presented the following concluding arguments for its
production:

I think *Fox*, properly developed, could have a lot of potential. It has

99

the audience attraction of running over a period long enough for them to relate to and get involved with the central characters. It also has enough dramatic flexibility never to become predictable. Within its dramatic scope could be the family saga, the love story, the thriller, the court drama, the cockney comedy, cops and villains, villains and villains, etc.

Usually in a serial a number of writers and directors are used. This often results in a confusion of styles, a blurring of characters. *Fox* would have *one* writer and *one* director. (Jim Goddard is convinced this is quite practicable after his experience on *Out.*) This would give a one-hundred per cent continuity in both the writing and the interpretation.

It's difficult putting an idea like *Fox* down in a few pages. All I can say simply is, I think it could have all the appeal, excitement and humour that *Out* has, plus a much greater range of story telling. In a way it is a natural extension of *Out*, a larger canvas, a sort of South London Godfather.

'FOX' OUTLINE

Billy Fox is a legend in his lifetime. King Billy they call him in his South London manor and at Covent Garden where he worked for nearly fifty years. Stories are told about King Billy's practical jokes, his boozing, his fights, his capacity for work and his generosity.

Billy has been married twice, first to Ruby who gave him two sons, Vin and Ray. When Ruby died prematurely, Billy married Connie, who was much younger than himself. They had three sons, Joey, Phil and Kenny. The five Fox brothers all have elements of their father's character: Joey the joker and ladies' man, Vin the grafter, Ray the hard man, Phil the clever one and Kenny the fighter. From the Elephant to Fulham King Billy and his boys are known and respected, they have many friends; there are also enemies, not the least of these being the Macey brothers, Frank and George, who have had to play second fiddle to the Fox family all their lives and never miss an opportunity to have a go at them.

Vin is forty-three. He lives with his wife Renie and his three kids in Battersea; the youngest, Andy, was born profoundly deaf. Vin runs a small scaffolding company. When Vin left school he worked the markets, selling anything he could buy cheap and knock out at a small profit. When he married Renie she pushed him toward his own business, she's bright and very ambitious for Vin, without her he'd still be stuck in the markets. Vin is not an aggressive man, he has learned to use his street intelligence to make his way through life, but if he is pushed into a corner he can handle himself.

Ray is thirty-nine, divorced. His ex-wife Sheila married again and now lives in Leicester with their sixteen year old daughter Jenny. Ray runs a club in the West End and lives in a flat just off Clapham Common. Ray is a hard man and moves easily among the villains who come to his club. He also knows a lot of police and accepts the fact of life that you have to put a bit of money about to stay healthy in his line of work. Ray has been to prison twice, a two and a four. After the last little lot he decided that was it, no way was he going back inside. His regular girlfriend Carol helps keep him in order. Ray loves to dress well, eat expensive, drive a nice motor and have an attractive woman with him, in a word he's a tiny bit flash.

Joey is thirty-four. Everyone loves Joey, there's something about him. Joey can walk into a drinker with an atmosphere like an embalming parlour and ten minutes later people are laughing and buying each other drinks. Joey is a taxi driver. He rents a small flat overlooking the common. Joey is a bit of a puller, his natural charm and cheeky good looks do the pulling for him. But Joey's emotional life tends to get a bit complicated. For the past eighteen months he's been obliging a married woman. At first it was just a giggle, but it seems to be getting serious, at least on her part, she's talking about leaving her old man and moving in; this Joey is not best pleased about but doesn't quite know how to tell her.

Phil is twenty-six, the bright boy of the family. He went to the local comprehensive, got nine O's and three A's and seemed a certainty for university, but Phil didn't want to go. He left school and went to work. But nothing seemed to interest Phil, nothing seemed to stretch him, and as he slowly drifted from job to job he started to realise he had made a mistake. He applied for a mature student entry to university to study philosophy, and got in. There he met Anna; her family are loaded and don't care much for her association with Phil. Emotionally Phil finds himself in a growing dilemma, increasingly torn between two cultures, the South London working class where he was raised and the academic, professional class to which he aspires. Phil finds himself drifting away from his family, which causes all of them a lot of unhappiness. One of the main reasons for Phil's problems is his maturing political awareness. Billy, like many working-class Londoners, is a confirmed conservative and Phil's left-wing views are anathema to him.

Kenny is just twenty-one, the baby of the Fox family. At school he was always scrapping. An intelligent games master channelled this aggression into the boxing ring. Kenny was National Schoolboys Champion at fourteen, ABA Champion at seventeen, a full international with twenty six appearances for Great Britain before he signed professional forms with Eddie Chapman, the most respected of the younger managers. Eddie is convinced that he has a British, European and possible World champion in Kenny Fox, and is guiding him carefully toward international boxing honours. Kenny lives at home with Billy and Connie in a neat little house in Clapham. Boxing is his life, all he cares about apart from his family. He trains almost too hard, doesn't smoke or drink and has a steady girlfriend, Nan, who he intends to marry as soon as possible. As Kenny's professional boxing career has blossomed he has become something of a local celebrity and Billy and the brothers love showing him off.

A father and his five sons, five brothers, five individuals, their lives all different but with the strongest family bond tying them inexorably together. In a serial of thirteen one-hour films shot entirely on location, we show the interaction of their lives, a complete spectrum of drama, the humour, the sadness, the achievements, the setbacks, the ambitions, the innermost fears, the loves and infidelities, the violence and villainy, the pleasures and the pressures of a rather special family living in London today.

101

Some incidents in the Fox family story
Billy's seventieth birthday when the Maceys let a sack of rats into the party, and Joey learns that his married girlfriend has tried to kill herself.

Kenny's fight for the Southern Area title when he sees his opponent carried unconscious from the ring and later learns that he has died.

Phil suspended from university for organising a demonstration at which an eminent right-wing politician is badly injured by a flying milk bottle.

Billy's heart attack while out fishing with Andy. The deaf child's dilemma to find someone to help him. Billy's death. The family shock.

Billy's jazz funeral. If it's good enough for New Orleans it's good enough for Clapham. Billy leaves strict instructions for his musical funeral.

Connie discovers that Billy had a daughter, the daughter she always wanted to give him, by another woman.

The gunfight at the O.K. Corral South London style. The Fox mob decide to sort the Maceys out once and for all. They meet for a 'straightener' in Big Albert's boozer one Sunday morning.

Phil leaves for America to try and sort his life out. After Billy's death the family starts to fall apart.

Fox was put into production very quickly with the result that Trevor Preston had to write the last five or six episodes when shooting had already started. This was obviously not an ideal situation for the writer but nor was it for the director Jim Goddard, who had agreed to direct all thirteen episodes (a Herculean task) and who, for economy's sake, was shooting *Fox* as if it was a thirteen-hour movie. The continuity problems alone are enormous if one follows this procedure but clearly it is cheaper to shoot all the scenes that take place in any one location consecutively.

Verity Lambert loved every single episode of *Fox* but she did feel that the large number of episodes and the size of the family made for difficult viewing. It was this complexity and the almost inevitable fall in audience ratings that sequential series experience (an exception being *Widows* – something we will return to later) which resulted in *Fox* not getting the viewing figures for which everybody hoped.

Fox took three months to plan, six months to shoot and a further three months for post-production work. It was clearly a huge project for Jim Goddard to undertake but being the sole director meant that, as with *Out,* he could control everything. For example, we asked him about lighting the two projects:

For *Out* I wanted a razor-blue light. It was lit with a north light which is colder and clearer and will burn the windows out more. I told the camera operator that I never wanted to see anything out of a window unless somebody looks out of a window and then I'd take their point of view. I wanted to burn the windows out because it increases the intensity of what's happening inside, because it's about one guy, his

102

obsession and lunacy.

In *Fox* there wasn't one burnt-out window and I wanted a goldy, nicotine effect as you would find in a pub – not one of those reconstructed Covent Garden pubs but as you find in a real old South London pub. So it was lit with a south light which will change all day and be much warmer. And in *Fox* you could always see right down the street and all the cars and everything because as Trevor said, *Fox* was as much about London as it was about that family.

Fox and *Out* were recently bought by, and repeated on, Channel 4 because, as Jeremy Isaacs said, on a limited budget he always knew he wasn't going to be able to afford all the new drama he wanted to commission, so he has a policy of going for repeats of a few things of 'supreme quality'. And until the repeat of *The Far Pavilions* the repeat of *Out* achieved Channel 4's highest audience ratings.

'STAINLESS STEEL AND THE STAR SPIES'

Stainless Steel and the Star Spies is a Sci-Fi comedy programme about small metal creatures from another planet who come into contact with Earth and find human beings to be most peculiar. This programme also marked another departure for Euston Films for although it was their second foray into the field of science fiction it was their first film which used puppetry and pixillation mixed with live action (in a ratio of about 2:1). This sort of project would have seemed to have belonged far more naturally with another of Thames' wholly-owned subsidiaries, Cosgrove Hall Films.

The one-hour pilot was screened on New Year's Day 1981 and although it was transmitted at 4.45pm it wasn't necessarily designed specifically for children. According to Johnny Goodman this was one of the unresolved problems of the project – it could have been popular with adults as well if it had worked; the failure, he felt, was due to the lack of definition of the audience that was being addressed. The pilot was not considered a success (an interesting experimental failure perhaps) and the planned follow-up thirteen part half-hour series was never made.

EUSTON FILMS – NOT JUST A MAN'S WORLD

The Flame Trees of Thika marked another new departure for Euston Films. It is a serialisation of a book by Elspeth Huxley which offers a child's view of going to Kenya in 1918 with her parents to start a new life as coffee planters. Initially it was a project set up by an independent production company called Consolidated Productions. This company was established in 1978 by John Pringle, John Whitney (then Managing Director of Capital Radio and now Director-General of the IBA) and

103

The Flame Trees of Thika: 'the women in it were strong and courageous.' Tilly Grant (Hayley Mills), Elspeth Grant (Holly Aird).

John Hawkesworth, who had already worked for Euston. The company is 25% owned by CLT and Radio Luxembourg and has been very successful in America. They have co-produced with Home Box Office and CBS and they were the first non-American company to be licensed by an American television network for a prime-time series. A number of people who had worked for Euston, including Ted Childs, went to work for Consolidated Productions. Consolidated didn't put any money into the project once Thames/Euston decided to go ahead but they had already optioned the book, Hawkesworth had written one script, they had

104

recced the locations and Hawkesworth produced (with Christopher Neame). In return Consolidated received a credit and a percentage for providing the package.

Verity Lambert:

It appealed to me, I suppose. It seemed that if you did have a very strong London identity, which I think we did have at Euston, then you could afford to be flexible if something comes up, and the idea of Kenya and the animals and the child and everything were just very appealing. And I also thought Euston is a very male-oriented company and I thought it was a rather good story about women – the women in it were strong and courageous and I felt that it rang the changes a bit from the rather sort of macho stuff that we were making. And in fact I think it's quite interesting that I was travelling through Kenya at one point with John Hawkesworth and we were talking about it and I said, 'Of course, you know this is really a very feminist story'. And John said, 'What do you mean?' And I said, 'Well if you examine it all the women are the people who get things done in it and come to terms with their life'. And he said 'I've never thought of it like that but you're right.'

The Flame Trees of Thika was very expensive to produce; ideally Euston would have liked to have had some co-production finance to go on location but that couldn't be raised. Nor did Thames manage to pre-sell it, so there was a period when it was very uncertain whether it would be made at all. Eventually it sold rather well.

'WIDOWS'

The one thing that I would say about *Minder* is that the women who appear in *Minder* – as opposed to 'Er Indoors who never appears – are not stereotypes on the whole. If you examine the women, for example the stripper that Terry had the relationship with, they're all rather good characters. But I accept the fact that it is male-oriented and I suppose that *Flame Trees* was the first thing where I thought 'Hmm, well this is about women'. And it made me conscious of the fact because one or two of my feminist friends had made some quite, well if not derogatory remarks, had at least asked me questions about it and I had become conscious of the fact that I really should try and do something about women. Which is how – well when *Widows* came in I was very specifically trying to look for something that had women as the protagonists as opposed to men. (Verity Lambert)

Widows is the story of four women, three of whom are suddenly widowed when their husbands are killed in a horrific car chase following

105

a robbery attempt. But the women are on to a potential goldmine because the ledgers of Harry (one of the husbands), which are wanted by both police and rival villains, hold the key to a robbery fortune and to the future of half the criminals of London.

Widows also marks the major writing debut of Lynda La Plante, who is better known as the character actress Lynda Marchal. She had the idea for the story and submitted it to London Weekend Television who turned it down, at which point she submitted it to Verity Lambert and Linda Agran. What happened next is best recounted in Linda Agran's own words:

> Well, Lynda came in with an idea which she claimed she couldn't write. She said it's a six-parter and outlined it. She's an actress who has written little bits and bobs but certainly nothing as ambitious as this. And she said she could probably write the first one but after that she wasn't sure. So I said, well I'll commission the first script and if it's any good I'll commission the remaining five. And then you'll have to do it unless you want to be really embarrassed and start returning the money. So that's exactly what happened. Now the first one came in and it was terrific – I mean it would probably have run for about two hours – but it was terrific. It had great energy. So I set her off to write the remaining five and I realised that if I held her up – because in fact it's quite complicated in terms of its structure – if I gave her any rewrites at any point I would hold her up and she'd have to go back and start writing again and would probably get lost. So as she delivered the first drafts I would ring her up an hour and a half later and say, 'Terrific. Terrific, keep going.' And she'd go, 'Nothing . . .?' 'No, just keep going, just great.' And so when she worked right through we had this huge file this big and then I said, 'Right, now we'll start again.' So she and I virtually locked ourselves away and went through it and I remember picking up the phone in the middle of the night and saying, 'Listen, how the hell did Harry know, etc.' because it really is quite complicated.

We asked Linda Agran both about the experience of working on a women-controlled production and about the representation of women:

> I really think that it needs a woman, not necessarily a woman producer, but it needed a woman there all the time in terms of casting, attitudes, in terms of the women's attitudes to each other, and so I decided to produce it myself. Well I'm delighted with the success and I'm pleased that I did it. It was a real labour of love, though; I enjoyed doing it. It was also lovely casting blokes to do bits on the side. I used to fantasise with Lynda about having casting sessions with blokes – telling them to take their clothes off, you know – but of course we

Widows director Ian Toynton, surrounded by (clockwise from extreme left) Maureen O'Farrell, Ann Mitchell, Fiona Hendley, Eva Mottley, Linda Agran, Lynda La Plante.

didn't do any of that!

I think one of the reasons that *Widows* was as successful as it was, was that it was the first time women – real women if you like – were in the front, driving it on, casting the right way, looking the right way. And written the right way. You see the problem with series writing, and the problem with a lot of the differences between men and women and the way they're perceived and the way they're portrayed, is that

107

male writers can't write women – or they think they can't, so they tend to avoid writing them. So they write a lot of men because they understand blokes and they know how they work and they don't want to get the women wrong. Very often it's through very good motives. Trevor, for example, used to say to me on *Out* and on *Fox*, 'Do you think . . . how do you think she would respond to that?' Almost as though dealing with Martians. Men, because they don't want to get it wrong, leave them out.

On *Danger UXB* for example, it was very hard to work women into it and very often in the script readings with Hawkesworth and the Technical Adviser or whoever, I would say, 'Listen, don't you think we should have a woman in here somewhere?' – 'No, absolutely not.' I would like to see more women and more black faces and a black hero. . . .

It was very strange on *Widows* too because when I was working on it right at the beginning people used to say, 'Oh, it's about women. Nah, won't work, people won't watch it.' – 'Who won't watch it?' And they would say, 'Well, women won't watch it because they won't be interested enough and it will turn men off because they won't want to watch a lot of heavy dykes holding up a . . . .' And it was interesting that they were proved to be absolutely wrong. Women loved it.

In fact, the success of *Widows* is unusual in being one of the few serials we can think of that has actually *built* an audience. The problem with serials is that once people miss an episode they tend not to go back to the production, fearing that they have missed too much of the plot. We also asked Linda about the attitude of the Thames hierarchy to the project:

Well, first of all they don't read scripts. And I can get quite angry about the fact that they're either buying my judgement or they are not. Other people's views of scripts are interesting but they are not going to affect my view of them. So when I told them about *Widows* they were in fact very supportive about the idea. I softened it a bit, but they saw it as a sort of crime thriller/mystery/twist and turn story and they felt also that there was some strength to my argument, I think, that women are not seen as often as they should be on television and not in the right roles. So there was a fair amount of enthusiasm for it.

In the original treatment the women don't get away with it but Verity Lambert said that she didn't want to do it unless they did: 'They'd worked very hard and got it all planned – why shouldn't they get away with it?' Linda Agran was similarly firm on this point despite Lynda La Plante's hesitancy:

108

I know that some people think that the end is morally very questionable and Lynda said to me they can't get away with it, can they – the IBA wouldn't allow it. And I said, 'Nuts. Sure I'll talk to the IBA if necessary. If people are really going to get involved with it – and it is fiction – of course they're going to want them to get away with it.' After all, they show *The Italian Job* on television and I don't think you have people sitting there thinking, 'Oh I hope the police are going to come soon and nab these baddies.'

The director of *Widows* was Ian Toynton, a man who had worked for Euston Films from the beginning. He was approached by Linda when four of the six scripts were finished. He said yes immediately: 'One of the bonuses for me was the strength and depth of the characterisation. One-hour series episodes don't give the scope for such development.' The major problem of the project for him was that he felt that the serial was terribly ambitious for the time and money budgeted but he made the same comment as Chris Burt did about *Reilly*: 'At least you knew the money was going up on the screen.'

Mike Phillips mentioned that in the United States theatrical producers were interested in a movie version of *Widows* for television. Thames, he said, wouldn't do a format deal but would be interested in taking the project to a screenplay stage. This was mentioned because he said that they had received a firm offer 'on the table' from the American cable service *Showtime* to do a TV movie version but that this had been decided against.

There will, however, by the time this book is published, be a follow-up serial, *Widows II*. We asked Linda Agran about this project:

Well, it was very difficult because neither Lynda nor myself had any idea that we had not ended it. They've gone to Rio, you know, and Dolly just says, 'I still love him'. Finish. Now I didn't realise that people were going to get that involved with it. You know, where's Harry gone, etc? So, Thames started to make noises about doing six more to tell what happened. And I said, 'No! I don't want to do that'. So then they said, 'Come on, come on, should we talk to Lynda, is she being difficult about it – doesn't she want to . . .?' And I said, 'Look, I tell you what, I'm prepared to sit down and talk to Lynda and see if there is any chance'. And it was really just to go through the motions so that I could say, right I've been down that path and it can't be done. And what happened was that we sat down and started to talk about what might happen. And we became rather sort of caught up in it. So we started getting involved in discussing it and so now we're working – I've got the rough first drafts on all of them and we're re-writing now.

It's slightly worrying because I think people's expectations are

109

raised and therefore – whereas going for *Widows* the first time was relatively easy because it was all unfamiliar – now that they've seen the
first six (and I'm sure that Thames will now repeat the first six and
then go rocking on into the new series) this one will be more difficult.

MONEY BEFORE PRODUCTION – DIFFERENT HORSES FOR DIFFERENT COURSES

Reilly – Ace of Spies, based on Robin Bruce Lockhart's book, was Euston's
most ambitious and expensive project to date. It cost £4.5 million and
Verity Lambert – who was extremely keen to do it – spent three years
arguing for it and trying to encourage co-production deals in order to
finance the project. This was fairly difficult to achieve given that Verity
Lambert is also keen to maintain a high degree of control over all of her
projects. This she would certainly seem to have achieved with *Reilly* in
that it was both pre-sold to Mobil in the States and to Australia, French-
speaking Canada and Dutch TV, yet Jim Goddard, one of the two directors on the project, said that he experienced no outside interference as
far as those deals were concerned.

   In fact, *Reilly* as a TV project has a history as long as Euston's own.
The series is based on fact and concerns the exploits of a mystery man
of Russian birth who worked for British Intelligence in the 1890s and
early 1900s. He retained his love of mother Russia but tried to bring
down the Bolshevik regime. The property was originally owned by Stella
Richman who was Controller of Programmes in the early seventies at
London Weekend Television. She left to become an independent producer and then offered it with Troy Kennedy-Martin to Brian Tesler as
soon as he arrived at LWT in 1974. Interested as he was in the package,
the problem for Brian Tesler was that it was clearly going to be too expensive to make. LWT didn't (and still doesn't) have a film subsidiary,
much as they would like one, which meant that if they were going to
make it they would have to do so 'in-house', still on film but made under
the ITCA agreement, which would have made it too expensive.

   Thus LWT turned the project down and it was offered to a number
of other companies, who also rejected it. As Brian Tesler expressed it:
'And then, one of the ironies of our business, Stella Richman's hold on
the rights expired and Troy Kennedy-Martin was free to offer it elsewhere.' So Troy Kennedy-Martin approached Verity Lambert:

   Well, *Reilly* I just wanted because I thought Reilly was a wonderful
   character and I thought that it was a real opportunity to do something about an extraordinary charismatic character against a fas-
   cinating historical background. And it was quite popular – it got
   about eight and a half to nine million people each week, which I don't
   think is at all bad. I thought it was an opportunity to get that kind

110

Reilly – Ace of Spies. The Port Arthur set. '*Reilly* represents the first time that Euston really got into large-scale set construction.'

of an audience and also to have some kind of a serious underbelly at the same time.

We talked to Chris Burt, the producer, at length about the project:

In fact Troy mentioned it to me when we were cutting *Sweeney II* – but then it was still Stella Richman's – it had a very long gestation period. And then Verity picked it up and took it to the Thames board – and she looked at a lot of people to produce it and she picked me, thank goodness!

At that time we had 12 scripts, of which one was in some sort of working order, really – they were written at that stage for a video production (it was thought that it was going to be part video and part film) so there were huge long speeches. And also it was out of date because what had happened since then was that once one really got into it, one got information which totally changed the whole concept of the serial and so we really had to re-write the whole lot.

When we started I suppose we had 6 scripts which wasn't really enough so it was a constant battle because the only way you can make that work on that money is, for example, if you have one set and

111

you've got twelve scripts and you know that you've got this set in episodes 1, 3, 5 and 8, you shoot 1, 3, 5, 8. I mean, I had a director coming on for half a day and then the other for a day and a half and then back to the first for a quarter of a day – I mean the continuity problems for the directors, for the actors, lighting – for everybody, were tremendous but I must say that I think that everybody did a very good job.

The serial was initially out of date because once we started work there were all sorts of books we discovered and people, like Michael Kettle who also brought out a book on Sidney Reilly, and bits and pieces of information we discovered about Reilly. I mean, we had so much information by the end of it that we could actually make an accurate guess about when Reilly was killed, which we did – it was a guess and we put it actually in the last episode. And it's very interesting that *Iszvestia*, three months later, came out with the full story of his death and I think we were one month out.

This research hadn't been done because the books weren't around – Troy was working in a vacuum by himself in a room in Notting Hill Gate but once the word gets around and it's an actual go project it passes round an enormous group of people by word of mouth. For example I got a phone call, 'I hear that you are making a film about Sidney Reilly, well I was hoping to do a film for Universal about Sidney Reilly and I've got all the letters and all the photos and all the rest', so off we went to the Screen on the Green and there was David Eady who supplied us with information that we simply didn't have – letters which gave us character descriptions and all those sorts of things. Which if the thing hadn't been going and word of mouth hadn't . . . – I mean that particular contact came because we had chosen a location manager and David Eady was married to his mother!

At this stage Troy, Verity, Chris and Jim Goddard (at the beginning) worked together (Martin Campbell was working on another project at this time so couldn't join them). Then it was just Troy and Chris on the scripts:

We had two directors on this project because when you are dealing with period as well and all the rest of it, it is terribly difficult. I know that Jim is built like an ox and had done *Fox* but there he had all the scripts and Trevor and he had worked on them together and they knew them inside out before they started but even then it was a terrific thing for him.

Despite the scale and cost of *Reilly* projects like this have got to be done because – well, in terms of sales of course *Reilly* has done extremely well and, for instance, Cannes last year was full of *Reilly* and it attracts other business – I think the *Hornblower* series is going to be one that is the same kind of size if Euston do it – and the fact is that there is a need for what I would call 'event' television or big productions. They are terribly popular with audiences, you can sell them around the world – provided that you can get the price right to make a profit.

I was on *Reilly* for two years and that's starting with the scripts, then the extraordinarily complicated scheduling of it – I mean it's the toughest thing I've ever done, in the sense of trying to do it on the money. It was an enormous canvas. We couldn't afford to go to Dundee or Glasgow which we knew was perfect for Russian scenes and we had to shoot it within the limits of people going backwards and forwards from their homes every night – although we did go to Malta of course to shoot the battle sequences and the Port Arthur sequences, and to France to shoot bits of Paris, but that was as much as we had. We had the money to go away for four weeks and that was it. And the Kremlin and all the rest we couldn't afford to go and do.

The locations were found by a combination of Roger Hall, the Production Designer, and two extremely capable Location Managers. But we operated out of a base in Elstree. And the real complications on that was because of the length of time and the difficulties of finding locations – you know you can't find the Kremlin overnight and then even if you do finally get the permissions – and remember you are not just getting the permission, you have to repaint things, take down telegraph poles, you've got to stop the traffic, you've got to put down cobble stones, you've got to burn fires here and there, all sorts of things – to get those permissions at a time when we also had a very strict construction budget which meant that they only had certain days to get things up and down and we had to go out on location shooting in between and there were the contractual arrangements with the artists – it was all an enormous problem.

When hiring Elstree all you get is the space and a telephone and a rather good management. We had to provide all our own equipment. (For instance Elstree has 35 mm editing tables not 16 mm.) In terms of money we weren't in a position of breaking down the scripts, analysing them and then saying this costs that, as most people do with a feature film. You were given a sum of money – 'you're not going to get any more, there's no contingency and now you go away and make it'. The money had to all go up on the screen. We had to allocate the money as we saw best and make the books balance.

In fact it was cast and construction which constituted the largest part of the budget; it is interesting that *Reilly* represents the first time that Euston really got into large-scale set construction, ironic for a company whose whole *raison d'être* was the importance of location work.

113

The long history of the *Reilly* project is a complex and at times acrimonious one between a number of people and of the project files we looked through at Euston Films it was much the largest and certainly the most interesting. Originally we had hoped to analyse and quote from some of the documents in order to offer a case study. Unfortunately however, Thames felt that the documents were too confidential and sensitive to be discussed in print – perhaps a not inappropriate response for a project about such a secret man as Reilly!

'THE NATION'S HEALTH'

The Nation's Health is thus far the only Euston production made specifically for Channel 4. It came about as a result of Tony Garnett leaving the BBC to go into independent film production. He talked to Bryan Cowgill and Verity Lambert about the possibility of him being placed on a retainer to present to Euston Films those projects which might not be particularly suitable for the cinema. As far as we know this didn't happen but he did initially present Verity with a project from Gordon Newman, a fictionalised piece about the Krays and about growing up with their sort of background. She wasn't very keen because she felt that Euston had been over that ground so much with *Out* and *Fox*. Having said no, however, Verity did say that she might be interested in something else that Gordon might do. Tony Garnett returned saying that Gordon wanted to do four drama-documentaries about medicine and the National Health system in Britain today, presented in the style of *Law and Order* and called *The Nation's Health*. This Verity jumped at.

Verity thought it a perfect drama for Channel 4 – 'Exactly the kind of drama Channel 4 should be doing' – and sent it immediately to Jeremy Isaacs, who commented:

> *The Nation's Health* was the first set of scripts that David Rose read that he knew instantly he wanted to do. And he came to me in some excitement and said to me, 'At last we've got something and it's marvellous. This is what we should be doing.' And I read them and I'm the most squeamish man alive – I can't bear operations – and I said yes, we'll try to do this. And then I spent a year trying to persuade Thames to make them. And the reason they didn't want to make them was that we couldn't afford to pay the entire cost of them. Anyway, in the end they did agree to make them for the price we agreed to pay and so they got made. And we were very glad to have them.

At the time of writing, *Reilly* and *The Nation's Health* were Euston's most recently completed projects. In our conclusion we discuss forthcoming productions and possible future developments.

114

PART II
READINGS

1 Anxious Moments: *The Sweeney* in 1975

James Donald

And again, there are those who hold it a virtue to say: 'Virtue is necessary'; but fundamentally they believe only that the police are necessary. (Nietzsche, *Thus Spoke Zarathustra*)

Every affect belonging to an emotional impulse, whatever its kind, is
transformed, if it is repressed, into anxiety. (Freud, 'The "Un-
canny"')

'Abduction', written by Trevor Preston, directed by Tom Clegg, produced by Ted Childs, was first broadcast on 27 March 1975 at ten past
nine in the evening.[1] It was watched by over seven million people, which
made it tenth in the audience ratings for that week. It was also the
episode that closed the first, highly successful series of *The Sweeney*.
　How to flesh out these bare facts so as to get some sense of the programme's resonance at that time? How to account not only for *The
Sweeney* as a particular type of commodity, filling that slot in the Thursday night schedule, but also for 'Abduction' as a topical narrative fantasy in which contemporary anxieties about a supposed breakdown of
'law and order' were visibly being played out? How, in short, to break
into television's elusive circuits of meaning-production and entertainment in order to identify the conditions in which the narrative strategies
of (for example) 'Abduction' could make sense and be enjoyable?
　I should perhaps acknowledge straightaway that 'Abduction' was in
some ways an atypical episode of *The Sweeney*. Coming at the end of the
run, it seems to have been more concerned than usual with the underlying thematic of the series – the paradoxical meshing between an an-
tagonism against authority and a passion for justice within the figure of
'Regan'. At this fairly early, potentially malleable stage of the programme, this condensation had not solidified into the gestural clichés
of later series: the thematic still retained at least the potential for explo-
ration and development. 'Abduction' therefore provides a useful way
into thinking about *The Sweeney* in general.

117

To understand how 'Abduction' works – a more interesting and less de-
lusory question than what it means, it seems to me – it will be necessary
to approach the programme from a number of angles: institutional,
economic, historical, generic and ideological. Some of these deal with
The Sweeney as a series, and it is only really when I deal with the question
of narrative that I focus exclusively on 'Abduction'.

I'll start, conventionally enough, with the production context. The
working methods of Euston Films are dealt with elsewhere in this
volume. My concern is how these informed the narratives of *The Sweeney*
in general and 'Abduction' in particular. At one level, the process is well
illustrated by the Outline Format for the programme (see Part I). What
is particularly striking about the document is the precision with which
the formal requirements are detailed – the need to tailor each narrative
pattern primarily geared to the breaks for advertisements, for example:

> The overall episode screen time (ex. titles) is 48.40. We expect the
> final draft script to read about 53 minutes. Each film will open with
> a teaser of up to 3 minutes duration, which is followed by the opening
> titles. The story is played across three acts, each of which must be
> no more than 19 and not less than 8 minutes in length.

Such constraints posed real difficulties, especially for the writers. 'One
felt very restricted on 52 minutes each week', according to Trevor
Preston, 'having to think up a new story, get the characters established,
get through to the *dénouement* at the end: I just used to feel like I was writing with my legs crossed most of the time.'

The decision to shoot *The Sweeney* on 16mm film rather than video
pushed it, according to Ted Childs, towards an emphasis on action
rather than dialogue and a particular focus on the three main characters,
Inspector Jack Regan (John Thaw), his sidekick George Carter (Dennis
Waterman) and their bureaucratic boss Haskins (Garfield Morgan),
with space only for two or three other major speaking parts per episode.
But the comparative freedom that film allowed was hampered by the
production schedule of only ten days for each film. This meant shooting
an average of five minutes edited screen time a day; no more than ten
locations (and those to be no more than half an hour's driving time, at
the speed of the generator, from the crew's base in Hammersmith); two
days scheduled for shooting inside the series' interior set at Colet Court,
a disused school building; and no more than three minutes exterior night
shooting.

The novelty of using 16mm film for a drama series, and the suspicion
with which it was regarded, also led to a rather conservative *mise-en-scène*.
As a result, as Childs now admits, many of the shots that finished up

on screen were 'a little too prissy and Christmas card-like', lacking 'the gritty, grainy quality they should have had, and could have had.' Certainly, *The Sweeney*'s treatment of London lacks either the realist edge or the mythologised quality of the city in such near-contemporary Hollywood films as *The French Connection* (which Childs claims as a direct stylistic influence) or Siegel's *Dirty Harry*, with its play on voyeuristic long shots and sometimes vertiginous helicopter shots. Whether this can be attributed wholly to the need for cheapness is doubtful, as later television crime dramas on film have shown – think of Euston's own *Out*, the BBC's *Law and Order* and *The Chinese Detective*, or MTM's *Hill Street Blues*.

Childs' emphasis on the need to produce *The Sweeney* according to a standard format – a commodity built to precise specifications – underlines the need for repetition in a series like this. Advertisers and audiences want to know what they're getting. But they never want exactly the same story – they want both the repetition of familiar elements (the structure, the characters, the narrative form) and also the novelty of something different in each episode.

For those working on the series, this duality often seems to have presented itself as a conflicting need to be both entertaining (which was taken to mean sticking to the formulae) and also to attempt something different – to be stylish, realistic, instructive, topical or whatever. 'What I try to do is *use* the genre,' says Trevor Preston, 'because it is a thing that people understand. They know what a crime series is, they know the format, therefore they feel comfortable with it.' Or again, 'I really do believe in entertaining people . . . but I also believe that the other fifty per cent can be all sorts of things. As far as subject matter and narrative go, I don't see why series and serials couldn't blossom enormously.'

So what did the makers of *The Sweeney* see themselves as doing? Technical and economic constraints may rule out certain options, but they cannot in themselves determine what does go into a narrative. What counts is the way contraints and demands are perceived as operating – the unconsidered assumptions and collective folk wisdom that constitute the ideological baggage of television professionals. It is from these that their intentions and decisions are woven, and they clearly affect the programmes that emerge. In the early stages of *The Sweeney*, there was, in fact, a serious disagreement about the form and direction of the series between Ian Kennedy-Martin, who wrote the pilot *Regan* and devised the series, and Ted Childs, whom Euston brought in as producer.

This seems to have revolved around two main issues. One was the method of production, with Kennedy-Martin taking exception to Euston's movie company-style use of freelance crews under the managerial control of a 'line producer' and the consequent down-grading of the writer. 'I always felt the particular area we were in was very much a director's medium,' says Childs. 'Some writers responded to that better than others. Trevor Preston did, obviously; Troy Kennedy-Martin

119

did; Ian less so.'

Tied in with this conflict about management and control was the other bone of contention – the purpose and style of the series. This sometimes took the form of a dispute about conflicting perceptions of *realism* within a popular genre. Childs saw this in terms of a particular shooting style associated with a current cycle of crime movies and, to a lesser extent, the *vérité* documentaries he had worked on previously. Realism, in this view, was a device for adding an extra frisson to the fiction:

> Those of us who were concerned with the production and direction, as opposed to the concept and the scripts, were influenced by *The French Connection*. That was the genre piece current at the time we made the pilot and the first series. We were all taken by that sort of realism – the much quoted shot was Gene Hackman with his paper cup standing across the street while two drug peddlers are having a slap-up meal in a Manhattan restaurant.

Ian Kennedy-Martin's conception was diametrically opposed to this. For him, realism meant telling the unvarnished truth about the Flying Squad in the mid-seventies. His original idea had been to explore the impact of Robert Mark's appointment as Commissioner of the Metropolitan Police on a detective in the Flying Squad whom Kennedy-Martin knew:

> He was an uncorrupted cop – I knew this by personal experience. There were the great shadows starting to come over the Flying Squad, which would end up with the arrest of Commander Drury. This friend of mine in the Flying Squad, a man of great experience, was now being told by Commissioner Mark that he had to work in a different way – that he was not to go to pubs in Fulham and talk to villains, that he must not make those contacts. It could all be done from a desk in an office on the third floor of Scotland Yard.

For Kennedy-Martin, schooled in the traditions of BBC naturalism, all that was needed for *The Sweeney* to be both entertaining and realistic was to knock the stories into dramatic shape with as few frills as possible added:

> It was taken over by Euston Films and they made a series out of it. I can't hold myself responsible for what happened then. I will say that the characterisation, the delineation of the situation that was in the pilot lasted the entire four series of *The Sweeney* – if anything, it is a criticism that they didn't change enough of my pilot. But I think they were influenced for the worse by watching television around them and there's obviously large chunks of *Starsky and Hutch* in the series,

120

and other influences. I kept saying things like, 'This series has got to be about real people and real situations. We don't have to invent anything. If the writers just go down and meet some of these people in Scotland Yard, they'll find out what's actually happening. So let's not have diamond robberies at London Airport and attractive females getting laid. It'll work the other way: just real people in real situations.' But very quickly it became about unreal people in unreal situations.

The point of raking over the embers of this ancient spat is simply to indicate the peculiar currency of the notion of realism within entertainment television. It involves certain assumptions about the status of a popular genre like crime fiction; it displaces the very problematic arguments about its relationship to the real world it purports to represent; and it is used to justify a preference for a particular dramatic style – in this case, imitations of *The French Connection* or *Dirty Harry* vs. *Z-Cars* naturalism. To get to grips with this range of questions, we have to move beyond the limited context of Euston Films to consider the historical preconditions for the narrative structures of *The Sweeney*.

LAW & ORDER

What was the relationship of *The Sweeney* to changes in English society in the mid-seventies? Even to pose the question in this way seems to invite the common sense answer that popular art *reflects* what is happening in society. It is true that crime fiction can be read (carefully and sceptically) as symptomatic of certain aspects of the popular culture of which it has been such an enduring ingredient. Also, it would be perverse to deny that there is a connection between the appearance of a programme like *The Sweeney* and the contemporary political concerns about, on the one hand, law and order and, on the other, police corruption and brutality. But the one was not simply a reflection of the other – changes in policing (or criminality) are no more a sufficient explanation of changes in crime fiction than changes in the rates of vampirism would be for the periodic popularity of Dracula films.

At one level, the incorporation of contemporary concerns into *The Sweeney* was not at all a mysterious process. To bolster its claims to be a realistic representation of crime and policing, the programme simply 'pinched' newsworthy incidents and attitudes to give a gloss of topicality to its cops-and-robbers formulae. In 'Abduction' for example, Jack Regan delivers this monologue on London:

I sometimes hate this bastard place. It's a bloody holiday camp for thieves and weirdos . . . all the rubbish. You age prematurely trying to sort some of them out. You try and protect the public and all they

121

do is call you fascist. You nail a villain and some ponced-up, pin-striped amateur barrister screws you up like an old fag packet on a point of procedure, then pops off for a game of squash and a glass of Madeira. He's taking home thirty grand a year, and we can just about afford ten days in Eastbourne and a second-hand car.

Such ideas about the unhappy lot of the policeman had already been given wide publicity, especially as certain chief constables and police representatives were taking an unprecedentedly active role in political debates at this time. Some of the complaints mouthed by Regan in 1975 had been expressed two years earlier, in more sober terms, in the BBC's Dimbleby Lecture by Robert Mark – the most vociferous cop of the decade. On the disillusionment policemen felt with the workings of the law, and their sense of unrewarded self-sacrifice he had this to say:

Some people cling to a curious, old-fashioned belief that there is something vaguely improper in a policeman talking about the law, the courts or lawyers. No doubt the General Staff felt the same way about the infantrymen on the Somme. But as Lord Devlin has said, the police have a right to demand that the path they must tread should be clearly designed to lead to a just result, for the community for whom they act, as well as for the accused. You simply cannot ask men to do one of the more difficult and dangerous jobs of our time and expect them not to reason why.

Mark also alluded to the idea that niceties of judicial procedure, especially when manipulated by (sometimes bent) defence lawyers, tipped the scales of justice too far in favour of the accused. (In doing so, he also seemed almost to disavow the corruption rampant within the Met, which he had energetically attempted to stamp out.)

The criminal and his lawyers take every advantage of these technical rules. Every effort is made to find some procedural mistake which will allow the wrong-doer to slip through the net. If the prosecution evidence is strong, the defence frequently resorts to attacks on prosecution witnesses, particularly if they are policemen. They'll be accused, as a matter of routine, of perjury, planting evidence, intimidation or violence.

Although specific echoes of Mark's lecture may be discernible in 'Abduction', the ideas and attitudes he was expressing were not limited to the police. They were apparent in the moral panic about mugging that started in 1972, was fanned by the press and the courts, and exploited by certain politicians in the years that followed.[2] Mrs Whitehouse and her supporters were speaking in the same terms when they denounced

122

the evils of permissiveness. So were the *Black Papers'* attacks on 'declining standards' in education. What they shared was a conviction that social, political and economic problems – the drift to anarchy, as they often
saw it – could be ascribed to the erosion of moral discipline, respect for
authority and a clear sense of right and wrong. This broader shift away
from the consensual politics of 'Butskellism' in the 1950s or Harold
Wilson's increasingly desperate appeals to 'the national interest' and towards more abrasively confrontational forms of politics gave special
prominence to the questions of policing and social order. This, then, was
the historical moment in which *The Sweeney* was conceived. It did not,
as I have already stressed, reflect that moment. It was an integral part
of it, working its ideological tensions, anxieties and fantasies into fictional forms.

The Sweeney should therefore be seen as part of the cycle of 'rogue cop'
movies and programmes that were produced between the late sixties and
the mid-seventies. The central image in these – from Siegel's *Madigan*
(1968) to the absurdities of a geriatric John Wayne lumbering around
London in John Sturges's *McQ* (1974) – was of the policeman who is
forced to cut through bureaucracy and the complexities of civil and legal
rights, even to break the law himself in order to see that justice is done.
The fictional policeman as moral, even existential hero was nothing
new, of course. Nor was the idea that he might have to tackle the legal
and political establishment as well as the criminal – that is part of the
populist tradition in the gangster movie. But whereas in a film like Fritz
Lang's *The Big Heat* (1954), the honest cop, in order to avenge the murder of his wife, has to step outside a law that has been bought and cor-
rupted by a city's gangster boss, in films like *Dirty Harry* the enemies had
become squeamishly liberal lawyers, unprincipled politicians and the
spineless placemen running police departments. (This vision was taken
one step further in the vigilante movies, like Michael Winner's *Death
Wish* (1974), which to some extent superseded the rogue cop films.)

The political implications of these developments within crime fiction
did not pass unnoticed at the time. Indeed, it may be that Jack Regan's
complaint that 'all they do is call you fascist' may refer less to police/
public relations than to this critical reception. In a scathing review of
Dirty Harry in the *New Yorker* (15 January 1972), for example, Pauline
Kael wrote:

> In the action genre, it's easier – and more fun – to treat crime in the
> medieval way, as evil, without specific causes or background . . . the
> basic contest between good and evil is as simple as you can get. It
> makes the genre piece more archetypal than most movies, more
> primitive and dreamlike; fascist medievalism has a fairy-tale appeal.

In this country, Troy Kennedy-Martin, Ian's more radical brother and the creator of *Z Cars,* had expressed similar fears about the phenomenal popularity of Stratford Johns's bullying detective Barlow in the early days of that series:

> The avidity with which the press greeted the concept of Barlow as the stern face of authority, the vengeful father, surprised me; I felt it was a stereotype which would have been automatically resisted in the production office. After all, it seemed an amazingly old-fashioned concept. But this love affair with authority, this identification with power. . . . If there are psychological roots for British fascism – they are here.[3]

In quoting these comments, I am not for a moment attributing any particular beliefs or motivations to the makers of *The Sweeney.* Indeed, like Troy Kennedy-Martin, Trevor Preston has expressed some concern about the possible outcome of his earlier work:

> The major criticism which I find to have a certain element of truth in it is that *The Sweeney* reinforced the police's view of themselves. I tend to agree with that now, but . . . I'm being a bit of a hypocrite because I'm only agreeing in retrospect, after *Law and Order.* I think that was bad. Had I had my time over again, I wouldn't have written some of the scripts I have written, to be quite truthful.

Certainly the anti-authoritarianism of *The Sweeney* was populist, in that it invoked an opposition between the interests of the people (us) and the actions of a self-serving power bloc (them).[4] It was also reactionary, in that its villains were usually stereotyped deviants or outsiders. But an account of the ideology of *The Sweeney* which simply identifies in the programme certain attitudes and values that also characterised the 'politics of resentment' or 'backlash against permissiveness' in the early seventies would be begging the chicken-and-egg question. The terms of Jack Regan's diatribe in 'Abduction', for example – its semantic content, to use a grammatical analogy – was certainly drawn from a political discourse that had a currency beyond the limits of crime fiction. But that does not tell us *how* – formally, syntactically – they were worked into the fictional form of *The Sweeney,* nor how these fictions might have helped to shape its viewers' ideas about authority and deviance.

This is where Pauline Kael's comments about the fairy-tale appeal of *Dirty Harry* and Troy Kennedy-Martin's observation about the relationship between police series and the authoritarian image of the father are relevant. It was less the explicit political content of *The Sweeney* that made it reactionary, than its narrative form, its reliance on stock figures and structures. This is a point Umberto Eco has made about Ian Fleming and the James Bond novels:

The user of such [stock] figures which personify the Manichean dichotomy sees things in black and white, is always dogmatic and intolerant – in short, reactionary; while he who avoids set figures and recognises nuances, and distinctions, and admits contradictions, is democratic. Fleming is conservative as, basically, the fable, any fable, is conservative: it is the static inherent dogmatic conservatism of fairy-tales and myths, which transmit an elementary wisdom, constructed and communicated by a simple play of light and shade, and they transmit it by indestructible images which do not permit critical distinction. If Fleming is a 'Fascist' it is because the ability to pass from mythology to argument, the tendency to govern by making use of myths and fetishes, are typical of Fascism.[5]

What all these observations point to is the way that popular narratives like *The Sweeney* create (to use Fredric Jameson's phrase) a 'mapping fantasy' for the viewer – a *fantasy* in the sense that they give shape to unconscious wishes and anxieties (rather than the external actuality of crime and policing), a *mapping* fantasy in that the co-ordinates of their representations are drawn from a historically specific stock of imagery. If we are to understand the ideological force of *The Sweeney*, then, we should study the mechanics of its narrative. To do this, I shall look in some detail at 'Abduction'.

NARRATIVE

The narrative structure of 'Abduction' sticks to *The Sweeney*'s usual format. In the teaser before the credits, Kate Regan, Jack's ex-wife, discovers that their daughter is missing from her school. The main body of the story is divided into three 'acts', interrupted by two slots for advertisements. In the first act, we learn that the kidnapping of the child is linked to Regan's tenuous leads on a planned jewel robbery. In the second, as the result of finding a vital clue on the body of Regan's murdered informant, he and Carter identify a lesbian couple as the kidnappers and recover the girl. In the third, one of the women, who is also involved with a member of the gang, puts them onto their trail; the robbery is foiled and the gang caught red-handed.

The plot turns on a conventional thriller device, in which the solution of one mystery (here the jewel robbery) depends on the solution of another, apparently unrelated mystery (Susie's abduction). 'Abduction' is certainly no whodunnit. The identity of the villains is of barely formal interest. Their leader 'Kenny Jarvis', when revealed, is just a name attached to a face with the right physiognomical connotations. Neither he nor the lesbian kidnappers are given any psychological motivation or social explanation. They are stereotypes of criminality or deviance. The episode is no heist movie, either. The robbery is reduced to a few men

125

tiptoeing across a dark roof, and there are none of the spectacular action sequences that were one of *The Sweeney*'s trademarks. Nor is it a police procedural: the plotting of the detective work is pretty perfunctorily done.

What gives the episode its interest is not these conventional generic elements but, I think, the explicitness with which it reworks *The Sweeney*'s basic narrative tensions: Regan's individualistic anti-authoritarianism and the personal price of being a policeman. These are set up quite clearly in the programme's opening scenes. The pre-credits sequence follows Kate Regan into Susie's primary school, and it is her teacher who states the enigma that organises this strand: 'Can I have your attention please, children. Has anybody seen Susie Regan this morning?' This centering of Kate also invokes the serial theme of Regan's broken marriage, destroyed by his obsessive commitment to his work, and may also imply the question of whether their daughter's disappearance might bring them together. The first scene after the credits poses the crime/pursuit/arrest enigma: who are the jewel thieves? This is explicit in Regan's conversation with his informant, Stan, but is also conveyed by the *mise-en-scène*. In a couple of inserts, Regan and Stan are seen in long shot, framed first through a car window and then as if through binoculars. This is a conventional cinematic sign for 'being watched by an enemy'. Its clear signalling as a point-of-view shot, without telling us *whose* point of view it represents, establishes that, in this episode at least, Regan is the hunted as well as the hunter.

The second scene, in which Kate is interviewed by Inspector Knowles, the divisional policeman in charge of the case, picks up the kidnapping theme. In the third, very brief, scene, Regan takes Kate's phone call for help while Haskins, typically, pesters him about the details of the holiday rota. By this point in the programme, then, three strands have been established: the crime/pursuit/arrest narrative; the vulnerability of family life; and the conflict between Regan and authority.

In the bulk of the episode, these themes are developed and woven together. Each scene moves the narrative forward, meting out the information which edges it forward towards the resolution of the two crimes, the kidnapping and the robbery. At the same time as sketching in a range of possible developments, though, they also put obstacles in the way of Regan's investigation. We do not doubt that he will solve them in the end, and our continuing interest depends on delaying that resolution and seeing how he does it.

Both Kate and Knowles want him off the case, for example – Kate because she is afraid of his aggression ('. . . you'll go screaming in there like a stuck pig. Why don't you think of me for once, and Susie?'); Knowles for mixed motives of professional niceties and personal jealousy, or 'departmental politics and bullshit' as Regan characteristically puts it. Similarly, Carter's wife Alison tries to stop him from giving up his sick leave to help on the case – 'I'm beginning to know how your wife must have felt,' she tells Regan. Such domestic and procedural wrangles serve several functions. They provide a plausible context in which to establish or reiterate necessary items of narrative information - in the former, that the usual motives for abducting the child ('sexual or sick') do not seem to apply, in the latter that the kidnapping is probably linked to the jewel gang investigation. But, as I have said, they also put a retarding brake on this narrative momentum. They do so by referring outwards from the plot to the audience's assumed commonsense knowledge about crime, policing and the family. They show the difficulties police work is supposed to create for a marriage. In doing so, they also help to build up the bundle of ideological traits that make up the character of 'Regan' – his aggression, impatience, intolerance and self-righteousness – and so add a degree of psychologically plausible motivation to his function as the catalyst in the narrative's chain of events.[6]

The first narrative theme to be resolved is the abduction. In the scene before the second break for advertisements (a particularly lame action sequence, it must be admitted), the two policemen burst into the kidnappers' house, disarm the woman who threatens Regan with a pistol and rescue Susie. Regan sweeps his 'Princess' into his arms and promises her, 'It's all over now, love, it's all over.' The moment is marked by an uncharacteristically fluent camera movement, circling ecstatically around the pair as they embrace. This seems to resolve the fairy-tale aspect of the story – the princess abducted by the wicked witches has been rescued by the hero.

To point out the fairy-tale motif is not to dismiss it as trivial or irrelevant. On the contrary, the enigmatic figure of Susie, seen only in this fleeting glimpse, is at the symbolic heart of the story. In strictly narrative terms, her abduction motivates one of its major strands, and her rescue (and the capture of her abductors) opens the way to the resolution of the crime theme. She serves as a reminder of Regan's broken marriage. Perhaps most important, though, as Regan later makes explicit, she also stands for the idea of purity which is threatened in the world of *The Sweeney* by crime and moral deviance. She thus constitutes one of three fixed points in the programme's terms for representing female sexuality. First there is Kate, the wife, sympathetically presented but whose desire for a fulfilling family life and an active sexual relationship (if not with Regan then with someone else) is incompatible with his obsessive commitment to the law. Secondly, there is the lesbian Faye, whose inverted mirror of Regan's masculinity is a direct offence and/or threat to his sexuality – 'She stuck a .45 up my nose,' he whines. And finally there is Susie, the female child idealised as the embodiment of natural, asexual innocence. The other female characters oscillate around these representational terms – Alison's carping lack of sympathy for Regan's egoism;

127

The Sweeney: 'Abduction'. Regan (John Thaw) confronts his daughter's kidnappers 'whose inverted mirror of Regan's masculinity is a direct threat to his sexuality.'

the primary school teacher who supports Kate and becomes a momentary object of desire for Regan as her surrogate; the bisexual Brenda, whose involvement both with Faye and a member of the jewel gang is the pivot between the two crimes and who therefore combines sexual deviance with criminality.

Female sexuality is thus presented as both a threat to purity and the purity that is threatened. For Regan, clearly, it is mysterious and troubling. This aspect of the story therefore opens up a new way of look-

128

ing at what is at stake in the whole question of law and order in a programme like *The Sweeney* (and more broadly). It is not just the criminal law and political order: it is the very symbolic order of patriarchal authority which lies at the heart of our culture. That is why the Regan/Susie relationship, though scarcely visible, is crucial. In her discussion of the father/daughter relationship in *Feminism and Psychoanalysis*, Jane Gallop indicates how its psychic complexities are bound up with the question of law and authority:

If the phallus is the standard of value, then the Father, possessor of the phallus, must desire the daughter in order to give her value. But the Father is a man (a little boy in the anal, the phallic phase) and cannot afford to desire otherness, an other sex, because that opens up his castration anxiety. The father's refusal to seduce the daughter, to be seduced by her (seduction wreaking havoc with anal logic and its active/passive distribution), gains him another kind of seduction (this one more one-sided, more like violation), a veiled seduction in the form of the law.[7]

Here, perhaps, we can begin to comprehend what motivates Regan's obsession with the law. If Troy Kennedy-Martin is right, and the old Barlow in *Z Cars* and *Softly, Softly* was the vengeful father, then maybe we should see Regan as the Oedipal son, bridling against the phallic authority of the law, yet desiring to embody that authority himself, to *be* the law. In 'Abduction' Susie not only represents a fantasy of infantile release from the anxieties of the symbolic order, but her kidnapping also constitutes a threat to Regan's patriarchal status as the bearer of the law. (As Phillip Drummond has observed, Regan is 'almost a stereotype of the law-giver whose castration is the price of his symbolic potency.')[8]

I know that many people will be sceptical of such a reading; but it is borne out, I think, by the scenes in the final act of 'Abduction'. The first is a conventional narrative mechanism, the interrogation that produces the knowledge necessary to solve the mystery. The most striking thing about Regan and Carter's questioning of Brenda, though, is their hostility towards her bisexuality and its implicit subversion of the order of fixed sexual identities on which their authority depends:

Regan: '. . . we're the two biggest male chauvinist pigs in the Sweeney and if you don't start telling the truth we're going to throw the lot at you and your friend.'
Brenda: 'Faye?'
Carter: 'Is that his name?'

[. . .]

129

Brenda: '. . . we didn't harm your little girl. I like children. She's a nice kid: pretty, intelligent. The three of us played Monopoly together.'
Carter: 'What – Uncle Faye, Auntie Brenda and Susie?'
Regan: 'Have you any idea what you've done to her mother? She could end up in a psychiatric ward because of you.'
Brenda: 'Sorry.'
Regan: 'Sorry! It's too bloody late for that. If you were Alan Foss [her boyfriend in the gang], I'd take you somewhere quiet and make sure you never walked straight again.'

This aggression is unleashed in the beating Regan gives Kenny Jarvis, whose function is simply to embody the threat both to the criminal law and the family in a form that can be the legitimate target of Regan's violence. Or rather the figure of Jarvis serves a dual function: it both gives expression to the unconscious fears underlying the perception of that threat, and at the same time hides their social and psychic roots.[9] Regan's violence therefore acts both as a simple resolution to the narrative, restoring the formal order disrupted by the crimes, and also as a metaphor for the possibility of a simple solution to the anxieties the programme plays on. In arresting and punishing Jarvis, Regan is reasserting not so much the criminal law as the symbolic order.

When Carter drags Regan away, his words echoing Regan's to Susie ('It's all over, Guv, it's all over'), that does in a sense conclude the narrative of the episode. But two scenes remain. These act as a coda which returns to the continuing themes of the series. In the final scene, Kate admits that she still loves Regan, but hates his job. 'You can't separate a man from his job,' he replies, confirming the 'natural' order of male/active: female/passive. When the phone call to the next case comes, we know he will go. So does Kate, who leaves the room and closes the door, literally and metaphorically, on their relationship. This therefore leaves the enigma of Regan's sexuality and the theme of the private cost of his public duty open for further development.

In the preceding scene, Regan's uneasy position within police politics is treated in a similar way. The scene turns on the figure of Haskins, who is initially sympathetic to Knowles' threat to bring a complaint against Regan. The viewer is already predisposed to Regan, of course, if only because Knowles, all the way from his petulant performance to his greasy hair, is set up as such a creep. Haskins, though, is won over in two stages. First, Regan challenges Knowles' competence as a detective – 'You couldn't find an Irishman in a harp club.' Knowles, who sticks too closely to the 'good Policeman's Manual' for Regan's taste, does not count as a real policeman – which seems to amount to the same thing as a real man in this context: 'There are two kinds of jacks: some do, some talk. He's a talker. That's why he couldn't get on in the Sweeney, and he knows it.' In the second stage, Regan reveals that his crusade

130

against crime is not based on judicial, professional or even moral princi-
ples. As he commented earlier to Alison Carter, it is above all *personal*.
This is how he justifies his actions – in a speech shot, significantly, from
Haskins' point of view:

> . . . Don't you think my guts turned over every time the bloody phone
> rang? What do you think I am? I did it *because* she was my kid. You
> let these animals get away with it once, just once, and every copper
> and his wife will be living on a knife edge, scared to let their kids out
> of their sight. Susie's all I've got left, she's the only thing in my life
> that's clean and simple. I don't give a damn what you and Knowles
> think. I know why I did what I did, and you can damn well think
> what you like.

What drives Regan, it seems, is not a desire for justice so much as the
fantasy of a world that is 'clean and simple', an infantile, pre-cultural
world devoid of anxiety and threat. Indeed, although it may seem
paradoxical, crime and the law do not really figure very largely in *The
Sweeney*. As I have already mentioned, little interest is shown in the character or motivation of criminals, or the detailed logistics of crime and
detection. The processes and principles of law-making, complex issues
about legal rights and responsibilities or civil liberties, the procedures
of courts and prisons – none of these figures in the series. Even other
policemen like Knowles generally appear only to underline the authenticity and authority of the Sweeney and, in particular, Regan.

We are back, in short, with the fairy-tale simplicities of Good and Evil
that Pauline Kael identified in *Dirty Harry*. What was particularly interesting about these rogue cop heroes was that they were no knights in
shining armour, but the secret sharers of the corruption they battled
against. Regan might revile criminals as 'animals', but Kate knows he
can behave 'like a stuck pig' himself and there is a measure of truth in
Knowles' accusation that he is 'sick'. This was the ambiguity that Ian
Kennedy-Martin had orginally wanted to explore: 'What *The Sweeney*
shows is that there are two kinds of villains on the scene. There are the
police and there are the villains, and often they're interchangeable.'

Why should this have been such a notable feature of police fiction in
the seventies? Certainly, this ambiguity is connected to other representations of the police then in circulation. But, like them, it also tapped
a widespread sense of anxiety and insecurity which was, for many
people, the way the political crisis was actually experienced. It was to
such feelings, born of the clash between popular aspirations and an
economic recession, that the politics of Thatcherism were so finely attuned. Thatcherism too relied on certain mythologised images to focus
resentment on the idea of an unholy alliance between the state and a
number of scapegoats – muggers, scroungers, immigrants, terrorists and

131

so forth. These stereotypes are part of the same cartography as the characterisations and contemporary references in *The Sweeney*; they provide the co-ordinates on which its narratives are mapped. But what made it popular? What did it offer its audiences that was so enjoyable? To understand that, I think we need to look at the other half of Jameson's definition of narrative, at *The Sweeney* as fantasy.

PLEASURE AND FEAR

I have tried to show how the empty narrative scheme of *The Sweeney* could be fleshed out with historically specific social references. The basic narrative structure of disruption/quest/restoration of stasis became the general pattern of crime/pursuit/arrest that is evident in 'Abduction'. The narratives of *The Sweeney* can therefore be seen as variations on a particular fantasy-structure,[10] which, I have suggested, both invites and must be capable of bearing the projections of viewers' desires and anxieties.

Now, I don't suppose that is what it felt like for the average punter watching 'Abduction' in 1975. (I am trying to get at the preconditions for the programme's popular reception, not to repeat it.) The experience of popular involvement in fictions like *The Sweeney* or in other forms of mass entertainment, the desire for active participation in their illusions, has been well described by the French sociologist Pierre Bourdieu:

> The desire to enter into the game, identifying with the characters' joys and sufferings, worrying about their fate, espousing their hopes and ideals, living their life, is based on a form of *investment*, a sort of deliberate 'naivety', ingenuousness, good-natured credulity ('we're here to enjoy ourselves') which tends to accept formal experiments and specifically artistic effects only to the extent that they can be forgotten and do not get in the way of the substance of the work.[11]

That seems to me to capture the communal pleasures of 'watching telly' - thief-taking as spectator sport. But although Bourdieu explains the conditions in which the transaction of entertainment takes place and the enjoyable return on the audience's investment, he does not really tell us what it is that is being invested.

What if the investment is considered in terms of identification? This is quite a complex notion,[12] and means more than that viewers of 'Abduction' would have been rooting for Regan or wanted to be like him. Fictional narratives draw us into shifting identifications with a number of representations of figures. So in 'Abduction' in this formal sense, we have to identify not only with Regan, but also with Knowles, Kate, Carter, even Brenda and Jarvis, to make the narrative work. Indeed, narratives are actually constructed by weaving these diffused identifica-
132

tions into a particular pattern – imagine, for example, the narration of the events in 'Abduction' organised not around the functions of Regan-as-hero, but with Brenda, Kate or Jarvis as the central protagonist. It is doubtful whether that plot could be contained within the crime genre; its ideological impact would clearly also be different.

Here we can begin to see how the viewer, the narrative form and the symbolic order are stitched together. The viewer's investment in *The Sweeney*, his[13] identification with the figures in its narratives, can be seen as a form of projection – an operation, in psychoanalytic terms, whereby feelings or wishes which 'the subject refuses to recognise or rejects in himself, are expelled from the self and located in another person or thing.'[14] This throws an interesting new light on the moral ambiguity of the figure of Regan. Fictional narratives, like dreaming and fantasy, deal with 'fragmented and contradictory figures'[15] – in other words, repressed desires and anxieties are not projected onto a single figure, but their affect is reproduced through the interaction of the range of figures within the narratives. Here, in place of the conventional split between desire/good/hero and fear/bad/villain, the two are discomfortingly condensed within Regan. The effect of this is similar to a characteristic the Italian critic Franco Moretti notes in the Frankenstein and Dracula stories: 'The literature of terror is studded with passages where the protagonists brush against the awareness – described by Freud – that the perturbing element is *within them*: that it is they themselves that produce the monsters they fear.'[16] It is this play between the internalisation of political crisis and the projection of repressed fears, I would argue, that was tapped by *The Sweeney* and the rogue cop movies. In political terms, in this country at least, it did not lead to the fascism predicted by some commentators, but to the peculiar 'authoritarian populism' of Thatcherism.

This brings us back to my original question: how does *The Sweeney* work? It works as a commodity within the circuit of production and consumption of the entertainment industry. At the same time, it works by playing out in narrative form some of the political fears and resentments of the time (and in doing so helps to prepare the cultural ground for the growth of Thatcherism). But to be effective in both these ways, its narratives must plug into the mechanisms and processes which tie the subject into the symbolic order. At that level, the series is as much concerned with the crisis in male self-confidence that marked many films of the period, from pornography to Hollywood's buddy movies, as with the politics of law and order.

All this doesn't exactly make the programme sound like fun, and it is certainly true that for it to work in any of the ways I have suggested, it had first of all to entertain people. But that is only really a problem if entertainment is taken to mean anaesthetising viewers, rather than engaging their attention. The entertainment offered by *The Sweeney* is not

133

the spectacular glamour and carefree abundance of a Hollywood musical, for example, but its moral tales of crime and retribution are just as much fantasies. What they provide, like many forms of popular culture from Victorian melodramas to video nasties, is not a utopian promise of otherness but the fantasy experience of fear – precisely the playing out of repressed anxieties. It is this entertaining fear that is the investment made by the audience. As Moretti observes of the monstrous terrors of Frankenstein and Dracula, 'it is a fear one *needs*: the price one pays for coming contentedly to terms with a social body based on irrationality and menace.'[17]

That is not to say that *The Sweeney* works either as a form of catharsis or as the new opium of the masses. What popular television drama does, at its most successful, is to represent in engaging topical forms some of the basic tensions within the culture, providing narrative solutions to these irresolvable social and symbolic contradictions. If that makes *The Sweeney* sound like our disenchanted version of myth, I think that is probably not too inaccurate.

Notes

This article is largely based on work done for two television programmes prepared for the Open University's course *Popular Culture*. I would like to thank the other people who worked on them, particularly Alan Clarke and Janet Woollacott, on whose ideas I have drawn freely (however much they may disagree with my conclusions); Vic Lockwood, the producer; Ted Childs, Ian Kennedy-Martin and Trevor Preston for giving me interviews in Spring 1982, from which I have quoted here; and, finally, Equity, Euston Films and Thames Television for their co-operation in enabling the programmes to be made.

1. This was ten minutes later than usual because of a party political broadcast.

2. The best account of this 'move to the right' is given in Stuart Hall, Chas Critcher, Tony Jefferson, John Clarke and Brian Roberts, *Policing the Crisis: Mugging, the State, and Law and Order* (London: Macmillan, 1978). This movement was not without its own nuances and contradictions, of course. Judging from the number of invitations Thaw and Waterman received to speak at police dinners, for example, *The Sweeney* offered an image of the police that many people in the force found attractive. Mary Whitehouse, on the other hand, thought its violence and bad language might undermine respect for the police.

3. In H.R.F. Keating (ed), *Crimewriters* (London: BBC Publications, 1978), p.123; quoted in Alan Clarke, 'Television police series and law and order', Unit 22 of U203 *Popular Culture* (Milton Keynes: Open University Press, 1983), p.50.

4. This definition is based on Ernesto Laclau, *Politics and Ideology in Marxist Theory* (London: NLB, 1977), especially chapter 4.

5. Umberto Eco, 'The narrative structure in Fleming', in Bernard Waites, Tony Bennett and Graham Martin (eds.), *Popular Culture: Past and Present* (London: Croom Helm, 1982), p.261. This is an extract from Eco's *The Bond Affair* (London: Macdonald, 1966).

6. It is perhaps worth noting that this bundle does seem to add up to more than the sum of its parts, in that it bears a striking resemblance to the ideal type of 'the authoritarian personality' proposed by members of the Frankfurt School in their research into the psychological syndrome that typified the potentially fascist character. This was characterised by nine basic personality variables:

Conventionalism Rigid adherence to conventional, middle-class values.

Authoritarian submission Submissive, uncritical attitude towards idealised moral authorities of the in-group.

Authoritarian aggression Tendency to be on the look-out for, and to condemn, reject and punish people who violate conventional values.

Anti-intraception Opposition to the subjective, the imaginative, the tender-minded.

Superstition and Stereotypy The belief in mystical determinants of the individual's fate; the disposition to think in rigid categories.

Power and 'toughness' Preoccupation with the dominance-submission, strong-weak, leader-follower dimension; identification with power-figures; overemphasis upon the conventionalised attributes of the ego; exaggerated assertion of strength and toughness.

Destructiveness and Cynicism Generalised hostility, vilification of the human.

Projectivity The disposition to believe that wild and dangerous things go on in the world; the projection outwards of unconscious emotional impulses.

Sex Exaggerated concern with sexual 'goings-on'.

This summary is taken from David Held, *Introduction to Critical Theory* (London: Hutchinson, 1980), pp.142-3.

7. Jane Gallop, *Feminism and Psychoanalysis: The Daughter's Seduction* (London: Macmillan, 1982), p.70.

8. Phillip Drummond, 'Structural and narrative constraints in *The Sweeney*', in *Screen Education* no.20, Autumn 1976, p.25.

9. Franco Moretti makes this point about the double function of the rhetorical figure in his essay on the literature of terror: 'Taking away one or the other would mean eliminating either the problem of the unconscious (by asserting that everything in literature is transparent and manifest) or the problem of literary communication (by asserting that literature serves *only* to hide certain contents).' Moretti, 'Dialectic of Fear', in *Signs Taken For Wonders* (London: Verso, 1983), p.103.

10. 'Fantasy-structure' is a term used by Fredric Jameson, *Fables of Aggression* (Berkeley: University of California Press, 1979), p.11.

11. Pierre Bourdieu, 'The aristocracy of culture', in *Media, Culture and Society* vol.2, no.2, 1980, pp.237-8.

12. For a useful introduction to identification in cinema, see John Ellis, *Visible Fictions* (London: Routledge & Kegan Paul, 1982), pp.41ff.

13. I say *his* deliberately, because the narratives of *The Sweeney* do undoubtedly place the viewer, of either sex, *with* Regan as hero/active/male. To stress these powerful symbolic equivalences does, of course, beg difficult questions about (a) the bisexuality of identification and (b) the pleasures that *The Sweeney* offers its female viewers. See, for example, Ellis, op.cit. and Laura Mulvey, 'Afterthoughts on "Visual pleasure and narrative cinema" inspired by *Duel in the Sun*', in *Framework* nos. 15/16/17, 1981.

14. J Laplanche and J-B Pontalis, *The Language of Psycho-Analysis* (London: The Hogarth Press, 1973), p.349.

15. Ellis, p.43.

16. Moretti, p.102.

17. ibid., p.108.

2 *Out* and *Fox:* Better Popular Television Than We Deserve?

Jim Cook

INTRODUCTION

Despite Colin McArthur's lone voice in *Tribune*, arguing between 1971 and 1978 for more committed, intelligent and *popular* reviewing practices,[1] journalistic coverage of cinema in this country, and even more so of television, still remains unexcited and unexciting. Characteristically, it is tied to an extremely narrow range of concerns – bounded in the case of fictions by bits of plot summary, assessments of authenticity and musings on the morality of it all.

My argument here is not the ingenuous one that overnight the journalistic institution should suddenly release additional column inches for serious media coverage, nor even more certainly is it the disingenuous one that the press gives the 'general public' what it wants and if fractions within that composite want more, then specialist publications like this exist to cater for them. Rather, it is to re-assert that part of any left cultural struggle must be to try to dent the massive hegemony exerted by dominant institutions in their agenda-setting of what constitutes appropriate and useful knowledge.

Writing about reviewing in *Framework*, Autumn 1983, the Australian critic Meaghan Morris concludes: 'It [reviewing] should not indulge in the fantasy that reviewing directly changes or influences film: changing film is the business of film-makers. Political reviewing is a matter of changing what can be *said* about film, and how: and if this has any importance at all, it is that filmic discourse and discourse on film are inextricably related in and by the institutions of the existing economy; and because film – and the cinema – matters for reasons other than and beyond itself.' To which I would only wish to add that, *mutatis mutandis,* the above holds equally good for television, and that one way of both starting to challenge dominant reviewing's own institutional space and to avoid any other space being academically marginalised is to set the two in tension; to use each as a critique of the other.

These general considerations were brought into sharp focus when, having expressed my pleasure in, and enthusiasm for, *Out* and *Fox*, I was asked to write a piece for this book. Together they constitute nineteen hours of collaborative film-making on the part of Jim Goddard and Trevor Preston, and have been seen by audiences of several millions; and yet there does not exist a single 'serious minority' piece on the two series, while popular reviewing hugs the impoverished parameters described above.

'OUT' & 'FOX': SELECTED CRITICAL COMMENTS

Out

For: Although '*Out* is blatantly aimed at the *Sweeney* market'[2] it is also recognised 'more as a superior drama series than a classy thriller'.[3] 'Very believable because the cast were different from the crop of familiar faces we see all the time',[4] it came as a relief to conclude 'with Frank Ross' character much more unredeemed than one had feared'.[5] There were, however, problems of what level to take it at: is Frank Ross just like you and me, 'a human being with bills to pay . . . not too different from most of us outside'[6] or is his story 'a powerful fable? . . . It has the very stench of life going rotten. Can there be a more self-corroding instinct than revenge?'[7]

Against: Not all reviewers were prepared to stand by and see life go rotten. For some the pleasures had to be nervously qualified because 'the social stance of the series is somewhat ambivalent'[8] with only 'traces of a social conscience lurking within it',[9] while for others 'it would be tolerable if Frank was depicted as an out and out nasty. But Tom Bell, twitching his jaw with steely determination, gives us a villain with whom we are supposed to sympathise'.[10] Some did indeed find it intolerable, apparently to the extent of going off and watching an entirely different series: 'I don't give a toss about Frank Ross and I refuse to participate in the romanticisation of men who wear stocking masks and carry pick-axe handles and sawn-off shotguns in order to perpetrate brutal crimes'.[11]

Another strand of criticism of *Out* focuses on a scatter of more directly 'aesthetic' points: 'the acting, though not a patch on *Law and Order*, is reasonably good, yet the important faces are calculatedly upmarket'[12] (cf. note 4 above on the cast's plausibility); 'the familiar conventions of ritualised violence';[13] 'the plot fell back on clichés . . . [relieved only] by Pam Fairbrother's performance as the mentally disturbed wife, Eve Ross. Miss Fairbrother seemed like a character out of another and vastly superior play'.[14]

137

Fox

<u>For</u>: 'The story of a modern urban extended family [in which] the ensemble acting is quite extraordinary'[15] is 'heart-warming, occasionally bawdy, and often very strong stuff.'[16] While 'everyone involved is proud of the realism of the series'[17] its appeal is seen as one of acceptable fantasy. 'I don't suppose for a minute that life in South London or anywhere else for that matter is really as action-packed, as poignant or as cosy as we are to see it in this ITV serial but it ought to be.'[18] 'In a society with fewer and fewer genuine outlets for self-advancement, the Foxes combine a street-wise grittiness with a fighting spirit reminiscent of the dark days of 1940.'[19]

<u>Against</u>: Such appeals, however, were found by a number of reviewers to be eminently resistible. 'Dedicated to the proposition that the upper working-class denizens of South London are all warm and prosperous people',[20] the series 'was sometimes more maudlin than sentimental, wearing emotions on its sleeve rather more than would be acceptable to working-class families'.[21] Its style, 'the kind that used to send middle-class voyeurs flocking to East End pubs on a Saturday night',[22] is 'more like an updated version of *Laburnum Grove* than an anglicised *Godfather*'.[23]

For some reviewers the series' attitude to the family is seen as positively disturbing: 'they are made to look as if they're just defending a God-given right to domesticity, rather than carving up London and belting the hell out of whom they choose'.[24] Indeed, 'one has the horrible suspicion that author and director would like us to approve of these people';[25] and 'to some extent it succeeds; but in the last resort it remains a triumph of virtuosity over virtue'.[26]

An 'aesthetic' slant to this criticism is offered in a comment about the series' combination of 'a very comfortable standard of living with a sentimental attachment to less affluent days.'[27] The same review continues: 'It [i.e. the combination] exists all right. But packed into one family and sliced up into neat hourly units, each with its obvious dramatic climaxes and cheap emotion, it becomes merely one more pathetic capitulation by British television to the style of American soap opera.'

Less blatantly on the run from the ideology and the form of the series, other reviewers comment also on the diffuse structure – ('most of the time I can't see the people for the effects')[28] – and a particular problem is identified as 'the desire to make each episode self-sufficient and yet fit into a wider plot'.[29]

The difficulty with criticisms like these, whether 'for' or 'against', is that they rest unproblematically on sets of assumptions that are implicit, never spelt out, and frequently contradictory. In the case of the conventions which the works adopt, for example, the reviewers fail to recognise the construction in *Out* of a deliberate (and for television quite rare) tension between the conventions of the thriller form and the conventions of 'Play For Today' or 'art' television. Instead, reviewers merely note the, to them, unacceptable mix, while characteristically praising Pam Fairbrother's 'art' (i.e. intense, individual) performance at the expense of the thriller elements.

In the case of the narrative structures of these works, instead of recognising the flexibility offered by the extended series format, the reviewers invoke the unity of the one-off play as their yardstick of coherence and formal perfection. Having constructed the essentially middle-class well-made play as the norm, reviewers then expect all television drama to conform to this model.

The limitations of the reviewers quoted may owe as much to the fact that they have to abide by the criteria of mass circulation journalism as to their own inherent deficiencies. But the reason why a serious minority criticism has not been able to deal adequately with *Out* and *Fox* needs to be sought in a different direction. In a review of Ken McMullen's *Ghost Dance* in the *Monthly Film Bulletin* for February 1984 Steve Jenkins unwittingly offers a clue as to why the work of such as Preston and Goddard has been neglected. Adhering broadly to the familiar realist/anti-realist dichotomy, Jenkins writes: 'Works such as *Looks and Smiles*, *Boys From The Blackstuff* and Mike Leigh's *Meantime* are linked, despite their differences, by a tendency to confront the symptoms/effects of decay with a fairly blank, predominantly naturalistic stare. In absolutely refusing this option, Ken McMullen opens up an infinite range of possibilities.'

The trouble is that not all consumers of drama have the same amount of cultural capital available to them when it comes to exploring these possibilities. The kind of avant-garde work which Jenkins is reviewing and which he opposes to the realist drama of Loach, Bleasdale and Leigh is simply not accessible to the working-class audience addressed by Preston and Goddard. The audience's capacity to follow anywhere the 'possibilities' may lead is severely limited.

On the other hand the 'realist' work which Jenkins opposes to that of McMullen, work which in fact does have its supporters within minority film culture, isn't necessarily the best model for understanding Preston and Goddard either. For example, though there are some obvious overlaps between *Out* and *Fox* and what Alan Lovell has characterised as 'British social drama', there are also some obvious differences. Lovell has this to say about the 'tendency' of writers and directors such as David Mercer, John McGrath, Ian Kennedy-Martin, Dennis Potter, Trevor Griffiths, Jim Allen, Ken Loach, Alan Plater, G. F. Newman, Alun Owen and Colin Welland:

In the broadest sense they share a realist/naturalist approach to art. Two characteristics of the tendency mark it as belonging to realism/

naturalism. The first is the conviction evident in the plays that ordinary people's lives are worthy of dramatic attention. The protagonists are miners, dockers, building workers, the lower ranks of the police, working-class teenagers, Rugby League supporters, teachers, political activists. Following the naturalist/realist impulse, an important part of the drama is a description based on a familiarity with the day-to-day routines of ordinary life, speech patterns, social interaction and relationships, the physical character of homes, work and leisure places.

The second characteristic is a belief that ordinary lives have a representative quality. Observation of such lives will provide insights into the nature of the whole society, its attitudes and values. As a consequence of this belief, art is seen as a form of social criticism, a way of exposing social injustice. The plays frequently concern themselves with unemployment, strikes, homelessness, the effectiveness of political action, crime and racism. [. . . .]

There is clearly an *a priori* commitment to a view of working-class life being rich and vital. [. . . .]

The tendency inevitably has its limitations. They might be summed up in an overall way as a limited imaginative power. The social analysis which inspires the drama doesn't probe deeply enough (there is a too easy acceptance of the social forms of working-class life, especially the family and marriage). The curiosity about aesthetic forms seems limited and a little timid; the uncertainty about the value of naturalism is indicative of this.[30]

While the work of Preston and Goddard conforms to some of the characteristics which Lovell identifies (Preston strongly insists he is writing from a working-class point of view) what is distinctive about it, and surprisingly ignored by a criticism well acquainted with popular cinema, is its base within the genres of the thriller and the melodrama. And it's worth noting that it is these very elements, demanding strongly active and reactive characters, which prevent *Out* and *Fox* falling into the miserabilist variant of social drama favoured by some of the writers Lovell lists, as well as by the critics. The presence of elements of the thriller in *Out*, with its 'quest' narrative and closed world of recognisable locales, characters and values, is presumably obvious enough. Indeed, in their construction of what Jim Goddard has described as a 'sharp, clean, hard, threatful' world, he and Preston have given Britain a work which, though unannounced and unapplauded, is as highly wrought and achieved as anything in films directed by Jean-Pierre Melville.

The deployment of forms of melodrama in *Out* and *Fox* perhaps needs further comment, since it is a model normally invoked only in relation to 1950s Hollywood and late 1970s American TV series. In his influential article on melodrama, 'Tales of Sound and Fury', Thomas Elsaesser has described it as 'an emotional dynamic whose social correlative is a network of external forces directed oppressingly inward and with which the characters themselves unwittingly collude to become their agents.'[31] Although this dynamic is to an extent, and interestingly, undercut by the thriller elements, the melodramatic elements – the circumscribed society, the family, the flawed characters, the external pressures, the violent conflicts – are indubitably there. Unfortunately they seem to have been simply misread as out of place in a thriller such as *Out* or as merely productive of a loss of focus in *Fox*. Whereas it is surely the interplay between thriller and melodrama, and between these generic elements and the more 'realist' aspects of the dramas, which is one of the major sources of pleasure.

'OUT'

From its opening moments in Episode 1 – credits over a sepia-blurred set of actions – *Out* announces its twin concerns: Frank Ross' memory of what happened at the moment of his gang's capture by the police while committing a robbery, and need to seek out why it happened. *Privately* affected by that past moment he needs *publicly* to nail it and the central narrative of the six episodes becomes that of a quest to understand that moment eight years ago even if this means running counter to and ignoring all that's happened in the intervening years. There is therefore a double structuring tension in *Out*: the public thriller one – will he discover who betrayed them? – and the private melodramatic one - will this do him any good in so far as the obsessive search is not helping his family Evie and Paul and is in danger of alienating his friends/lovers Chris and Ann?

Inside this basic tension a range of generic elements are afforded a *controlled* play (cf. McMullen's 'infinite range of possibilities'). In terms of 'realism' the locations are worth noticing – the 'scabby drinker' where Frank meets Vic Lee, now working as a potman; Chris' anonymous modern flat; Frank's family house, etc. – along with the heightened realism of the language, recognisably working-class in idiom but also capable of being pared back to expressive essentials as when, again in Episode 1, Frank violently attacks the police who have mistaken him for a burglar in his own home: 'You're *contaminating* my house.' As for the thriller and melodramatic elements, as indicated above they centrally operate in tension with each other – Pam Fairbrother's 'superior' performance as Evie being precisely a critique of Frank's thriller quest – and at certain points become diverging plot directions between which Frank must choose; as for example in Episode 3 when he postpones seeing his real tearaway son Paul to help out Billy, his surrogate 'son' from his former gang.

141

Out. 'I wouldn't take your hand if I was drowning.' (L. to r.) Frank Ross (Tom Bell), Hallam (Bryan Marshall), Veneker (John Junkin).

In relation to these two strands it's interesting again that the reviewers draw attention, although with mistaken emphasis, to the in fact highly melodramatic 'superior' scenes with Evie while ignoring, i.e. regarding as merely formulaic, equally 'superior' thriller scenes. For example the sequence in Episode 2 when Frank, desperately in need of cash for Evie and to pay back Chris, uses Anne's loan to play at an exclusive gambling club, is pure genre, easily the equal of Melville in its con-

142

struction of a complex world of allusion, nuance and indirect pressures where style equals power. It is also of course a class allegory as Frank insinuates himself into and takes on the upper class at their own elegant, violent and corrupt game.

In terms of representations of class, *Out* is generally interesting for the extent to which it is consistently a *working-class* thriller. From the cabby in Episode 1 who recognises that Frank is just out – 'my brother went down for a couple of years last year' – and forgoes his fare, and the engineer re-installing his phone who remembers Frank – 'the whole manor's talking about you' – through the intense loyalty and love of Chris, Billy and Big Ralph to the equally intense hatred of Bryce, Eddy, Tony McGrath and Lou Wilson, a central connecting link is their common background. It is a background in which issues of loyalty, commitment, and self-respect (equally as 'relevant' as the more overtly political ones featured in social drama) are debated and acted out. However, and this arguably is a problem in *Out,* since these issues are developed in terms of the individual versus authority – the final confrontation between Ross and Bryce is very directly concerned with this – it is finally unclear what weight the loyal class-specific 'lieutenants', Chris and the straight policeman Rimmer, are meant to carry in relation to Ross and Bryce – the former have the right values but dramatically they're less interesting than the central protagonists who verge on being 'tragic individuals'.

In this context the issue of *Out's* class base and the values it explores creates problems for the series' portrayals of women, less so with Evie and Paul's step-mother, Lucy, who in different ways function as critics of Frank and his actions, but certainly with the faithful sufferers Ann, Alison, Cimmie and Angela. At one level these portrayals can be rationalised as staples of the thriller genre but this doesn't get round the problem of the effect of such representations when they're offered in a realist mode with a dominantly masculine working-class address. At another level of course this is no more than to say that the problem of the representations of women here is no different from that in the majority of social dramas – Bleasdale, Loach/Garnett, etc. – and that as such it shouldn't be a contributory factor to the critical dismissal of *Out* when in the case of these latter it is guiltily acknowledged and then quickly passed over.

'FOX'

With both a much greater length and looser plot and generic base *Fox* foregrounds those issues of class and gender which underlay *Out* but were kept 'in place' as a result of its tighter structure. Given *Fox*'s structure, however, this foregrounding is by no means regular and indeed inside the basic family melodrama of the family unity held together by

143

King Billy, fragmenting after his death and then gradually re-composing, there is once again space for a limited play. Whereas in *Out* this was a play of forms here it is more a realist play, a display even, of social attitudes to family, relationships, sexuality and work. As in *Out* the realist pleasures are those of 'South London' location and language along with a loose inter-twining of the five brothers' stories, into each of which are variously set the concerns listed above. Unlike *Out* however, where descriptive reference is made easy since everything relates to the quest, here instancing becomes difficult without a comprehensive account of all 13 episodes. Since this is impossible what follows refers basically to episodes 2 and 9.

Episode 2, 'Arched Fingers for Bach, Flat Fingers for Love', (the arcane titles are a minor delight) opens on the morning after Billy's 70th birthday party and features in quick succession:
— Billy's patriarchal rage at Joey for his involvement with a married woman who has tried to kill herself: 'You've had your feet under some poor bastard's table and that ain't right, Joey – you know that.'
— Phil noticing the difference between his student girl-friend Anne's screwed-up parents and his own.
— Ray fixing up a criminal friend with an alibi.
Of these three story-lines Joey's is the most developed, with the aggrieved husband hunting him down and him being rescued by Billy, Vin and Kenny. As they stop the fight Billy, while no less aggressive to Joey, tells the husband 'You take one Fox and you take us all.'

In Episode 9, 'Fox Big F – Family', Billy is dead and the brothers and Connie, his widow, are faced with problems:
— Phil is being spied on by his girl-friend's father and wants to leave London despite Connie's accusations of selfishness.
— Vin is refusing Renee's promptings for him to sell up his scaffolding business and leave London for a pub in the country.
— Kenny is still traumatised about going back into the ring after causing a fighter's death.
— Joey is still agonising over whether he can handle his girlfriend Bet's bisexuality.

For someone who has not seen the series such brief descriptions can presumably indicate the episode structure, but what they cannot convey is the range of contradictory attitudes shown in the episodes: Jack-the-lad promiscuity severely critiqued but from a position of authoritarian patriarchy (Joey); the allure and limitations of family (Phil); friendship and loyalty against the law (Ray); divided responsibilities and loyalties (Vin); adolescent uncertainty (Kenny); challenges to macho sexuality (Joey again). What needs to be said positively about this range is that it is working-class based *and* wider than most realist TV representations, and although a direct feminist or radical address is outside its remit it *is* dramatically putting under scrutiny a range of conservative values.

144

Indeed, given its overall masculine address it is difficult to imagine a dramatic context better able to problematise macho sexuality than the 'realist/melodramatic' one in which Bet explains the nature of her sexuality to Joey: 'So what do I do?' asks Joey confusedly. 'What do we do?' replies Bet wearily. Despite Phil's subsequent advice to Joey to break with Bet and given that he subsequently finds a more conventional happiness with Peg, the issue of Joey's inadequacy to the occasion is not avoided and Phil continues to be a profoundly ambiguous figure especially in his final recomposition of the family.

To develop these remarks further would lead to a fuller account of *Fox* than is appropriate here. The point of them is rather to reassert (yet again) that a popular serial form misread by reviewers and ignored by serious criticism exploited a rare televisual space to address itself uncondescendingly and pleasurably to working-class values and to problematise them by dramatising a whole range of questions about social identity. That said its relegation of women to reactive roles in relation exclusively to (white) men remains a severe limitation, but until their precise function in the series has been critically debated with a 'corrective' weighting being given to its other strengths (as has been the case for example with Bleasdale and women) I remain agnostic as to whether this should be regarded *a priori* as a crippling limitation.

CONCLUSION

For anyone who admires *Out* and *Fox* as much as I do, reading only intermittent comments about them will possibly have been as frustrating an experience as I have found writing about them in this way. My reasons for so doing are nothing to do with a principled resistance to telephilia but rather because detailed analyses of material not currently available are of limited value and also because for the purposes of this essay *Out* and *Fox* are being considered very much as a case in point.

The terms of this case briefly are that, for reasons described at length in this book, Euston Films has enabled a particular type of product to be produced. Two examples of that product, *Out* and *Fox*, seem to me worthy of consideration and this is because, to echo Meaghan Morris, TV like cinema 'matters for reasons other than and beyond itself'.

These programmes matter not only because in their uncompromisingly popular address, both aesthetically and referentially, they offer a range of representations arguably of equal complexity and commitment to those of social drama, but also, and symptomatically, because they have on account of their popular form been largely ignored or dismissed by critics. Both of these considerations should give left cultural commentators pause for thought.

Notes

1. A selection of McArthur's writing is published as *Dialectic* by Key Texts, London, 1982.
2. Emma Soames, *Evening Standard* 24.7.78.
3. Peter Knight, *Daily Telegraph* 1.8.78.
4. Richard Afton, *Evening News* 27.7.78.
5. Julian Barnes, *New Statesman* 1.9.78.
6. *Daily Express* 1.8.78.
7. Jack Tinker, *Daily Mail* 22.8.78.
8. Stewart Lane, *Morning Star* 2.8.78.
9. John Wyver, *Time Out* 21-27.7.78.
10. James Murray, *Daily Express* 25.7.78.
11. Kevin Cully, *Tribune* 4.8.78 – proof indeed of how fragile was McArthur's tenure there.
12. Craig Raine, *The Observer* 20.8.78.
13. Richard Last, *Daily Telegraph* 8.8.78.
14. Stanley Reynolds, *The Times* 1.8.78.
15. Chris Dunkley, *Financial Times* 12.3.80.
16. Margaret Forwood, *The Sun* 11.3.80.
17. Gordon Blair, *Sunday Mirror* 9.12.79.
18. Patrick Stoddart, *Evening News* 11.3.80.
19. Kevin Cully, *Tribune* 25.4.80.
20. Richard Last, *Daily Telegraph* 11.3.80.
21. Stewart Lane, *Morning Star* 11.6.80.
22. Peter Dunn, *Sunday Times* 16.3.80.
23. Clive Hodgson, *TV Today* 20.3.80.
24. Russell Davies, *Sunday Times* 22.6.80.
25. Andrew Davies, *Times Educational Supplement* 21.3.80.
26. Roy Shaw, *Times Educational Supplement* 30.5.80.
27. Peter Keating, *Times Literary Supplement* 28.3.80.
28. William McIllveny, *Glasgow Herald* 3.5.80.
29. Julian Barnes, *New Statesman* 18.4.80.
30. 'The Context of Social Drama', pp.25, 26, 29 in BFI Dossier 20, *Boys From The Blackstuff* (London: BFI, 1984).
31. Thomas Elsaesser, 'Tales of Sound and Fury', *Monogram* No.4, 1972, p.14.

3 In Production: *Minder*

Michael Winterbottom

How are we to describe *Minder*'s relation to the crime series, or for that matter any other possible generic category: thriller, *policier*, screwball comedy? Linda Agran, the commissioning editor and the current script executive of *Minder*, acknowledged the difficulty of any categorisation, while offering one possible version: 'People still have problems categorising it. It's an hour-long film-drama that has comedy in it.' Such a description, however, begs more questions than it answers, in that it avoids those generic descriptions which begin to define a programme. For categorisation is not a *post facto* irrelevance, a process which arbitrarily allocates an already determined object to a particular ideal class. It is employed by the audience in consuming (or re-producing) the programme. It is used by the promotions industry (in this case *TV Times* billings, adverts, reviews). And it is used by those within the industry who make the programmes. By allocating a programme to a particular genre a set of expectations and conventions are set up, for the producers as well as the audience.

Steve Neale's description of genre as organising 'repetition' and 'difference'[1] pinpoints the contradictory impulses that structure a TV series. This suggests an analysis of *Minder* which situates the series as marginal to the dominant genre against which it was initially produced (the TV crime series), and the production team as marginal to the two industrial blocks of 'TV' and 'Film', which have not only different methods of exhibition but also different budgets, different methods of working, different aesthetic criteria and different cultural and professional prestige.

'Repetition' and 'difference' also inform the organisation of personnel at Euston. Ironically, despite the freelance nature of employment, there is more continuity of technical crew at Euston than there is on in-house productions at Thames (see *Hazell: the making of a TV series* by Alvarado and Buscombe on the difficulties in achieving continuity of technicians on that production).[2] At Euston the crew are employed for the whole series, although certain functions such as editor and lighting cameraman are filled by two people in alternation.

There is also considerable inter-series employment. George Taylor, the producer, pointed this out:

> Tony Dawe [sound recordist] worked on the very first show [at Euston] – he's still with us today, eleven years later (strictly freelance, but still with us). Dusty Miller, the lighting cameraman on the floor today eleven years later, lit the very first show. The camera operator John Maskall was the camera operator on *Special Branch* – he's on the floor today.[3]

Similarly, Roy Pointer was lighting cameraman for all of the first series of *Minder* and has since then worked in alternation with Mike Davies, then Dusty Miller. Roger Wilson, the supervising editor, has worked on all four series, cutting alternate programmes. Mike Murr, the dubbing editor, has worked on three of the four series. George Taylor's explanation for this was the need to have people who knew their job and were, above all, reliable.

Against this continuity, the differentiating factor within the crew is that of the director. He is employed on a six week contract for each episode, and although certain directors have built up a considerable track record on *Minder*, fifteen directors have so far been used,[4] and this variation is more clearly visible when looking at the first series, where seven directors worked on the eleven episodes.

This places the director in a position of relative insecurity *vis-à-vis* the technical crew, and one consequence of this was suggested by Roy Pointer. He felt that if the director was asking for something which fell outside the style of *Minder* he would be justified in consulting George Taylor directly: 'George Taylor's my boss, not the director.'

The function of the producer provides the other fixed reference point in relation to which the director's role is defined. On any series the producer has responsibility for ensuring that individual episodes fit in with the rest, and therefore must have ultimate control. George Taylor and Lloyd Shirley originally co-produced (George Taylor is now producer, whilst Lloyd Shirley is executive producer). Although both were employed on a freelance basis they had previously been founder members of the board of Euston, and had worked on previous series. The pressure of time on the directors, combined with this status of the producers, can be seen to militate in favour of continuity.

The second differentiating function is that of the writer. Fourteen writers have worked on *Minder* so far, six having worked on the original eleven episodes, and Linda Agran commented that she liked to introduce one or two new writers each series. But the writer's position cannot be delimited very clearly in terms of employment conditions because the writer works at one remove from the production team, and outside the rigours of a predetermined production timetable. Their work is, however, supervised by the script editor, originally Linda Agran and now

148

Frances Heasman. Her role for the writer is analagous to that of the producer for the director. In fact, due to the lack of a pilot before the first series, and because of the illness of Leon Griffiths (the format 'originator') during the second series, the job of script editor was particularly crucial: co-ordinating script production, preventing duplication of plots, advising on the characters of Arthur and Terry and suggesting re-writes. Again, the personal status of Linda Agran as one of the few permanent Euston employees cannot be discounted as a factor contributing to this centrality.

What is being suggested here is not that *Minder* as a series is merely repetition and that the organisation of the production team is constituted to contain or repress creative individuals. Rather, that the two roles marked as 'authorial' by both the industry and critics, those of director and writer, are constituted within the production team as variables. Clearly writers such as Leon Griffiths and Tony Hoare (who has written thirteen of the episodes) operate with a certain independence due to their experience of the show. Tony Hoare commented:

> The nice thing about starting at the beginning of the series is that . . . you've been partly responsible for creating those characters. Whereas, if you come into a series midway those characters are already there, and you've got no choice but to conform to that.

And directors such as Roy Ward Baker, Terry Green and Ian Toynton have a similar stake in the show, but that independence stems from their familiarity with the conventions to which the programme conforms.

Although two of the people interviewed, Tony Hoare and Terry Green, have worked together on a number of episodes, it is not normal practice to encourage writer/director teams. There were differences of opinion as to whether this was due to the difficulty of arranging contracts, or was deliberate policy. Tony Hoare also felt that writers are not encouraged to discuss their work with the director:

> There's some peculiar, mysterious conspiracy that goes on that no one can tie down or explain, or they choose not to, where they keep writers and directors apart . . . And I think that's divide and rule, I really do . . . Obviously, they're two quite important elements, the writer and the director, if they got together, they're going to have more control than the production side would want them to have.

Whether or not there is a deliberate policy of keeping writers and directors apart, the pressure of time within the two weeks of pre-production and two weeks of production must prevent too much discussion. The director's six-week contract also means that re-writes will already have been done by the writer, on the basis of discussions with Frances Heasman and Linda Agran, before the director has been employed. For these reasons the production team mediates between the director and writer, and is able to interject its own conventions and expectations.

The selection of writers and directors is also a factor in ensuring the 'flow' of the series, and this applies equally to the technical crew where it is highlighted by the schedule forcing two lighting cameramen and two editors to alternate. Because of this, the producer closely controls the choice of crew. George Taylor:

> You have to, you see, because you can't leave it to individual whims, a particular director; he might like a particular lighting cameraman but that lighting cameraman might not be fast enough. There might be everything wrong with the guy, on the other hand he might be brilliant, but we've got to have somebody that we know we can rely on.

The choice of personnel articulates *Minder* within a particular generic tradition, Within the context of freelance production for television both directors and writers, like actors, are liable to be typecast. The backgrounds of Tony Hoare and Terry Green may not be typical, but they immediately place *Minder* within the context of the crime series. Terry Green has done 'all the cops and robbers', and Tony Hoare's credits include *Bergerac, The Sweeney, Hazell, New Scotland Yard, Hunter's Walk* and *Softly, Softly*. More specifically, their experience places *Minder* in a tradition of Euston crime series, the latest of which before *Minder* was *The Sweeney*. Terry Green's first job directing film was *Special Branch*, and both worked on *The Sweeney* before *Minder*. This experience is shared not only by other writers and directors, but also by Lloyd Shirley and George Taylor who were executive producers on *The Sweeney*, and by many of the crew such as Mike Murr and Roy Pointer, who felt that they had become associated with Euston Films.

The expectations that this origin produced, combined with the orientation of the original series format (which Leon Griffiths has said was aimed at filling the space left by the departure of *The Sweeney*) was to lead to difficulties in the reception of the first series of *Minder*, even though two stylistic variations upon the crime series were demanded by the format. It rejected action sequences:

> Violence is implicit in the character, but need not be explicit in the series. Terry is not a stunt driver so there won't be spectacular car chases that land everybody in the local Magistrate's Court the following morning. For Terry it is often enough to squeeze somebody's elbow and suggest that they stop being a 'silly feller' to avoid unrealistic shoot-outs and shattered balsa-wood bannisters.

and it also required 'a leavening of humour'. But Linda Agran felt that:

150

'The directors didn't understand what they were doing, the actors didn't understand . . . up until that point all film drama had been very heavy.' Certainly Euston's own crime output had been, and the expectations of another *Sweeney* were compounded by the casting of Dennis Waterman as Terry, both for the production team and the audience: 'It affected everybody. Because Dennis did come virtually straight off *The Sweeney*, he was Carter, then he goes on to this.' The contravention of this expectation was compounded by the lack of pre-publicity for the new series. *Minder* first appeared directly after the ITV strike of 1979, thus preventing TV promotions, and the *TV Times* strike continued to prevent Euston from priming its audience. The first series was a failure in the ratings.

Minder's relationship to *The Sweeney* can be examined from a different point of view. Verity Lambert has acknowledged that they were looking for a series 'that would be popular and entertaining and would hopefully attract an audience of a similar size to *The Sweeney*' and like *The Sweeney* it has achieved the status of a long-running, relatively low budget and extremely popular series. But this has not always been the case, and the history of *Minder* as Euston's 'banker' uncovers not only aspects of Euston's relation to Thames, but also the 'space' that *Minder* occupies within Euston's production.

Linda Agran commissioned the series format after initial discussions with Leon Griffiths and Verity Lambert. The money for this came directly from Euston rather than Thames. On the basis of this document – a fourteen-page outline of characters, style and suggested plots – Bryan Cowgill as Programme Controller at Thames gave the financial go-ahead for the first eleven-episode series. There was no pilot.

The lack of popularity of the first series meant that the decision of whether to produce a second series or not was again Bryan Cowgill's. Now the boot is on the other foot. Since series 3 there has been a reluctance at Euston to continue indefinitely with *Minder*, which may go some way to explaining the eighteen-month gap in production before series 4. This was originally to consist of thirteen episodes, but was then talked up to twenty and when Manuel Alvarado and John Stewart interviewed Verity Lambert she commented: 'twenty and that really is it'. Euston are now prepared to do another six, bringing the total number of episodes to 63 (production of the 'final' six begins in January 1985). Linda Agran described this process as horse trading, and the bargaining involved gives Euston the credit with which to go ahead with higher risk projects.

Richard Paterson, in his article '*The Sweeney*: A Euston Films Product', remarked on the difficulty of giving exact financial information:

It has not been possible to acquire information about the financing of the series . . . without information on cost and expected revenue it is

151

not possible to acquire a basic understanding of the cycle of capital reproduction in the media industries.[5]

This information is, however, not simply being withheld. Because of Euston's particular insertion between the film and television industries, cost can be calculated to the last penny, but no accurate revenue figures are possible. For television companies, the fixed costs of the studios and personnel make any total costing a rather arbitrary process. Revenue is also difficult to assess, as it is the advertising between the programmes, rather than the programme itself, that earns the income. These indirect revenues and costs contrast with the film producer's ability to detail both exactly. So any profit and loss account with reference to *Minder*, or Euston Films generally, would have to be treated with scepticism. But this does not mean to say that the traces of Euston's economic situation are not to be found within the production set-up.

As has been explained elsewhere in this volume, one of the attractions of setting up Euston Films was that it could operate under the BFTPA agreement. This has enabled Euston to produce 50-minute films within television budgets, i.e. for the same price as an equivalent 50-minute studio drama (approximately £200,000). This entails the arduous production schedule first implemented on *Special Branch*: 2 weeks pre-production, 2 weeks production, 4 weeks picture editing (2 of which are during the shoot), 2 weeks sound editing and 2½ days dubbing.

The two weeks of pre-production are used mainly for finding locations and casting. This compares with the six weeks allowed by the BBC for *The Chinese Detective*. They can often still be looking for a location or an actor on the Friday before shooting begins on the Monday. Under this pressure of time the director is unlikely to be able to discuss the script carefully with the writer, or ask for any complicated re-writes. Nicholas Ray's comments on the Hollywood system reveal the difficulties inherent in such a production set-up, and re-emphasise the need for reliable crews, writers and directors, and indeed, programme format, brought out by George Taylor:

> If writers were able to work more closely with directors from the beginning of a film's conception, the results and the mutual understanding would improve. Most directors, when they start making films, are handed complete (though often impracticable) scripts a few days before shooting is due to start. Later they will have to fight to work with a writer of their own choice. Often the difficulty is that the studio likes to use one of its own writers, for obvious economic reasons.[6]

Having to shoot five minutes of programme time per day causes similar pressures. The director's relationship with the editor is affected

152

by this. George Taylor, the producer, always views the rushes, but the director is often unable to spare the time. Terry Green:

> I only go and see the rushes if there's a problem, if there's a report that something's wrong, or if the editor doesn't think that we've got it, or whatever. Because I know what I've shot. And the next day they're broken down and the editor starts cutting. That is the one thing I don't like, but there's no way round it in the schedule that we work to. Because ideally what we should do is to shoot everything and nothing gets broken down, and then you sit down when you've finished it and look at all the rushes with the editor. So I've got no chance of re-shooting something that I don't like – it's only if there's a technical fault or if the editor thinks we need an extra shot.

The director may only see the material after the first cut, on the Thursday or Friday after the shoot has finished. The production timetable is therefore effecting a stricter demarcation between editor and director, leaving the editor a personal autonomy within the confines of the conventions of the series.

This strict demarcation is apparent in other areas of the production team, and both determines and is determined by the production's rather hybrid status between television and film. Using a smaller crew than would be possible either in studio television drama productions or on a commercial film, there is nevertheless a four man camera crew: clapper / loader, assistant (who pulls focus, sets aperture, etc.), camera operator and lighting cameraman. Similarly in the cutting rooms, the functions of picture and sound editor are divided, whereas at Thames they are usually supervised by one editor. This difference is much more clearly marked in relation to TV productions on tape. There not only does the director have immediate access to the pictures being offered to him during the shoot, via monitors, but he is also present throughout the videotape editing process and supervises the dub, at which the tape editor is not present, unlike the film editor at a similar stage. This is not to argue that because of these differences (simply the result of 'custom and practice') the director has more 'creative' freedom on tape, or that the result is 'truer' to his intentions, but simply that there are more autonomous contributions to the end product on a highly demarcated film production.

This demarcation expresses both the demands of the timetable, as it enables the 8½ week turn-around to be achieved, and the demands of the crew, most of whom move between production for television and production for the cinema. They therefore see their job as making low budget films, and expect the 'industrialised' working methods associated with the cinema. (This even extends to the type of equipment used. Editors at Euston use Moviolas, which are upright and often associated with
153

American practice, instead of Steenbecks, which are flatbed and often associated with Europe. Without going into the different cutting methods these machines entail, what is significant here is that Steenbecks, in Britain at least, are almost universally used in TV cutting rooms, whereas Moviolas are standard in 'film' cutting rooms.)

This 'industrialisation' helps resolve the seeming paradox between the autonomy of crew members and the production of a 'formula' series such as *Minder*, a type of programme often pejoratively described as mass-produced. Given the need to produce a regular product within the series, each contributor must work towards the same objectives. Hence the difficulties encountered on the first series. Once this style is agreed upon, and given the continuity of the crew on *Minder*, this becomes a constraining factor on the amount of variation which the use of different directors builds into the system.

Production constraints also impinge upon writers through the number of actors who can be used, number of scenes, types of locations and so on. The use of the 'Winchester' as a standard set is a case in point, suggesting the gradual definition of the series conventions. In series 1 a number of different pubs and clubs were used, including the 'Winchester'. It was then decided to build a set for the drinking club, therefore ensuring continuity of location from episode to episode, and providing what Tony Hoare described as a focal point where different elements of the narrative can be brought together.

Richard Paterson has commented on the Rovers Return being the principal example of the importance of place in *Coronation Street*; 'Here the narrative is made coherent and almost all narrative strands are discussed in this main place of exchange in the Street.'[7] Clearly the 'Winchester' fulfills something of the same function for *Minder*, and Dave, the barman, provides a regular foil for the humour of Terry and Arthur. Yet the rest of the series, filmed on locations, has no fixed milieu, although Leon Griffiths has pointed out that it was originally intended to be set in the East End. Both these seemingly contradictory movements can be understood through production requirements. The bases for *Minder* have been in the west of London (it is there that labs and studios are based, and where most of the crew live), and the cost and time involved in regularly sending the crew to the East End would be prohibitive. The organisational incentive for building a set of the 'Winchester' was explained by Linda Agran: 'a third of the show can be shot in the Winchester, that set's standing, it's your weather cover, it's also economically very good for the production.'

The trace of economic factors, mediated by the production timetable, can also be seen in the post-production process of sound editing. Because of the two-week programme shooting schedule George Cole and Dennis Waterman are not available for post-synching. This is the technique, standard in the cinema, where actors have their dialogue re-recorded

154

whilst watching the film being played back. It allows a greater flexibility in producing the soundtrack because the editor can add just those effects required to completely 'clean' voices. Unlike sound editors in film studios or TV companies Mike Murr does not have convenient, on-site access to a sound library for background effects and atmosphere tracks (except for his own personal collection of effects from previous *Minders*). And because of the cost of specially recording music for a programme, or clearing the copyrights on a record for a series that is to be sold internationally, very little music is used on the soundtrack. These three factors mean that almost all the sound used in *Minder* is taken from location recordings (a specially adapted blimp is used on the camera to ensure it is as quiet as possible) and the result is what Mike Murr described as a 'realistic' soundtrack. (A further point was made by Terry Green, who pointed out that the director's contract ran out before the dub, and therefore he is often unable to go.)

So far only one element of the double action of genre has been looked at in any detail – the way that production is organised so as to ensure continuity within the series. But *Minder* cannot be understood as a fixed ahistorical structure. Changes and developments have occurred, although the description of those changes varies, from Linda Agran's:

> They were the changes, if you like, to bring it in line with what was the original very clearly defined aim of *Minder* as set out by Leon Griffiths.

to Tony Hoare's:

> I think the series has changed . . . the overall concept wasn't that it would be the programme it has ended up as.

An analysis of the script format suggests that the specific changes in *Minder* have been conditioned by the oblique relation of the series to the precedents it is articulated against. Within the play of 'repetition' and 'difference' it is difference that is explicitly foregrounded by the format:

> Most successful series feature two running characters. *Minder* is no exception, but the relationship is more complex than in most series.

The particular set of variations chosen by Leon Griffiths places *Minder* in relation to the crime series:

> The series is predicated on several prejudices shared by most viewers and a lot of writers and directors:
> a) They're getting sick of seeing cops chasing robbers through the streets of San Francisco and Belgravia.
> b) The freelance do-gooder is only believable if you place him in the

155

Minder: 'Gunfight at the OK Laundrette'. The first episode – 'much closer to the traditions established by *The Sweeney.*'

unreal world inhabited by the Saint and the Avengers.
c) The criminal as a hero is not acceptable as the protagonist of a long-running series.
d) One British private eye is enough.
e) Heroes employed by strange unknown 'trouble-shooting' agencies are unbelievable and they'd rather have Starsky and Hutch anyway.
[. . . .]
It will become clear that there is no 'police' or 'private eye' story that cannot be adapted to the format of *Minder.*[8]

'Gunfight at the OK Laundrette', the first plot outline in the series format (under the title 'Siege at the OK Corral') and the first episode of the first series, defines Terry's relationship to the police. He's minding Arthur Cavallo, the owner of a chain of laundrettes, and a friend of Arthur's. Through a conversation with Cavallo we find out that Terry has done time, as has Cavallo himself: 'I was bad company. I did all my bird 20 years ago.' So both Terry and his client are placed as ex-criminals. Terry's job, however, is essentially one of policing. When they arrive to collect the week's takings from the laundrette, three black guys with shooters hold them up. Terry fights to try and save the money, this being intercut with the arrival of the police. During the struggle Cavallo is shot and he, Terry and a woman are taken hostage. Terry acts as a go-between. His sympathies are shown to lie with the criminals, but it is he rather than the police who eventually disarms Stretch and his friends,
156

thereby ending the siege. His ambiguous position is commented on by the attitude of the police when he brings them out. He is forced to spread-eagle on the road while they check to see if he is armed, then he is taken to the station where Chisholm, making the first of many appearances, acerbicly comments that it will make a change for Terry to be a prosecution witness.

This plot places the episode closer to *The Sweeney* not only in terms of content but in its narrative structure and strategies of engagement with the audience. A comparison between the plots of 'Gunfight' and the later 'If Money Be the Food of Love Play On' emphasises the linear development of the narrative of the first episode, leading to the 'inevitable' denouement of Terry releasing the hostages, in the same manner as the police series concludes with the capture of the criminal. There is also a considerable number of action sequences in this episode, and these are combined with traditional strategies of suspense. Part two ends with a threat by Stretch to shoot the woman hostage; the police presence outside is intercut with the danger for the hostages inside, where Cavallo is slowly dying of his wounds. The choice of 'Gunfight' as the first episode of the first series could therefore be seen to be a deliberate attempt to attract a similar audience to that won by Euston's earlier successful crime series.

The simplicity of the narrative organisation of 'Gunfight' contrasts with that of 'If Money Be the Food of Love, Play On', where there are a number of subplots clustered around the main articulation of the narrative, Arthur's business deals. In this episode Dee, an Australian con artist, has come to England to get her share of a jewel haul from her ex-partner, Gary. Arthur supplies her with a fur coat and a car, at inflated prices. Those aspects that would normally constitute the central plot, such as Dee's revenge on Gary, are subordinated to the routine (every week) business of Arthur trying to make his crust, thereby de-centering the crime within the programme. Nowhere is this made more obvious than in the role of Rycott, the comic policeman who is a marginal irritation to the everyday running of the black market economy.

The change in narrative structure in turn allows Arthur and Terry to share more scenes, and so produces more comedy. Alternatively, the desire for comedy can be seen as the motivation for the change of narrative structure and move away from the crime series format. Lloyd Shirley felt that: 'It was clear at a very early stage on *Minder* that the comedy strand was going to become dominant.' Much of the comedy is generated precisely by playing with the rigid oppositions the crime series enforces between criminal and police, and especially by exploiting the hypocrisy of the 'straight' world. Arthur operates at a point where the distinction between commerce and criminality begins to blur. This is partly due to the writer's need to prevent Terry and Arthur being out

157

Minder: 'If Money Be the Food of Love, Play On'. (L. to r.) Terry McCann (Dennis Waterman), Mournful Maurice (Barry Jackson), Arthur Daley (George Cole). 'And I want your assurance that it is bankrupt stock.'

and out villains: 'One of the big problems with a show like *Minder* is that they're bloody crooks, but you've got to portray them as never being quite real crooks.' So, in 'If Money', Arthur, having done the deal with Mournful on the fur coat, concludes: 'Readies, cash in your claw, right now. And I want your assurance that it is bankrupt stock'. Here, as is generally the case, we know the goods are stolen. Arthur's deals are, strictly speaking, criminal, and Rycott and Chisholm's perpetual incompetent efforts to send him down reinforces this sense of criminality. But because Arthur is able to keep his hands clean, he can also keep up his rhetoric of supporting 'nation, family, duty, authority, standards'. This irony, which produces much of the comedy in *Minder*, also brings into question the legitimacy of *any* commercial deals: 'What we're really trying to show is that everyone's robbing each other blind, it's just that some manage to do it within the dubious law'. The 'dubious' law which Arthur operates within is that of supply and demand, and its effect is articulated most clearly in Terry's repeated exploitation. A recurring motif is Terry's incomprehension of why he stays with Arthur – an incomprehension articulated in both the episodes that have been looked at here. But this disingenuously ignores not only the demands of the narrative, and the commercial needs of Thames, but also the more general imperatives of labour selling itself on an open market. This is brought out in the opening sequences of 'If Money'. Arthur is lecturing Terry as they go into the 'Winchester', the camera concentrating on Terry's reactions to Arthur:

158

Arthur: You know your trouble, my son, total ignorance of the times we live in. No historical perspective, that's your problem, you know what they say about history repeating itself.
Terry: Shouldn't do it in company?
Arthur: Oh, very amusing, Terence, very droll, and here you are turning down gainful employment.
Terry: And here you are giving me GBH of the eardrum again.

After meeting Mournful they go into the 'Winchester'. Here in 3-shot with Dave and Arthur, Terry is placed centre frame, again focusing the audience's attentions on his reactions to Arthur's rhetoric. Arthur is talking about the Yarrow ('Er, Jarrow, Arthur') marches:

Arthur: There were no motorways in those days, Terry, no socks, holes in their daisies, but cloth caps at a dignified angle, in order they might demand their democratic right to do an honest bit of collar.
Terry: What do you know of . . .
Arthur: Sad days my son, but they will be back, Terry, stand on me.
Terry: Gawd help us.
Arthur: That is what they said, but He helps them that helps themselves.
Terry: Well you must have His undivided attention then.

This article has limited itself to an attempt to articulate the relationship between the organisation of the production of *Minder* and aspects of its generic operations. And Terry's comic deflation of Arthur can be understood in that context. But in attempting to address one particular absence within recent work on genre, I've ignored the ideological construction of the series, and in doing so have conceded that area to other analyses which have concentrated upon the conservative nature of Euston Films. The implied critique of Arthur's comic Thatcherism in Terry and Arthur's conversation offers an alternative reading.

Notes

1. Steve Neale, *Genre* (London: British Film Institute, 1980).
2. Manuel Alvarado and Edward Buscombe, *Hazell: the making of a TV series* (London: British Film Institute, 1978).
3. Interviewed by Manuel Alvarado and John Stewart.
4. Up until episode 11, series 4.
5. Richard Paterson, '*The Sweeney*: A Euston Films Product', *Screen Education* no. 20, Autumn 1976.
6. Nicholas Ray, 'Story into Script', quoted in BFI Dossier no. 11, Jim Cook and Alan Lovell (eds.), *Coming To Terms With Hollywood* (London: British Film Institute, 1981), p. 25.
7. Richard Paterson, 'The Production Context of *Coronation Street*', in Richard Dyer, Christine Geraghty, Marion Jordan, Terry Lovell, Richard Paterson, John Stewart (eds.), *Coronation Street* (London: British Film Institute, 1981).
8. *Minder* format, reprinted earlier in this volume.

4   Memory: *The Flame Trees of Thika*

Tana Wollen

Broadcast in the early Autumn of 1981, *The Flame Trees of Thika* did not apparently bear the signatures usually associated with Euston products. Although the 'lavish production values'[1] which could by now be expected of Euston films were still very much in evidence, they were lavished not on the construction of a contemporary locale but on the production of a past set in a distant place. The pleasures of recognition evoked by the dramatic 'here and now' of *The Sweeney, Out, Fox* and *Minder* were apparently replaced by the pleasures of recognising an 'elsewhere' that belonged to memory. The production of that memory might have indicated yet another sign of Euston's capacity to come up with projects that were new and different. *The Flame Trees of Thika* marked the constant refreshment of Euston's entertainment as the car-chased streets of South London opened out to the sun-drenched plains of East Africa. It is possible to make connections between such apparently diverse products as *The Sweeney* and *Flame Trees* in terms of what could be characterised as a 'Euston' sense and use of location. But there is more to connect them than filmic style.

The production of a memory validates constructions of the present. Euston Films productions represent a quintissential Britishness. That Britishness, often equated with 'maleness', is epitomised by Terry and Arthur's wit, in Carter and Regan's heroics, in Frank Ross' and Sidney Reilly's ruthlessness and cool calculation. The *New York Times*, reviewing *Flame Trees*, applauded it as an accurate portrait which managed 'to combine the colonialist arrogance and the spunky courage of the British'.[2] The memory of a colonial history which Euston Films produced in *The Flame Trees of Thika* was in fact no great departure from the company's construction of an urban present. Differences between the soft-focused, nostalgic representation of history and the hard-edged, dramatic construction of the present are only impressionistic. But it is by means of such impressions, ephemeral but constantly renewed, that television and film manage to create a consciousness of where we are, of
160

what we were. Euston Films, by combining in its project the dramas of street violence with an account of how a wild open space was tamed, refreshed a national identity. Britishness now, represented by the ruthlessness of working-class heroes, was once represented by the courage and fair play of the more genteel middle classes abroad. Where there is grit, there was pluck.

The British identity, represented in Euston productions, is structured by two significant absences.[3] The claim has been made here that in the Euston product what was characteristically British was also male. That maleness is structured by an absence of, or at least an indifference to, the female both before and even after *Flame Trees* and *Widows*. It can be argued that when the Euston woman is strong she is so because she is able to assume what have already been established as the strengths of the Euston male. But to be British is also to be white. The other absence which structures Euston films and their representation of a British identity is race. In the late summer and early autumn of 1981, the production of a memory in which a white middle-class family brought control and government to an unruly land inhabited by black, unpredictable people, was of no small significance. But the history represented in *The Flame Trees of Thika* could only make an ambiguous, even contradictory, sense of the present. The British could either rest assured in a hazy glow which their lingering ability to rule benevolently afforded, or they had to wake up to the fact that the past was the past and that things had gone disastrously wrong.

The absences of women and race were not seen as such by the producers at Euston Films – that in itself partly defines them as 'structuring absences' in this account. What Verity Lambert admired most about *Flame Trees* was what she recognised as its depiction of strong women characters. Tilly and Elspeth Grant were unusual in that their story could represent positive images of women in what is usually recounted as the history of rugged male adventure. Holly Aird, as Elspeth, was a newcomer to the screen but Hayley Mills, as Tilly, was not. John Hawkesworth, one of the co-producers of *Flame Trees*, introduced Hayley Mills to a screen career when she was 13 in *Tiger Bay* (1959). Her most famous role was in *Pollyanna* (1960), the orphaned child she played at the age of 14. She developed this child image in later Disney films and in spite of her nude scene in *The Family Way* (1967) it is fair-haired, wide-eyed childishness which the screen image of Hayley Mills connotes. The two women occupy strong positions in the narrative of *The Flame Trees of Thika* but they are not necessarily strong in themselves. One is a child and the other connotes childishness. They are strong and brave in spite of their gender but never, it seems, because of it.

Flame Trees was sold to thirty-three different countries which included Kenya, Zambia, Zimbabwe and Swaziland. Having purchased the product, the African countries banned it from their screens after the first few

161

episodes. It was denounced as 'unacceptable' by audiences in Kenya, Zambia and Zimbabwe. However, even knowing this, the executives at Euston could still not see anything 'problematic' about the ways in which Africans were represented. True to a sense of time and place, what they considered was 'good' about *The Flame Trees of Thika* was simply its faithful depiction of the way things had been. For the producers, depiction of past places and events in *Flame Trees* accentuated the difference from the present. Far from saying that black people are painted savages, their liberalism would hasten to show how different the present day African is from his/her grandparents. It could not be seen that the stereotypical representations of black people so visible in *Flame Trees* have their roots in and give rise to flagrant racism.

John Hawkesworth already belonged to Euston's past in that he had produced *Danger UXB*. He had also produced other memories of the past in *Upstairs, Downstairs* and *The Duchess of Duke Street*, so *The Flame Trees of Thika* can be contextualised within Hawkesworth's recurring television production of Edwardian or Georgian memories. An account of the production of *Flame Trees* was written as part of a double-page colour spread in the *TV Times* of the week the first episode was broadcast. The account was, therefore, popular knowledge. In 1978, so the *TV Times* related, John Hawkesworth went on holiday to Kenya, taking Elspeth Huxley's autobiography *The Flame Trees of Thika* to read on the flight.[4] Immediately struck by the book's possibilities, he set about persuading Verity Lambert to accept a dramatised version for Euston. In this respect, the production of *Flame Trees* was not very different from other Euston productions in that it centred around the ideas of a single writer and, in this case, a co-producer. The other co-producer, Christopher Neame, produced *The Knowledge* for Euston in 1979, while Hawkesworth started scripting *Flame Trees*. Filming started in 1980. Every episode was shot on location in Kenya, which took thirteen weeks. Two cameramen were flown out before the main shooting started in order to film wildlife.

It was the wildlife and other 'symptoms' of the location which posed most of the production difficulties. The sense of past time and place had to be 'accurately' evoked and, in a style similar to most television adaptations, the original book had to be as faithfully adhered to as possible. It is *mise-en-scène* which most immediately and strikingly signifies time and place, and one of the reasons why film and television is generally supposed to show so wonderfully history 'as it really was'. It was setting the right scene which caused so many problems. The Euston production team filmed during Kenya's dry season. Flame trees only flower very suddenly and for short periods of time after the brief rains in October and November. Episode 4, 'Friends in High Places', demanded the reconstruction of a thunderstorm. Most popular production accounts are also marketing strategies, dealing with the resolution of such difficulties so that viewers of the product can marvel all the more at

162

the film-makers' ingenuity and craft. The *TV Times* account was no exception to this. The thunderstorm was provided by paying most of Nairobi's fire brigade to open their hoses on the dry savannah and a film crew was rushed off to shoot some flame trees which had somehow managed miraculously to flower many miles away. Several episodes required the killing of wild animals, which is now illegal in Kenya. This the production team found easy to understand and so rather unconvincing cut-away shots and stuffed animals from the Nairobi Natural History Museum were used. Less easy to understand than the ban on the killing of wild animals was the Kenyan government's restrictions on dress. In Elspeth Huxley's autobiography, the Kikuyu women who build Robin and Tilly's house are bare-breasted. So conscious are the Kenyan and Tanzanian authorities of the West's racist depictions of the African in traditional dress as a primitive savage, an exotic anthropological specimen, that public display of nudity or semi-nudity is now strictly forbidden. The attempts by Africans to resist the force of racist images could not be understood either by the Euston production team executives or by Elspeth Huxley herself, who was invited to Kenya by Thames to ensure their fidelity to her original account. It was deemed 'a pity' that the African women had to have their breasts covered. This is hardly surprising given that the representations of African people in *Flame Trees* were not perceived as racist in the first place. The image of topless white women thatching a roof would be deemed scandalous if it was not recuperated by 'comedy'. The image of bare-breasted black women, thatching the mud and wattle house that Robin Grant thought 'Not bad for under £10', was simply part and parcel of what Western racist codes of representation claim unproblematically as the photogenicity of the wild.

The adaptation of a novel as a 'classic' television series lends television a patina of cultural respectability. By adapting novels, television brings out the best of the literary, what is dominantly considered to be 'better' culture. Television adaptations of novels depend on a memory of that novel, obtained either from reading or, as is more likely, from a memory which is generally circulated, part of a common cultural 'baggage'. This is more the case with the 'classics' of literature, of which most people have a knowledge, even if they haven't read them. However, the television adaptation not only depends on this memory but reconstructs it by producing another, televisual one. How many classical novels has television 'brought to life'? The moving image, more immediate than the printed word, brings a past memory more sharply into the present. The memory of the book is replaced by the memory of the adaptation. Publishers are well aware that books which have been adapted by television will be bought and read not for the literary representation to be enjoyed so much as the ways in which the literary matches what television has displayed. Paperbacks re-issued call upon the memory of the literary text by sporting scenes from the television adaptation on the front covers. The books are bought and read, often evaluated, in terms of how faithful they seem to the memory which television or film has reproduced.[5]

The most prestigious television productions are the adaptations of the classics. These have earned the BBC, especially, international renown. The representations of Britain which circulate through the world's broadcasting networks are those of a British history dominated by ancestral homes, landscaped vistas, yards of gathered silk and tulle. The serialised classic earns television respect in that television adapts work by a 'great' author, makes it accessible to the masses and meanwhile circulates respectable representations of the national heritage.[6]

The Flame Trees of Thika is Elspeth Huxley's autobiographical account of her childhood in the years when Kenya began to be methodically pioneered. It has never been a literary classic in the way that Dickens' or Trollope's novels have been. Nevertheless, placed in the television dramatic serial slot in the 'new autumn season', *The Flame Trees of Thika* was granted the same prestige as the more 'classic' television adaptations. This was made explicit by Thames' scheduling strategies towards the end of the serial's run. The last episode was broadcast the day after the first episode of *Brideshead Revisited*, the classic serial par excellence. As the last credits for *Flame Trees* were rolling, the continuity announcer told viewers that *Brideshead* would be taking the place of the 'truly lovely' serial that *Flame Trees* had proved to be. So *Flame Trees* was produced by television as a memory from literature, although it was probably not a memory widely shared. The title sequences claimed that the television serial was an adaptation of a 'novel', whereas Elspeth Huxley's book had been previously published as an autobiography. The press previews referred to the adaptation of a 'true story' and so *Flame Trees* was not only tinged with the authenticity of the literary but was also guaranteed, not by the author's 'greatness', but by autobiographical 'truth', a truth based on 'real' historical events which had happened in a real place within living memory. Elspeth Huxley herself revisited Thika to watch *Flame Trees* being shot, and serialised her account of how things in Kenya had changed and of how things had remained the same for the *Observer*. 'The seeds my parents and others like them planted and tended have not perished. Others have reaped the crop, but that is often so.'[7] The television adaptation of *The Flame Trees of Thika* represented, then, two kinds of veracity which television marketing strategies, scheduling and serialisation had already established. *Flame Trees* had the status and authenticity of the literary slot and it also had the autobiographical truth which was guaranteed both by the individual author and by History.

With these two veracities glossing *Flame Trees*, in producing a memory of colonial East Africa the 'truth' had to be constantly affirmed by the production's fidelity to the two 'reals' – the literary text and History. Television's meditations were taken as given so that the immediacy of the visual did not merely appear to stand in for the truth; it *was* the truth. The trouble and care taken over *mise-en-scène* has already been mentioned. Accuracy had to be seen, made visible. The house that Robin and Tilly Grant had had built was re-built according to the exact specifications of the original. Juma wears white robe and red fez, the recognisable garb of the African house servant, and Chief Kupanya, as befits a Kikuyu chief, is draped in a cloak made from the skins of rare colobus monkeys. This accuracy of *mise-en-scène* enables the viewer to recognise this representation of history as truth 'not by virtue of the "facts" being correct, but because the image looks right.'[8] Visual representations ensure a truth in themselves. The immediacy of images serves to confirm in turn that 'what we see is true and this truth confirms what we see'.[9] The Penguin edition, re-issued after the Euston production of this memory, shows Holly Aird (on pony) and Hayley Mills looking into the camera lens. The band across the cover claims the book as a spin-off from what is 'Now a spectacular Thames Television serial'. The word 'spectacular' is significant. It is not a 'classic' serial but one in which images compensate for cultural lack. It is the moving flow of images, the spectacle, which constantly affirms the 'truth'. What won *Flame Trees* such popular acclaim was the spectacle of the exotic. What nature and science programmes had shown were now incorporated into a human drama. *Flame Trees* was 'a beautifully photographed true-life adventure story',[10] the wildlife was 'spectacular'[11] and the photography was 'stunning'.[12]

This capacity to present spectacle as truth is one of the ways in which television and film can mediate the real. Euston products, filmed for television, can capture especially well subtle tones of light and colour for the small domestic screen. Television is able, through its various generic codes, to mediate the 'real' in many different ways. Television constructs and operates a number of different realisms. What is supposedly realistic has to measure up not so much to the 'real', as to the particular modes of realism which television has led us to expect in particular instances. In this respect, the complaints that *Flame Trees* did not adequately show the real hardships of pioneering life, that it was too idealistic, 'much too cosy',[13] were out of key. Hayley Mills' constantly-coiffeured hair and the spotless 'Laura Ashley' dresses *were* realistic in the sense that they belonged not to documentary realism but to the dramatic realism of a television adaptation. *Flame Trees* thus played on two forms of realism: the spectacle of real wildlife and African landscapes, *and* the realism of television drama. However, unlike television drama, *Flame Trees* did not have any strong narrative momentum. There were no intricacies of plot or unfathomable depths of character to keep viewers hooked. Whilst narrative threads did weave through various episodes (Njombo's curse

165

as a punishment for murder), individual episodes were fairly self-contained. There were no cliff hanger endings, and in this sense it wasn't narrative pull that kept the ratings consistently high. *Flame Trees* was neither series nor serial but rather what has usefully been defined as an 'episodic serial',[14] exploiting the codes and conventions of both. What provided the impulse to view were the ways in which various realisms mediated two 'reals' in their apparent fidelity to the 'original'. The 'spectacular' filming was one form of realism and the dramatic realism of acting out what it 'really must have been like', was another. The *New Statesman* reviewer was looking for a kind of realism which did not operate in *Flame Trees* when he complained that it was 'non-amatory crises and acts of good pioneer neighbourliness which provided this week's jerky narrative impulse'.[15] Spectacle, idealising history for television drama, compensated for the complete absence of convincing script.

In *Flame Trees*, Euston produced a spectacular memory of Britain's colonial past. It was not a memory produced as spectacularly as *Brideshead*, *The Far Pavilions* or *Jewel in the Crown*, but it preceded these, whetting the appetite for this kind of sumptuous reminiscence of far-flung places where the sun never sets, and constructed audience expectations of bigger and better. Memory necessarily involves the production of a past which pertains to the present. East Africa was not a lost adventure world – after all, as John Hawkesworth had discovered, it is possible to book a safari there even now; it was part of a history in which, as *Flame Trees* showed, the British were at their best. Elspeth Huxley's book, so the *TV Times* declared, 'draws the captivated reader into a world not so much lost as gone before'.[16] Euston's reproduction of this world that had 'gone before' reclaimed it for viewers as a memory so it could not be lost. Made so vividly 'present' by television it was a memory that could be all the more easily clung to.

The memory of Africa which *The Flame Trees of Thika* produced (a minute locality metonymically representing a vast continent) showed Africa to be at once romantic and unpredictable, even dangerous. There was nothing new about this. Racist stereotyping persisted in this memory for the present. Africa and Africans were startlingly beautiful to look at, but they were liable to bite the hands that fed them, ungratefully and without warning. However, the challenge which Africa presented to Europeans to 'make something' of such a beautiful but 'uncultivated' place persists. Africa continues to connote adventure, a testing ground where only the toughest survive. Like the American West for Europeans of the mid-nineteenth century, Africa offered the British in the early twentieth century a wilderness for taming. The theme music of *Flame Trees* (made available on record) employed the meandering whistle and orchestrated strings associated with Westerns. The thorn trees and dry grasses in the first few episodes might not have been all that distantly related to the open prairies.

166

Africa's mystique was described by Tony Osoba. The *TV Times* quoted him as saying 'It's the red earth, the scents, the feel of the place. I think we got closest to it during a week we spent filming at a camp called Lewa Downs. We were shooting deep in the bush, living under canvas, taking showers under buckets. In the evenings we could sit around an open fire and the Kenyans would roast chestnuts while the hyenas howled.'[17] Osoba played the mysterious Ahmed, Ian Crawford's Somali servant who, wrapped up in an endless red turban, helps Ian to smuggle horses across the border. Half Nigerian and half Scottish, Osoba had never been to Africa before shooting *Flame Trees*, but the role he played and his own 'unusual' racial background served to authenticate his description.

That Africa was, and is considered to be, untamable, contributes as much to the continent's mystique as its beauty does. In *Flame Trees* the savage or unpredictable are always lurking, but for the Grants at least they are obstacles which can be soldiered through. The fluffy chickens Tilly tries to rear are massacred by *siafu* (safari ants). One of Lettice's Pekes is snaffled by a leopard which at dark comes right up to the house. That these symbols of an English domesticity can be so 'tragically' menaced allows the serial to produce a memory of Africa as a dark and devious threat. However, the threats and difficulties can themselves be mitigated by the power of Africa's beauty.

At the end of the first episode, 'The Promised Land', Tilly rages. It is pouring with rain, the roof leaks and her husband has reprimanded her for using an old family heirloom as a medicine cabinet. She bursts into tears. 'The place is crawling with insects. The natives are all savages and I hate it.' The camera zooms out from the newly built house to focus on the newly planted trees that give the serial its name. The first bloom flames scarlet in the rain. As Elspeth gazes wistfully from the window of the train which takes her back to England she (the camera) sees herds of zebra, gazelle and wildebeestes grazing. A mother elephant and her baby drink from a muddy river, their trunks dipping in unison. A couple of giraffes twine necks lovingly. The 'wild' life of Africa is at peace. It welcomes Elspeth (and the viewer) back. It is unthreatening, almost tamed.

In *The Flame Trees of Thika*, it is how Africa and Africans are perceived that makes them peaceful or threatening. This is the lesson to be learned from the memory which Euston produces. Africa represents both the mystical and the dangerous for those who want to perceive it as such. The Grants do not. Robin and Tilly are more sensible, patient and sane than their fellow settlers, while the main point of identification for audiences lies in Elspeth.

Elspeth spends her childhood in Thika wondering and curious. These qualities are supposedly shared by the viewer, wondering at Africa's strangeness, at the intrepid 'courage' of people like her parents and

167

The Flame Trees of Thika. 'It is through Elspeth that Africa is "understood".'

curious as to their 'real' history. It is through Elspeth that Africa is 'understood'. She has the answers to several of the narrative's secrets. For her, as for the modern 'liberal' viewer who is constructed at this point of identification, Africa and Africans can make a certain sense. It is Elspeth who is told by her father's servant who murdered Hereward's headman. It is Elspeth who can provide certain explanations. Robin and Tilly wonder why the Kikuyu live in round rather than rectangular houses. Elspeth's explanation is the one European viewers would find sensible. It is because rectangular furniture, such as Europeans have, would not fit into round huts. Her father pushes her Eurocentric, but childishly appealing, explanation further, to reveal one which only confirms the Kikuyu's primitivism. 'They only have three-legged stools. Goats are kept under the beds. The smoke keeps out the lice and the

168

goats' urine keeps down the jiggas.' 'Ugh,' grimace Elspeth and Tilly. And what says the viewer? But Elspeth runs away from the bullying white girls who lock her up in a cupboard when she openly declares that some of her best friends are 'natives'. She refuses to call her pony either Guinivere or Cleopatra as Lettice suggests. Instead, she names it after the place from which it came, Moyale. Elspeth's understanding of Africa is plausible because she is a child. But she has to return to England from the land that has 'gone before'. She has to grow up.

Robin and Tilly Grant provide other points of identification as well-intentioned adult settlers. Other whites are to be recognised as types. The Grants are the acceptable face of colonial rule in television's terms. Roger Stillbeck, from whom the Grants buy 'their' land, refers to the band of black porters as 'a scratch lot'. Tilly at least wonders 'what they think of it all'. Roger's reply is 'Porters don't think'. Robin and Tilly's own racism is merely the result of benevolent naivety. As the Kikuyu warriors dance around their tent, the Grants' white faces show horror, fear and distaste. The camera movement not only shows this reaction but does so sympathetically. The dance culminates in a low-angle shot of a fearsome Njombo in tribal dress before he dons the Western-styled shirt and servants' shorts. The Grants' relief at the arrival not of a band of hostile warriors but of a willing labour force is the audience's too. The memory produced is one of the painted savage disguising the servile and courteous worker who simply needs education and tactful handling. When Sammy reacts violently to Mr Roos, the unsavoury Boer who abuses him at the plough, Robin intervenes. Robin might think Mr Roos is a cad but he does the right thing and drinks cold beer with him on the verandah after the leopard shoot. Over the blistered back of a Kikuyu baby who has fallen into a fire, Mrs Nimmo describes to Tilly the gentrified Scottish stock from which she springs. A jar of Vaseline and a jug of boiled water are the simple antidotes to a 'heathen' mother's ignorance and neglect. Her racism seems to be excused by her 'mumsy' affection towards Elspeth. There is the good-natured but unstable Irish Mary, the Australian Victor who waves the Nimmo soda siphon aside with 'I don't need no gas in my booze'. These are colonialism's more unreliable elements.

The other couple with whom Robin and Tilly are contrasted favourably are Lettice and Hereward Palmer. Hereward is a stuffy, stiff upper-lipped army type whose feelings are locked up for good. Lettice is the delicate flower for whom Africa's dark and potent forces, as she perceives them, only bring harm. Her lover's death is made Africa's responsibility even though it was in a European war that he fought and died, alongside East Africans. 'It's a cruel country. It takes your heart and grinds it into powdered stone and no one minds.'

Ian has come to Africa to enjoy the romance of wide open spaces before they disappear. Whereas Tilly believes that the British will make

169

dirt and disease disappear, Ian recognises the fact that history will not end tidily. 'And in a few years' time when you've got a few million natives working for a few thousand white men there could be big trouble.' To this, Hereward retorts, 'The Africans are fortunate to be under British rule.' Robin and Tilly exchange looks. But the discussion ends there.[18]

The Africans are friendly and grateful towards the Grants who are shown as having treated them fairly though firmly. Chief Kupanya is the wily patriarch behind an imbecilic smile. Sammy and Njombo persist in their 'primitive' feud. Their witchdoctors and 'corrupt' systems of justice provide narrative impulse only in that these incomprehensibles disrupt the business of farming coffee. It is through these few characters that Elspeth is introduced to the 'strange' Kikuyu beliefs. For the most part the Kikuyu are anonymous figures, carrying shields and spears; bedecked in feathers and paint they wail, sing and dance as 'natives' do, rhythmically. They are nothing more than 'ghosts in negative'.[19] The most ghostly African presence in *Flame Trees* is a drunk. As Elspeth stows herself in a freight carriage bound for Thika, the African lumbers indistinctly out of the dark. Identifying with Elspeth, the viewer fears for her safety. Fears founded on racist stereotypes produce expectations of the African raping or robbing her. Instead he offers her a drink. She politely refuses and he lurches out into the night. No doubt this confusion of racist expectations only goes to prove, by this additional example, the African's docility when confronted by a lack of fear. But what would be his story?[20] *The Flame Trees of Thika* only constructs a particular history, one which can be respectably circulated. The memories produced are particular ones of a colonial Africa, but they are not African memories because, it has to be presumed, the British have nothing to learn from such memories for the present.

Memories enable the past to live in and bear upon the present. The present in which Euston generated a memory of colonial history was 1981. On the one hand there were attempts to shed colonial history as the Nationality Bill restricted claims to British citizenship. On the other hand the consequences of that colonial history became dramatically visible. In that present, history as a process of struggle was seen on television.

Only months before the first episode of *Flame Trees* was broadcast, Britain's inner cities flared. The riots of 1981 were class riots in that those on the streets (and on television) were the young unemployed, the new dispossessed. They were race riots in that of those dispossessed, black people constituted the majority and in that the police oppressed them most severely. It was against the police, the faces of 'law and order', that these dispossessed young people fought. The riots were constructed as 'race' riots by the media and so the history of a particularly subjugated part of the working class was repressed. As 'race riots', the disaffection of a whole class could be minimalised, limited to particularly 'black' areas
170

of the inner cities. The forms of racism which had already existed for centuries made it especially easy to represent the deprived as depraved. Law and order had to be reinforced, had to be made respected, on the one hand. On the other, anger had to be smoothed.

Whitelaw's measures made the hand of the law heavier. The Police Bill, riot gear and plastic bullets were introduced. This was hegemony enforced. The media effected the hegemony of consent.[21] Television had been blamed as having induced 'copycat' riots. Conscious of its 'responsibilities' in these terms of influences and effects, television had to redeem its social and political role. Wounds needed healing, reassurance was being called for. In St Paul's cathedral, that very symbol of Restoration, all differences were forgotten. The nation was repaired by the Royal Wedding.[22]

It was in this context that *The Flame Trees of Thika* produced salving memories for a present that seemed so ravaged. *Flame Trees* taught such a lesson of history, which, as Keith Tribe points out, 'can be deployed in contemporary arguments'.[23] Production of the past does not simply recover history, it also fabricates it. The history fabricated in *Flame Trees* was a version which reviewers clutched at with relief.

The *Sunday Times* acknowledged the 'business' television was up to by claiming that in *Flame Trees*, television had 'started out on the long and tricky job of selling us benevolent agrarian colonialism at family level'.[24] To the *Daily Mail*, 'benevolent colonialism' had been well and truly sold by the end of the first episode. 'Today, when we hear nothing but abuse about the whites in Africa and their wicked colonialism, it is refreshingly new for many of us to learn how life was really like for so many of those Europeans. Some of them were, to be sure, contemptuous of and patronising to the Africans but many, like Elspeth Huxley's family, brought work, medical advances and, above all, agricultural husbandry, to areas that were a wilderness. And the relationship between the whites and the natives was in such cases friendly and co-operative.'[25]

Flame Trees not only produced a memory tinged with the pastoral nostalgia for wide open spaces. It produced a memory of Britishness, of fair play, of being in control. The Grants were ordinary, 'decent' people. Identifying with their story was easier than identifying with the lavish neuroses of *Brideshead*, though perhaps more boring when people were forever having 'to tighten their belts'. In *Flame Trees*, the Grants were part of a history that was made to stand for the whole. Their innocent open-mindedness was especially appealing for an audience that did not want to be told it had been extremely nasty. When they scolded their servants, it was only for their own good. 'They were an idealised family but British ex-patriots must mostly have been like them. Naive, resourceful, relatively liberal young couples repaired to unknown places like Kenya and worked hard for their own satisfaction and not much profit. In such good intentions, others may easily find repression'.[26]

171

Others easily did, but in *The Flame Trees of Thika* their history was repressed.

By producing a memory of colonial history in terms of the lives of individuals rather than in terms of one race dominating another, Euston conformed to conventional television constructions of history. But unlike the television costume dramas in which individuals (usually 'great men') make history, the Grants and Kenya seemed to be outside history, removed from it. Their romance was the escape. Tilly, Robin and Elspeth, along with other ex-patriots, were seen to be making a life for themselves in a place that was remote, unconnected with the real centres of power. Their lives were not 'real' history, but rather a luxurious experience, *hors de combat*. It is what is seen to be 'real' history that catches up with them, seizes them unawares and drags them back from a land of plenty. Narrated between fiction and fact, the Grant drama invites the viewer to experience history as an adventurous expedition, short lived but beneficent in its effects. In any event, the leaving of it was to be regretted. At the same time the viewer is invited to reminisce over the spectacular romance of the enterprise. 'Look, that is what it was really like!' Euston fabricated a comforting history for popular spectacle, to remember at a time when the consequences of that real history, the protests of the oppressed, had made themselves obvious. Memories such as those produced in *The Flame Trees of Thika* are incomplete.

Notes

1. Clive James in the *Observer* 6.9.81.
2. *New York Times* 31.12.81.
3. The idea of absences structuring a text was initiated and developed in the collective analysis on John Ford's *Young Mr Lincoln* by the editors of *Cahiers du Cinéma*. An English translation of the analysis appeared in *Screen* Vol. 13, no. 3, Autumn, 1972.
4. *TV Times* 29.8.81 – 4.9.81.
5. This argument is developed by John Ellis in 'The Literary Adaptation – An Introduction', *Screen* Vol. 23, no. 1: 'The adaptation trades upon the memory of the novel, a memory that can derive from actual reading or, as is more likely with a classic of literature, a generally circulated cultured memory. The adaptation consumes this memory, aiming to efface it with the presence of its own images.'
6. See Paul Kerr, 'Classic Serials – To be Continued', *Screen* Vol. 23 no. 1: 'The classic serial is thus left with "words of beauty and power which tells a story" and simultaneously reinforces a high cultural memory.'
7. Elspeth Huxley in the *Observer* 30.8.81.
8. Keith Tribe, 'History and the Production of Memories', in Bennett, Boyd-Bowman, Mercer, Woollacott, *Popular Television and Film* (London: British Film Institute, 1981).
9. Colin MacCabe, 'Memory, Phantasy, Identity: *Days of Hope* and the Politics of the Past', in *Popular Television and Film*, op. cit.
10. *Daily Mirror* 5.9.81.
11. *Daily Telegraph* 2.9.81.
12. *The Standard* 2.9.81.
13. *Daily Telegraph* 9.9.81.
14. John Tulloch and Manuel Alvarado, *Doctor Who: The Unfolding Text* (London: Macmillan, 1983), p.ix.

15. *New Statesman* 18.9.81.
16. *TV Times* op. cit.
17. *TV Times* 3.10.81.
18. Episode Two 'Hyenas will Eat Anything'.
19. *Guardian* 2.9.81.
20. Episode Seven 'The Drums of War'.
21. The distinction between the 'hegemony of coercion' and the 'hegemony of consent' is theorised by Antonio Gramsci, most notably in his essay 'The Intellectuals', *Selections from the Prison Notebooks of Antonio Gramsci* (London: Lawrence and Wishart, 1971).
22. The number of people who watched the Royal Wedding on television sets around the world was estimated to be 420 million.
23. Keith Tribe, op.cit.
24. *Sunday Times* 6.9.81.
25. *Daily Mail* 2.9.81.
26. *Broadcast* no. 1134, 16.11.81.

5   Widows

Gillian Skirrow

A green van waits near the Blackwall Tunnel. A driver, Terry Miller and Joe Perelli in the back. They wear overalls and ski masks ready to be pulled over their faces. A bread truck is followed by a security wagon; the green van pulls in behind and they all disappear into the tunnel. Terry Miller prepares explosives. Joe has a sawn off shotgun.

A police car chases a stolen Cortina driven by two boys towards the tunnel. As the green van approaches the tunnel exit, Joe and Terry pull their ski masks down over their faces. The Cortina and police car approach. The security wagon breaks and the green van slams into the back of it. The explosives jerk out of Terry's hand. The green van blows like a bomb. The bread van escapes.

Three days later it is announced that Harry Rawlins, Terence Miller and Joseph Pairellie died in the explosion . . .

OPENING TITLES

(from the synopsis for Act One, Episode One of *Widows* by Lynda La Plante)

There is a prophetic ambiguity about the opening of *Widows*. It looks like the closure of an episode in 'the male crime series', a neat genre, previously unadulterated by women, but though it marks the end of this neatness it also foregrounds the continuity of the constraints of the genre within which *Widows* develops its feminist approach.

Previous attempts to produce police/crime series with female protagonists resulted in separate series paralleling the men's: *Cagney and Lacey* for *Starsky and Hutch*, and *Juliet Bravo* for, well, *Dixon of Dock Green* perhaps. Although the women in these series were sometimes seen to have different values and assumptions about their work – which was refreshing – the separatist strategy left most of the conventions of the male crime series unquestioned. The contribution of *Widows* was to try to engage with these conventions, using them and questioning them at the same time; a constant process of negotiation with the expectations of both the audience and the institution of television. I hope to show how
174

Widows makes the constraints visible in the narrative, and by doing so opens up the possibility of a new kind of television criticism, done by television itself working on its own forms.

The kind of production which appears in the crime fiction slot on both ITV and the BBC is usually written, directed and produced by men. The most important relationships in the programmes are those between men, usually a father-son relationship between an older and a younger cop – though sometimes hinting at a homosexual element – and the most important issue is male identity, which in these series is often expressed through fast and violent action. The characters from whose point of view we see events are on the side of the law and do not change from week to week – unlike the stories, which are usually about a different 'case' every week in the series. In these stories women have very minor roles; even if they are the cause of the disturbance of equilibrium which sets off the narrative, the equilibrium which is restored in the end is a strictly male one. So, much of the pleasure in crime fiction is in its foregrounding of fast and violent action between men; but another aspect of crime fiction's appeal, which might seem contradictory, is its supposed relationship to reality. *The Sweeney*, for example, represented the Flying Squad's activities, so that the crimes dealt with seemed to reflect problems in contemporary society, giving the audience a sense of being up-to-date and street-wise. These, then, are some of the characteristics of crime fiction on television, characteristics which in their institutional moulds all too easily solidify into constraints, since any production line once set up is expensive to change, and good ratings for the well-tried pattern cannot be put at risk by something which does not meet audience expectations. It is such constraints which militate against progressiveness in representations of women in the crime series in particular and on television in general – and by 'progressive' I simply mean the achievement of more equal – i.e. at least a wider variety of—representations of women on mainstream television. I intend to investigate *Widows* in relation to the constraints on the crime fiction genre and to argue for its progressiveness in that it challenges those constraints and provides the audience with a different kind of pleasure.

Widows is a serial consisting of six 52-minute episodes first transmitted at 9.00pm on Wednesdays in March and April 1983. At Harry Rawlins' funeral his widow Dolly is given a key to his bank vault where she finds a box containing his ledgers – documentation of all the robberies he had done and had planned for the near future together with the names of a great number of London criminals and details of all the 'jobs' they had been involved in both for himself and for other people. A rival gang, the Fisher Brothers, want the ledgers so that they can inherit Harry's control over the underworld. They suspect that Dolly knows where the ledgers are and offer to buy them. Dolly calls a meeting of the other two widows, Shirley Miller and Lynda Perelli, to suggest that instead of selling the

175

ledgers to the Fisher Brothers they, the Widows, plan the next big job Harry had lined up. They agree to give it a try. The police also suspect that Dolly knows something, and Resnick (the officer in charge of the case, who has a personal motive for revenge against Harry and his system) has Dolly watched. However, the Widows make their preparations without detection. At a late stage they realise that the job calls for a fourth person and Lynda's friend Bella is recruited. During the dress rehearsal for the hold-up it becomes evident that the job they are about to do is very similar – perhaps a repeat? – of the one in which their men died. Now read on . . .

In *Widows* the functioning of certain structuring oppositions or tensions within television crime fiction are (some radically and some subtly) changed, and it is these changes that make the constraints and conventions become visible even to the point of producing contradictions. The main change is in the kind of characters who get the major roles and the minor ones. Major roles usually go to representatives of the law, who are generally male, leaving the bit parts to law-breakers, women and other deviants. When, as in *Widows*, the major roles go to women who are also law-breakers, the functioning of conventions that usually represent the male/female and law/law-breakers oppositions is immediately upset, which in turn upsets the balance of the reality/fiction tension in the genre, and indeed in the series format itself. Since the women have to learn how to be criminals and develop their organisation the serial is obviously a more appropriate format than that of the more common (in TV crime fiction) format of the series, in which the institutional framework and the roles of the major characters remain relatively static. (For present purposes we may define a serial as a narrative in which the main plot line only develops towards a conclusion in the last episode; in a series, on the other hand, each episode will have a narrative, resolved before the end of the 52 minutes or whatever. Only the characters and their general institutional setting will continue into the next episode.)

Although there have been crime serials (e.g. *Killer*, STV, *Out*, Euston Films) the series format seems to be preferred perhaps because the genre both relies quite heavily on novelty and claims for itself commitment to real social issues. 'Real social issues' seem not to include gender; but a variety of 'harder' issues, which are on the borderlines of social acceptability, can be raised individually and superficially, allowing any real threat they might present to be ejected at the end of each episode. Because the serial gives more time to one issue and more opportunity to relate it to other issues the threat presented by the women becomes a complicated one and gathers momentum so that it not only refuses to be ejected but eventually produces a resolution on a different level from that expected. In the end *Widows* is not only about a successful crime but also about loss and about desire.

The series format of the regular crime series suggests a comparison with current affairs series, which also deal with a social issue once a week and might well precede or follow the crime series in the schedules since both are often placed between 8.00pm and 10.00pm. The references of the crime series are to the real world, real police work, and its conventions of dialogue, lighting, shooting and editing are those generally accepted as 'realistic'. The allusions and style of *Widows* on the other hand are clearly fictional. Although it is unusual to talk about *mise-en-scène* in a television production, in *Widows* the *film noir*-style setting has to be taken into account because it not only draws attention to itself but functions as part of the serial's construction of meaning. There had been an attempt in *Hazell* to re-create some of the lighting effects of *film noir* but in so far as this was noticeable at all it served only to signal a sophisticated nostalgia for a lost genre, whereas in *Widows* the black and white motifs, the subdued colours and partially obscured images in the garage scenes help to give the women more power by evoking memories of films in which women were active and ambitious though finally destroyed by a male writer and producer. Since we know that *Widows* has a female writer and a female producer the references to *film noir* encourage us to hope that this time the women might not have to be destroyed.

There is also a discourse about disorder and change in the *mise-en-scène* of *Widows*. people's rooms are constantly being done over by the police or rival gangs; the Fisher Brothers gang not only re-arranges other people's rooms and faces but is itself moving to larger premises as it plans to take over Harry Rawlins' operation, and the new premises are littered with half-unpacked furniture at odd angles across the frame. Resnick and his team are seen much of the time in corridors, and half-way through the serial Resnick moves out of his traditional-style office into an open-plan space where he is reduced to stealing other people's potted plants to give himself cover. Harry's garage in which the Widows set up their headquarters is full of bits of cars, tools and junk. On one level the chaos represents the confusion which the women gangsters produce for the usual investigatory strategies and routines of both the police force and the institution of television – between which there are some interesting comparisons – and it is significant that Resnick, the character who is most shaken up by all that is going on around him, is also the one whose thinking goes beyond the routine and the obvious to an understanding of what is really happening. On another level the backdrop of disorder and confusion which represents the Widows' invisibility to the other characters serves to throw into relief for the viewers the women's highly organised execution of their plans.

The plot, in which the women have to learn to impersonate hardened male criminals, foregrounds performance. It is crucial to the women's success in the hold-up that they appear to be men: 'If they sus you're a woman, forget it!' says Bella. This leads to an investigation and a de-naturalisation of the signifiers of male sexuality, which as far as a

177

Widows: 'If they sus you're a woman, forget it.

hold-up is concerned turn out to be a large shape, a deep voice and a confident and threatening posture, even bordering on the monstrous as a gas mask solves simultaneously the problems of depth of voice and size of face. The signifiers of female sexuality are also investigated through the form of dressing-up and performance: Shirley in her bathing costume in a beauty competition, and Bella in the sado-masochist costume she wears when earning her living as a dancer. The success of the two women in these costumes also depends on an expected appearance and performance for the male gaze. Before the audience sees the performance of the beauty competition, the dance or the hold-up it also witnesses some elements of rehearsal in which the causes and processes of production of those roles are foregrounded. So whereas the crime series stresses its relationship to reality, and suppresses evidence of its own fictiveness, *Widows* takes the construction of appearances as its central concern, and is subtly self-referential, making several allusions to famous fiction images. For example, when the other widows first see Dolly one of them remarks that 'Lana Turner is alive and well and living in St. Johns Wood'; as Resnick's car screams up to a bakery one of the younger policemen quips that 'he thinks he's in a Sam Peckinpah movie'; and the death of one of the minor characters at the hands of a hit and run driver
178

appears to have been taken straight from *Wait Until Dark*.

The little scenes or segments which are a feature of television forms, serving both to diversify and to unify within a programme whether fiction or non-fiction, are in *Widows* given narrative significance. It is a feature of these segments in television of all genres that they rhyme with each other. In *Widows* this tendency is developed into a paralleling structure. It is used right from the beginning when we are introduced to each of the three Widows at the funerals of their respective husbands, each funeral at a slightly later stage thus moving the action on in time. In the first three episodes the paralleling structure is used not only to introduce new characters, but to show three rival groups, the Widows, the police and the Fisher Brothers, working out strategies as a result of the failed raid on the security van in which Harry Rawlins' gang was obliterated. It is also used to point out the differences (or not) between the way in which the police are organised and the way the Widows organise themselves. For example, when Resnick briefs his men in the police station he is shown in traditional posture – a low-angle shot from in front isolates him in frame as he stands up, leans forward over a table and shouts at and bullies his men.

Reaction shots of the men show them in rows in front of him, almost cowering, sometimes focusing on Fuller, a young policeman who is defiant but with whom Resnick is to develop a father-son relationship. Dolly's first meeting with the other Widows – to suggest that they take over Harry's plans – is set in a sauna; all the women are dressed in towels and are lying or sitting at various angles. Although Dolly has the highest position and her look is dominant, the women all interupt each other, bicker and share a range of emotions, including crying and laughing. At their first formal meeting in the garage, a scene which more directly rhymes with Resnick's briefing meeting, the composition of the shots emphasises the differences between the institutional relationships of the police and the more personal relationships of the women, particularly contrasting Resnick and Dolly as leaders. Resnick had commanded the attention of the camera but Dolly does not need to be privileged in this way. The sequence opens with a long shot in which Dolly's back is to camera, then goes into closer shots which isolate Lynda in frame showing Dolly mainly in two-shots with Shirley, with whom Dolly is beginning to develop a mother-daughter relationship. By the second episode, however, the parallel structure reveals that the women's behaviour is beginning to resemble the men's, culminating in Dolly slapping Lynda's face.

At this point the viewers may think that the male-like behaviour is the result of trying to write women characters into a male genre – which is indeed the case but it is a danger which the serial is also aware of, and around which its discourse is structured. In the third episode it is through the paralleling structure that the surprise revelation about a

179

fourth and very powerful interest group is made. There is a pivotal sequence of parallels in this episode – which is mid-way through the serial – after which the paralleling becomes not a vehicle for comparisons but a structure of control. The sequence begins with the Widows rehearsing the hold-up and getaway in an old quarry. The planned hold-up is very like the one in which their husbands died. As they begin the rehearsal the sequence is suddenly interrupted by black and white footage of their husbands at exactly the same stage of rehearsal in a similar location, after which both rehearsals merge into one time with the women and men alternating in carrying the action forward in matched shot/reverse point of views cutting between the colour/women/present and the black and white/men/past. It is apparent that this black and white footage, marked as 'the past', has some effectivity in the present even before the nature of this effectivity is revealed – namely that both Dolly and Harry were too old to make the final run in time, which in Harry's case meant that he ended up driving the bread truck. At this point the men's sequence switches into colour and repeats the sequence first shown as the pre-opening titles sequence in Episode One in which the three men had apparently been killed when their van had blown up. This time it is extended to show clearly that it is Harry who escapes from the flames. Through the paralleling structure the audience has always known more of the plans of the other groups than Dolly has, but the police and the Fisher Brothers have not presented any real threat. From this point on, however, though the institution of the police becomes even less important as Resnick resigns from the force and continues on his own, the parallels become more of a threat as they reveal Harry at work. The viewers are never party to his plans but only see the results of his actions, and, sometimes, his surveillance of the Widows, which creates more suspense than the police surveillance had, because this time the women are unaware of it. The police had the gaze of spectacle but Harry's look is voyeuristic.

From this point on it is not clear whether when we see the Widows we are getting our usual privileged view or whether we are implicated in Harry's point of view as he spies on them. The regime of the segments is thus used to reveal the threat which Dolly released when she opened the box in the morgue-like bank vault and discovered the ledgers. Unlike Pandora or the femme fatale in *Kiss Me Deadly* she did not find chaos but the word. Harry's ledgers resurrected his authority; they were a blue print for being like him, which would deliver those who followed his instructions into his control. The Widows who have followed Harry's plans to the letter as a way of becoming active and free now seem to have actually been reacting to Harry's initiative and have all but delivered themselves into his trap. In the same way, or as part of the same process, the pitfalls of a feminist attempt to overturn the constraints of the male-dominated crime genre while working within them are clearly
180

demonstrated. Fortunately, however, the Widows and the writer are destined with one bound to leap out of this particular pit.

Making the women also the law-breakers achieves two things. First it leaves the male police structures of the crime series intact, allowing these structures to be commented upon, and secondly it enables the questioning of women's relationship to the law and to consensus morality. A straight reversal of the men/women relationship in the crime series would have left few men in the story at all since women usually appear in the series only in bit parts in the office or the kitchen. Nor is there a reversal of the men/active—women/passive relationship which is characteristic of many fiction films. In *Widows* the women compete against three very active groups of men for control of the money, Harry's ledgers and the narrative. The iconography of masculinity is not changed, it is merely viewed, coolly, from a different perspective. Resnick is more subtle than simply a stereotype or a caricature, (which is often the fate of criminals in the crime series) but perhaps this is mainly because many of the police heroes of the crime series are quite close to being caricatures themselves. Resnick takes a personal interest in the Rawlins case because Harry Rawlins once framed him – 'castrated' is the word Resnick chooses to describe the experience, which had prevented his promotion. He is childless and his wife makes him feel inadequate at home and in his job. A lot of his drive and energy is seen to come from this feeling of shame and inadequacy, and this undercuts his control and his power. The viewers begin by almost totally despising him, believing they know more than he does because they have seem more and because in spite of the evidence Resnick is determined to believe in the continuation of Rawlins' controlling consciousness. As appearances turn out to have been deceptive, respect and sympathy for Resnick increase, especially when in order to prove himself right he puts himself – in the role of the lone investigator – in a very vulnerable position and is violently dealt with by Rawlins' gang. Resnick suffers badly at the hands both of the criminals and the regular police force – perhaps a more likely story than Kojak's unremitting success.

The regular police seem to represent the institution of male behaviour, with their emphasis on status and hierarchies, and their surveillance of Dolly can be seen as institutionalising the male look (with the difference that in this production Dolly leaves them gazing at the entrance to the hairdresser's and hurries out the back door). The police/men are shown to 'see' the women in only one way. They suspect that the women know something about the failed hold-up in the tunnel and that Dolly may have Harry's ledgers but they are blind to the possibility that the women might think of organising a crime themselves.

None of the women (or the police) is presented as an object of desire, but this role is given to two men in the serial – Carlos, the car mechanic desired both by Lynda and by Arnie Fisher; and Harry himself, desired

181

by Dolly but living with the young woman (whose man, Jimmy Nunn, had died instead of Harry in the fire in the tunnel) by whom Harry has a child. Both these men are destroyed by the women for whom they are objects of desire. Lynda betrays Carlos to the police when she discovers his homosexual relationship with Arnie Fisher and he is accidentally killed while trying to avoid arrest; Harry is not physically harmed but Dolly burns his ledgers which were his means of controlling the underworld so, although he escapes into the next series, his powers will have to be built up again from nothing.

The women take control of the narrative by being shown to have successfully achieved all their goals, at least up to the point where, after the hold-up Dolly and Shirley are under siege in Dolly's house with Harry's gang and Resnick outside. By this time, however, Dolly knows about Harry's trap and so has not lost control of the situation, and if their final escape from the house is a little unbelievable, the rescue by Shirley's mother is spectacular enough to suspend our disbelief.

Paralleling the father-son relationships in the police force by a discourse about mothers and daughters among the Widows is one of the major ways in which the functioning of the male/female opposition is changed. The men are never a help but mothers always are. Dolly, older than the other women, is a strong mother figure which makes her no less effective as a leader but gives a particular style to her leadership. She has lost a child and there is a suggestion that Harry's masculinity is threatened by the lack of offspring as well as by having an extremely competent wife. Dolly, whose image is otherwise quite hard, has substituted for her child a poodle which she carries around with her as a visible symbol of her loss and which one of Harry's gang eventually tramples to death. Dolly and Shirley fall into a mother/daughter relationship because it is shown to be what Dolly needs and what Shirley is used to. There are many scenes between Shirley and her mother showing the importance of that relationship, and it is Shirley's mother who fairy godmother-like gets the heroines safely up, up and away at the end. Even the mother superior at the convent school where Dolly is a voluntary worker has a part to play; she is left unwittingly guarding the balance of the haul as Dolly flies off to America with enough money to keep the Widows out of the country for a while. Lynda's behaviour is also structured round a mother but in her case an absent one since her mother put her in an orphanage when she was three. Of all the women, Lynda is shown to be the one who has most difficulty in forming relationships with other women – both Dolly and Bella hit her – but she is also shown to have a lot of courage in persevering with relationships, as well as initiative and a wonderful way with inanimate things like car engines. This discourse about women's relationships with each other and particularly with their mothers is certainly something new for crime fiction.

Widows shows women's relationship with men as a problem. Harry's

182

betrayal of Dolly becomes at least as important for Dolly as the robbery. She risks precious moments before they escape from the siege to rip up Harry's clothes and to burn his ledgers, leaving the burnt remains so that he can find them. Harry's relationship to the women he is living with is shown to be a bullying and unpleasant one. Carlos is shown to want to control the way Lynda dresses herself and addresses him. Tony Fisher, the brother who is not gay, threatens Shirley with sadistic sexual assault. Bella has to earn money as a prostitute to supplement what she makes as a dancer. Even her dance-costume, all studs and whips, is about sexuality as pain.

All the women are shown to be economically dependent on men either individually or in general for their livelihoods – they have no other choice. As in *Gangsters* (BBC Birmingham, 1976) the system that produced them as criminals is shown to be as much of a problem as they are. The way in which they are forced to use their bodies in order to live is more unpleasant, though more socially acceptable, than criminality, and almost seems to justify their law-breaking activities as a way of achieving economic independence. Perhaps this is why, contrary to the expectations of the police, Harry, the viewers, and even the writers, they were able to break the 'law' of television against successful crime and get away with it.

Having celebrated the successes of *Widows* so far, it must be said that its failures are also revealing. Its operation on the male crime series and that genre's ignorance of, and lack of interest in, questions of sexuality has changed people's ideas about what crime fiction can deal with, but if *Widows* were to be compared with, say, a feminist novel instead of a male television series it is likely to be read less progressively. *Widows* shows heterosexuality to be a problem but it doesn't offer any possibilities of new kinds of relationships. Homosexuality is shown to be an even bigger problem, with the gay men (no lesbians are in evidence) occupying their usual place in the crime series: the villains, the violence, and the comic relief. The ending too could be seen as something of a cop-out. While one might not want the serial to indulge in female triumphalism, if it had been a feminist novel it is unlikely that it would have ended with Dolly still in love with the very nasty Harry to the strains of Kathleen Ferrier's 'What is Life', which substituted for the generic title music in the closing episode. To show her shattered by his betrayal is one thing, but for her actually to be in love is quite another. The battle between them in the next series should be interesting, but if, as one suspects, they both have to die then Dolly will have been punished for her transgression in the way of all heroines and law-breakers before her. The threat of the women will have been contained, and we shall have to wait for more 'different' productions to test the limits for female heroes on television.

It is of course debatable how far an ending lasting five minutes can actually affect the reading of a serial which has lasted for six hours. In the male crime series the resolution is important. The pleasure seems to come from the humour, male cameraderie and competition, the 'star' police heroes, but most of all from the fast and violent action and the mystery of 'whodunnit' and 'willecatchem', which come together in the resolution. *Widows* I think institutes a different kind of pleasure, at least for women viewers. Although there is fast action and some very violent scenes there is much more emphasis on dialogue, on performance, and on the *mise-en-scène*, which brings out the close relationship of the women and positions us with them. We want them to pull off the robbery not out of a need for resolution but because of our identification with them. We have been positioned with them and not with the mystery, and no ending could resolve that. It would be interesting to know if men read the serial differently, or were able to take up a different position. The paralleling structure might allow it. It would not be difficult, for example, to identify with Resnick, whose rule has the rudiments of the lone investigator of *film noir* and who has a grasp of a (limited) version of the truth from quite early on. Harry is also a force to be reckoned with and his discourse is all the more powerful for being resurrected from the dead and only discontinuously revealed. Perhaps men would be able to identify with him; indeed it is from such a position that Dolly's grief-stricken resolution makes most sense.

Widows is certainly not women's counter-television in the sense that it sets out to destroy familiar pleasures as women's counter-cinema has done. Much of the pleasure of *Widows*, as well as its progressiveness, is in its operation of the familiar. It invites comparison with the male crime series not only by its position in the schedules but by containing within it many of the conventions and pleasures of that genre. The possibility of containing the mainstream conventions within a practice that is also a feminist criticism has only arisen since the recruitment policies of the institutions have been relaxed – in response to social pressures – to allow women who share many of the positions of the women's movement into decision-making and creative posts. Even if this trend continues it does not mean, of course, that feminist criticism can pack up and go home, but it does mean that criticism can actually be directed at film and television programmes without being entirely negative or without its having to be a reading against the grain. It might even have some hopes of affecting that practice.

The main achievement of *Widows* is that it is the first television production to bring feminist debate about representations in film and television from out of the margins and into the mainstream.

Conclusion

In tracing the history of Euston we have identified two distinct periods. In the first, under the control of Lloyd Shirley and George Taylor, the company established its reputation for action drama and police series. In the second, marked by the involvement of Verity Lambert and the arrival of Johnny Goodman and Linda Agran, a wider range of programmes were made.

Euston would now seem to be entering on a third period following the departure of Verity Lambert, though at the time of writing it is still difficult to assess whether this will lead to a change of direction. One important feature of the company to which we have already drawn attention has been an avoidance of projects deliberately tailored for the international market. Despite flirtations with the feature film and the exotic settings of *The Flame Trees of Thika* and *Reilly – Ace of Spies*, Euston productions have been generally imbued with a deep sense of 'Britishness' and in some cases have been unashamedly parochial, though as we have seen this has not necessarily inhibited foreign sales. Verity Lambert is on record as favouring a distinctive style of quality popular drama, often with its roots deep in British social life.

Whether with her departure this policy is maintained remains to be seen. Euston's two most recently seen productions (at the time of writing), excluding the new series of *Minder*, have been *Reilly – Ace of Spies* and *The Nation's Health*. These represent markedly different options open for the future. The former is a large-budget, historically detailed and glamorous project; the latter is much less expensive and more closely attuned to contemporary social issues. Indications are that the company will continue to pursue both options, as well as capitalising on past successes. Television executives are often reticent about their future programme-making plans, but on the basis of conversations and newspaper reports it is possible to indicate what Euston will produce over the next twelve months. (Though even after press announcements plans can change; Euston were reported to be planning a film based on Andrew Boyle's *Climate of Treason*, but it remains unmade.)

It now seems that yet another series of *Minder* will go into production in 1985, though perhaps limited to six new episodes. A *Minder* feature film produced by Euston has also been announced. As we have already noted, a sequel to *Widows* is in progress, again scripted by Lynda La Plante and this time produced by Irving Teitelbaum. This is scheduled for transmission in July 1985. Euston have also announced three completely new projects, two for the ITV network and one for Channel 4. John Mortimer has written a ten-part serial entitled *Paradise Postponed*, about a family living in Oxfordshire and charting the social changes in Britain during the 50s and 60s. Paul Theroux is currently working on adaptations of his *London Embassy* short stories about an American diplomat, for production in 1985. Before that Euston will be making *Prospect*, a major series for Channel 4. This project for a 12-part series was brought to Euston by Alan Janes and according to Muir Sutherland it is to be 'heavily funded' by Channel 4, though the exact extent has not been specified. The series is set on the Isle of Dogs and concerns the lives of two unemployed youths, one white and one black. Euston have also apparently acquired the rights to C.S. Forester's *Hornblower* stories, though no announcement of production plans has yet appeared.

It seems likely that decisions on future projects will be made more collectively than has been the case in the past. Formally speaking, of course, it is the Board of Directors of Euston Films who decide, though the views of Euston's Chief Executive and of Thames' Director of Programmes have carried considerable weight. Responsibility for running the company is now divided between Johnny Goodman and Linda Agran, the former taking charge of administrative matters and the latter dealing with the creative side. In practice this distinction is not always easy to make, but put very simply it means that Linda Agran seeks out new projects and supervises the development of scripts and Johnny Goodman makes the arrangements for filming.

Johnny Goodman has spent his whole working life from the age of 14 in the film industry specialising in production management. His background in making feature films and filmed television series such as *The Saint* and *The Persuaders* has given him a wealth of experience in the efficient organisation of production and an understanding of films as commodities:

The thing about production people like myself is that we're not on the side of the business where you get that wonderful satisfaction of sitting in a theatre and saying, 'Look at that photography, isn't it something – that's me' or 'Isn't the sound fantastic, I've just got a BAFTA award'. The kicks that people like myself get are in saying, 'What you've got up there was made for the amount of money the company allocated and doesn't it look great – I've helped to put all the factors together.' I take terrific pride. My kicks are in looking at the bottom line figure at the end of the day and saying, 'We brought it in OK.' I don't want to give you the figures, but in seven years here I have obviously been responsible to the Board for the manipulation of quite a few millions of pounds and I can tell you that I am very nicely minutely under budget across the whole spectrum. Now, to find any production company or executive who can say that they've been working on production for seven years and they are under budget across the board is unusual. That is presumably why I'm still here! And I get my satisfaction from that.

Linda Agran has also spent a great deal of her working life in the film industry, on the 'creative' side of the business. Before coming to Euston she was European story editor for Warner Bros. She feels strongly that her skill as a reader of scripts and her personal judgment of projects is what she is paid for:

I ask myself three questions. Do I want to spend a year of my life doing it? Do I want to watch it? And do I want my name on the end of it? If you can answer all of those questions with a yes, then rock on and do it. I think you're lost if you say to yourself – and I know other drama producers do it – 'it's not for me, but I think that *they* will like it.' I don't know how you can even begin to judge scripts or assess rushes or do anything when you're not working on your own judgment. You've got to work on your own judgment and your own tastes. And you've got to do what you're doing to please yourself because you have to believe that if you want to see it then there's a good chance that a fair number of other people will too. It sounds arrogant, but it isn't. It's the only way of working. And that's why – there's a certain amount of horse trading that goes on – I'll say I want to do this serial about whatever, and they'll say what about some more *Minders*, and I'll say OK, we'll do some more *Minders*, but only if. . . It's the only way. No one knows what's going to work, so all you can do is to commit yourself totally to what you're doing. If you do, there's a fair chance that it will come off.

On the future of Euston Linda Agran had this to say:

I think the future of the company is to expand. I would like to make a lot more than we make. I would like to do more one-offs. I would like to do the odd feature film. There's no reason why we shouldn't. And keep looking for new and fresh forms of drama. I just loathe thinking of things as being simply the replacement for something successful we've done before. Because then you're narrowing your vision, you're thinking there ought to be this in it or that in it.

Over the years there have been a number of attempts at emulating the success of Euston. Various ITV companies have tried to set up film-making subsidiaries operating under the BFTPA agreements. For reasons explored earlier in this book not all these plans have got very far. Although the ACTT say they are not in a position to prevent companies

187

from establishing such subsidiaries, they assume that any company wishing to do so would, in the interests of good labour relations, discuss the matter with their permanent staff. In some instances the workforce has taken a dim view of such proposals. LWT have long nurtured a desire for a Euston-type operation, but have experienced difficulties in getting if off the ground. Both their attempts at BFTPA film series co-production, *The Professionals* eventually and *Chandlertown* (retitled *Marlow: Private Eye*) initially, ran foul of union opposition. Happily a formula regotiated during the dispute over *Chandlertown* should prevent further difficulties, and under a mixed permanent staff and freelance crewing agreement LWT recently shot a production entitled *Blue Money*.

Possibly the best known of the film subsidiaries which have been established are Southern Television's Southern Pictures and ATV's Black Lion Films (formally a subsidiary of ITC). Starting up within weeks of each other in 1979, these two companies were very much in the Euston mould. Southern Pictures was headed by Mark Shivas, who was reported as saying:

> I am joining Southern's company because I believe it will give me plenty of room and time to develop really unusual projects for both the domestic and the international market and the opportunity to make single films and film series with congenial people and decent budgets.

Southern Pictures enjoyed only a brief period of production before its parent company lost its franchise in 1981, after which Shivas and other key Southern Pictures personnel joined former Southern Programme Controller Jeremy Wallington in establishing the independent production facility that was to become Limehouse Studios. Black Lion's head was former Thames and Euston producer Barry Hanson. Its aim as described by ATV Programme Controller Charles Denton was: 'to make television films and film series which through ATV will be designed for network screening on ITV.' More specifically, Denton went on:

> If we sell them abroad, well, fine, it will help claw back some of the cash. But if we wanted to make films that appealed initially to an international audience then we could have made them under one of the existing ITC companies, just as *The Return of the Saint* was made. Black Lion Films is going to encourage British film-makers to make television programmes for British audiences. The quality of the production will sell them abroad, but that's not what they are designed for.

Unfortunately Black Lion was a casualty of the crossfire between ITC and ACC Board members, who took different views on the company's production policies.

More recently Channel 4's policy of encouraging filmed drama has led to a proliferation of enterprises modelled on Euston's methods, if not necessarily on its content, and often using co-production finance from companies such as Home Box Office and Metromedia. Even the BBC has been considering setting up a film subsidiary. But the most important new development would seem to be Zenith Productions. Established in March 1984 as a wholly-owned subsidiary of Central Television (the inheritors of the ATV franchise in the Midlands), Zenith is headed by Charles Denton, with Margaret Matheson as Director of Programmes. Since Denton was previously Central's Programme Controller and Matheson its head of drama, Zenith can be seen as simply a development of Central's activities in filmed drama. And given that Ted Childs is the new Controller of Drama for Central it seems likely that Central will continue to offer some drama on film to the network. According to a press release Zenith will 'operate on a strictly commercial basis, making films for Central, Channel 4 and for other customers both in Britain and abroad'. Though the company is financed by Central it will seek co-production money. It will have a maximum of 'about a dozen' employees and 'will never seek to own a single facility'. It will of course operate under the BFTPA agreements. Clearly, it is too soon to predict how Zenith will fare, but the success of Central's filmed series *Kennedy*, produced by Margaret Matheson and directed by Euston stalwart Jim Goddard, can be taken as a strong indicator of the new venture's potential.

Far from fearing the emergent competition, Euston may well feel that imitation is the sincerest form of flattery; certainly Johnny Goodman feels that the company is in pretty good shape for the future:

I frequently remind people that Euston Films was a successful and efficient operation before Verity Lambert, Johnny Goodman and Linda Agran. It was Lloyd Shirley and George Taylor's 'thing' and after Lloyd and George went 'independent' it would have been reasonable to assume that Euston's fortunes would go into decline. Of course, the fact of the matter is that when Verity stepped in, followed by Linda and me, we developed and expanded a going concern. By the same token it's my firm belief that if or when the present management team disappear 'up the Swanee' the company will not falter. The pattern has been firmly set. I've sometimes observed other film or television companies trying to emulate the Euston Films operation, but they always seem to fight shy of giving any real muscle to whoever is awarded the title 'in charge of production'. My colleagues on the Board hold me responsible for the smooth and economical operation of both the company and the productions, and, what's more important, they give me the kind of backing that makes it possible to function efficiently. Without that I would be on a hiding to nothing.

Appendix 1 Audience Measurement in the UK

Lucy Douch

Making TV drama is like having a child, I should imagine, and to put that child out into the world and have someone say, 'Oh, it's a bit ugly!' hurts, and you feel terribly protective towards the programmes. Nice reviews are smashing. Huge ratings are even more smashing. (Linda Agran, Head of Scripts and Development, Euston Films)

The following information is presented with the intention of indicating the popularity of the Euston Films product in the United Kingdom both in relation to the rest of broadcast television and in a way that allows comparison between different Euston Films series and one-off productions. It is the result of the most basic research (i.e. the reproduction of published viewing figures) and is offered as a starting point. Further consideration needs to be given to a multiplicity of variables. Among the supplementary questions that need to be answered are: what was being shown on the other channels at the time of transmission? What qualitative research exists to establish the audience's appreciation of the programme? How much of the audience, in the case of series and serials, continued to view the programme throughout its run? Viewing figures of repeat transmissions would also provide an interesting comparison.

Even research as basic as this, however, is subject to conditions that render its outcome in need of qualification. The explanatory notes required to make these qualifications provide an interesting historical illustration of the problems besetting the whole notion of audience measurement, as well as helping to explain inconsistencies in the information given.

Until August 1981, television audience measurement (i.e. the counting of heads viewing a particular programme at a particular time) was undertaken separately by the BBC's Audience Research Department and, on behalf of the commercial television companies, JICTAR (Joint Industry Committee for Television Audience Research). The different systems used by the two bodies reflected the difference in the operating priorities of the two services. JICTAR, providing information for a commercial operation dependent on advertising revenue, produced statistics about the specific audience available within a 15-minute segment for each advertising break. This information was used to calculate advertising rates: the greater the audience, the more expensive the air time. Additional demographic information, giving details of the type of viewer watching television at any given time of the day, allowed television advertisers to target

190

their product accordingly. The BBC, however, was solely interested in the number of people who had 'seen' a programme, and counted in the total those who had watched more than half, but not all, of it. The pressure on the BBC to compete with the ITV companies for high ratings and a respectable share of the audience is exerted by the Corporation's reliance upon a statutorily imposed licence fee that requires regular justification – to licence-holders and Government – particularly if an increase is proposed.

The two systems of audience measurement regularly threw up discrepancies in their findings and the Annan Report of 1977 included a recommendation that a common system be implemented. In July 1980 it was announced that BARB (Broadcasters' Audience Research Board), a limited company owned jointly by the BBC and the ITCA (Independent Television Companies' Association), would be established to commission both quantitative (i.e. the size of the audience) and qualitative (i.e. the reaction of the audience to particular programmes) research. BARB commenced this undertaking in August 1981. AGB (Audits of Great Britain), who had previously been contracted to supply quantitative statistics to JICTAR, continued to produce information relating to audience size. The BBC Research Department undertook to extend its qualitative research to include ITV output.

It was a feature of the new shared system that it was considered undesirable to expose either of the television services to Fleet Street's desire to exploit the 'ratings war' between them. Such delicacy may be difficult to appreciate, but it would seem that the BBC, in particular, was anxious to avoid the kind of headlines seen in some national newspapers in the week before the unified system took over when it was declared that Ken and Deirdre's wedding in *Coronation Street*, if the viewing figures were to be believed, meant more to the nation than that of the heir to the throne. It hardly needs explaining that the Royal Wedding figure was averaged over six hours, *Coronation Street* over just half an hour. However, such unseemly practices on the part of Fleet Street resulted in the withdrawal from public circulation of a weekly television Top Twenty. Instead, a weekly Top Ten for each of the three channels (ITV, BBC1 and BBC2) was produced, without supporting figures, and a Top Twenty was issued for each month. Comprehensive statistical information was available only to BARB subscribers.

In January 1982, *The Times* bought access to BARB figures for £50 a week, on the condition that the newspaper did not publish a Top Twenty as such and did not make any reference to a numerical listing in any editorial coverage. Righteous indignation abounded amongst the other national newspapers. Not only was *The Times* buying information that had previously been freely available: it was buying information that it could not use, under the terms of a deal that was not open to other newspapers. The following month, despite resistance from the BBC, the BARB figures became publicly available again. The Top Ten television programmes for the week ending on 31 January 1982 featured not one BBC production!

Viewing figures are expressed in millions. To make sense of these figures in terms of what proportion of a potential maximum they represent, it is useful to know that in 1973 the ITCA (in its *Guide to Independent Television* for that year) was claiming a potential audience (aged four years and above) of 49 million (in 17 million homes), and that this figure rose steadily over the years to 51 million (in

191

20 million homes) in 1983.

In 1977, following the renewal of AGB's contract, JICTAR changed its weekly presentation of data. From the first week of August 1977, the ratings give audience figures in terms of millions of individuals, instead of millions of homes. This change was made to achieve compatibility between the commercial companies' data and the BBC's, at a time when the two were still collected separately.

AGB's quantitative data is derived from a representative sample or 'panel' of 3,000 homes. The sample is deemed to be representative as a result of an annual 'establishment survey' of 20,000 homes which establishes a national pattern of variables relating to population structure, colour television and VCR ownership, etc. The panel is constructed to reflect these variations. The television set in each home is fitted with a meter which records how long and to which channel the set is switched on. At the moment, AGB are conducting a staggered transition from the old-style JICTAR meter, which records the data on a wax-coated paper tape, despatched weekly by the panel members, to a more sophisticated microchip device capable of relaying information from every set in the home overnight via telephone lines. Panel members also fill in and despatch a weekly viewing diary, divided into 15-minute segments, which includes the demographic information required by advertisers. The information thus collected is compiled into weekly Network Reports which are sent out to BARB subscribers. This process of data collection and dissemination is an obvious subject for technological refinement, and there are many plans for computer-based and electronic improvements. (See 'The decline of television and the rise of ratings' by Karen Margolis and Mark Hosenball in *Broadcast*, 9 May 1983.)

NOTES ON THE PRESENTATION OF RATINGS DATA

Series and serials
Where possible I have shown:

a) the position in the weekly Top Ten/Top Twenty television programmes of the *first* episode of each series, in the context of a complete listing of the Top Ten/Top Twenty plus viewing figures;

b) the same for the *last* episode of each series;

c) details of the position and viewing figure of each intermediate episode.

When a programme has not achieved a Top Twenty rating, a viewing figure only is given, except in the cases of *Quatermass* (where the Top Twenty is shown to illustrate the dominance the BBC was able to establish and maintain when an industrial dispute had taken ITV off the air), the first series of *Minder* (which also went out soon after the dispute and never reached the Top Twenty), *Fox* and the second series of *Minder* (neither of which ever reached the Top Twenty). In these cases, the Top Twenty for the week of the first episode is shown.

One-off programmes
Only viewing figures and (where applicable) position in Top Twenty are given, except where the programme reached the Top Five.

The day of the week of transmission, the time of day and duration of each programme is indicated. All programmes were transmitted on ITV unless otherwise stated.

From January 1983, *Television Weekly* published a weekly Top 100 compiled from BARB/AGB data, and this information has been used with reference to programmes transmitted after that date.

The abbreviation ITV indicates bought-in, networked programmes, usually feature films. The following abbreviations have been used to indicate originating television companies:

ATV   Associated Television (Independent Television franchise area now held by Central Television)
ITN   Independent Television News
LWT   London Weekend Television
Southern Southern Television (Independent Television franchise area now held by Television South)
YTV   Yorkshire Television

Special Branch
Series 3
4/4/73 – 4/7/73. Weds, 9pm, 52 mins.
Episode 1 tx. 4/4/73

1	Eurovision Song Contest BBC	9.80
2	This Is Your Life Thames	8.75
3	Love Thy Neighbour Thames	8.25
4	Opportunity Knocks! Thames	7.55
5	Coronation Street (Weds) Granada	7.50
6	Coronation Street (Mon) Granada	7.35
7	**Special Branch Thames**	**7.15**
8	Justice YTV	6.80
9=	Crossroads (Weds) ATV	6.70
9=	Shut That Door! ATV	6.70

Episode	tx.	position	figure
2	11/4	6	7.00
3	18/4	9	6.70
4	25/4	4	6.90
5	2/5	17=	6.10
6	9/5	9	6.75
7	16/5	2	7.95
8	23/5	4	7.30
9	6/6	1	6.90
10	13/6	2	7.05
11	20/6	2	7.65
12	27/6	1	7.35

Episode 13 tx. 4.7.73

1	Thirty Minutes Worth Thames	6.45
2=	**Special Branch Thames**	**6.30**
2=	Hadleigh YTV	6.30

193

4=	Sam Granada		6.20
4=	Coronation Street (Weds) Granada		6.20
6	News at Ten (Weds) ITN		6.15
7=	Coronation Street (Mon) Granada		6.05
7=	My Good Woman ATV		6.05
9=	News at Ten (Tues) ITN		5.95
9=	News at Ten (Fri) ITN		5.95

Figures produced by AGB for JICTAR.

Special Branch
Series 4
14/2/74 – 9/5/74 Thurs, 8.30pm, 52 mins.
Episode 1 tx. 14/2/74

1	This Is Your Life Thames	9.85
2=	Opportunity Knocks! Thames	8.60
2=	The Val Doonican Show ATV	8.60
4	Man About the House Thames	8.15
5	Coronation Street (Weds) Granada	8.05
6	A Raging Calm Granada	7.95
7	Coronation Street (Mon) Granada	7.85
8	Within These Walls LWT	7.80
9	**Special Branch Thames**	**7.75**
10	Crossroads (Weds) ATV	7.45

Episode	tx.	position	figure
2	21/2	14	7.05
3	28/2	16=	6.75
4	7/3	16	6.75
5	14/3	7	8.10
6	21/3	11	7.50
7	28/3	9	7.45
8	4/4	7	7.65
9	11/4	6	7.75
10	18/4	2	8.15
11	25/4	4	7.85
12	2/5	3	8.40

Episode 13 tx. 9/5/74

1	This Is Your Life Thames	8.40
2	And Mother Makes Five Thames	8.00
3	**Special Branch Thames**	**7.75**
4	Coronation Street (Weds) Granada	7.75
5	My Name Is Harry Worth Thames	7.25
6	Hunter's Walk ATV	7.20
7	Coronation Street (Mon) Granada	7.15
8	Up the Workers ATV	6.95
9	A Little Bit of Wisdom ATV	6.90
10	Crossroads (Weds) ATV	6.85

Figures produced by AGB for JICTAR.

194

Armchair Cinema
'The Prison'
tx. 28/5/74 Tues, 8.30pm, 90 mins.

1	**Armchair Cinema Thames**	**7.85**
2	News At Ten (Tues) ITN	7.20
3	Sam Granada	6.95
4=	Justice YTV	6.60
4=	And Mother Makes Five Thames	6.60

Figures produced by AGB for JICTAR.

Armchair Cinema
'Regan'
tx. 4/6/74 Tues, 8.30pm, 77 mins.

1	Justice YTV	7.10
2	Sam Granada	7.05
3=	**Armchair Cinema Thames**	**7.00**
3=	And Mother Makes Five Thames	7.00
5	News At Ten (Fri) ITN	6.95

Figures produced by AGB for JICTAR.

Armchair Cinema
'Sea Song'
tx. 10/9/74 Tues, 8pm, 80 mins.
Rating: 5.30 (not in Top Twenty)
Figures produced by AGB for JICTAR.

The Sweeney
Series 1
2/1/75 – 27/3/75 Thurs, 9pm, 52 mins.
Episode 1 tx. 2/1/75

1	Love Thy Neighbour Thames	8.80
2	Bruce Forsyth & the Generation Game BBC	8.10
3	Coronation Street (Mon) Granada	8.00
4	This Is Your Life Thames	7.95
5	Opportunity Knocks! Thames	7.80
6	Coronation Street (Weds) Granada	7.45
7	**The Sweeney Thames**	**7.25**
8	Crossroads (Thurs) ATV	7.15
9	Haunted Granada	7.10
10	Topaz ITV	7.05

Episode	tx.	position	figure
2	9/1	*	6.80
3	16/1	15	7.10
4	23/1	13	7.40
5	30/1	15=	7.40
6	6/2	9	7.65
7	13/2	8	7.75
8	20/2	2	8.75

9	27/2	13	7.25
10	6/3	4	7.85
11	13/3	6	7.80
12	20/3	6	7.05

Episode 13 tx. 27/3/75**

1	This Is Your Life Thames	8.15
2	My Old Man YTV	7.95
3	Coronation Street (Weds) Granada	7.65
4	Coronation Street (Mon) Granada	7.60
5	Opportunity Knocks! Thames	7.55
6	How's Your Father? Granada	7.35
7=	Crossroads (Thur) ATV	7.30
7=	Man About the House Thames	7.30
9	Crossroads (Wed) ATV	7.25
10	**The Sweeney Thames**	**7.05**

Figures produced by AGB for JICTAR.
* not in Top Twenty
** transmitted at 9.10pm (Party Political Broadcast at 9pm)

Armchair Cinema
'When Day Is Done'
7/1/75 Tues, 8pm, 80 mins.
Rating: 6.95
18th in Top Twenty.
Figures produced by AGB for JICTAR.

Armchair Cinema
'In Sickness And In Health'
21/5/75 Wed, 8.30pm, 52 mins.
Shown in London region only
Rating: 1.52
Not in Top Twenty.
Figures produced by AGB for JICTAR.

The Sweeney
Series 2
1/9/75 – 24/11/75 Mon, 9pm, 52 mins.
Episode 1 tx. 1/9/75

1	Man About the House Thames	7.90
2	**The Sweeney Thames**	**7.20**
3=	Miss Great Britain 1975 YTV	7.10
3=	The Stars Look Down Granada	7.10
5	Upstairs, Downstairs LWT	6.95
6	Crossroads (Thurs) ATV	6.85
7	Crossroads (Weds) ATV	6.60
8	Crossroads (Fri) ATV	6.55
9	Sale of the Century Anglia	6.40
10	Crossroads (Tues) ATV	6.35

Episode	tx.	position	figure
2	8/9	2	7.10
3	15/9	6=	6.80
4	22/9	4	7.40
5	29/9	10=	7.05
6	6/10	1	8.30
7	13/10	1=	8.15
8	20/10	2	7.90
9	27/10	4	8.20
10	3/11	2	8.25
11	10/11	8	7.85
12	17/11	4	8.80

Episode 13 tx. 24/11/75

1	The Generation Game BBC		8.80
2	**The Sweeney Thames**		**8.70**
3	This Is Your Life Thames		8.60
4	Upstairs, Downstairs LWT		8.05
5	Crossroads (Weds) ATV		8.00
6	Crossroads (Tues) ATV		7.95
7	Crossroads (Thurs) ATV		7.85
8	Crossroads (Fri) ATV		7.80
9	Opportunity Knocks! Thames		7.75
10	Coronation Street (Mon) Granada		7.60

Figures produced by AGB for JICTAR.

Armchair Cinema
'Tully'
26/11/75 Weds, 8.30pm, 80 mins.
Rating: 7.20
18th in Top Twenty.

Figures produced by AGB for JICTAR.

The Sweeney
Series 3
6/9/76 – 20/12/76 Mon, 9pm, 52 mins.
Episode 1 tx. 6/9/76

1	George & Mildred Thames		8.80
2	**The Sweeney Thames**		**8.20**
3	Bruce Forsyth & the Generation Game BBC		7.90
4	Crossroads (Thurs) ATV		7.70
5	Pilger ATV		7.40
6	The Two Ronnies BBC		7.20
7	The Good Life BBC		7.15
8=	The Benny Hill Show Thames		7.10
8=	The Duchess of Duke Street BBC		7.10
10	Crossroads (Fri) ATV		7.00

Episode	tx.	position	figure
2	13/9	2	8.35

3	20/9	3	7.95
4	27/9	5	7.80
5	4/10	2	8.85
6	11/10	2	8.75
7*	19/10	4	8.30
8	25/10	5	8.25
9†	1/11	4	9.05
10	8/11	1	9.40
11	22/11	3	8.75
12	29/11	4	8.25
13	6/12	2	8.90
14	13/12	2	8.55

Episode 15 tx. 20/12/76

1	This Is Your Life Thames	8.70
2	**The Sweeney Thames**	**8.55**
3	Wednesday at Eight Thames	8.20
4	Coronation Street (Weds) Granada	7.95
5	Are You Being Served? BBC	7.90
6	Starsky and Hutch BBC	7.85
7	Crossroads (Weds) ATV	7.80
8	Porridge BBC	7.65
9	Opportunity Knocks! Thames	7.45
10	Crossroads (Tues) ATV	7.30

Figures produced by AGB for JICTAR.
* Repeat of Series 1 Episode 6.
† Repeat of Series 1 Episode 2.

Van Der Valk
Series 3
5/9/77 – 21/11/77 Mon, 9pm, 52 mins.
Episode 1 tx. 5/9/77

1	Bruce Forsyth and the Generation Game BBC	15.95
2	Starsky and Hutch BBC	14.95
3	Winner Takes All YTV	14.50
4	The Benny Hill Show Thames	14.40
5	Survival Special Anglia	13.85
6	The New Avengers ITV	13.40
7	The World of Pam Ayres LWT	13.30
8=	Crossroads (Thurs) ATV	13.05
8=	The Dick Emery Show BBC	13.05
10=	**Van Der Valk Thames**	**12.95**
10=	Crossroads (Fri) ATV	12.95

Episode	tx.	position	figure
2	12/9	12	12.25
3	19/9	5	13.75
4	26/9	4	14.50
5	3/10	7	14.30
6	10/10	7	13.95

7	17/10	19	12.80
8	24/10	18	13.30
9	31/10	11	13.25
10	7/11	*	11.15
11	14/11	*	12.20
12	21/11	*	13.50

Figures produced by AGB for JICTAR.
* Not in Top Twenty.

Out
24/7/78 – 28/8/78 Mon, 9pm, 52 mins.
Episode 1 tx. 24/7/78

1	Life Begins at Forty YTV	11.60
2	London Night Out Thames	11.50
3	Coronation Street (Mon) Granada	11.25
4=	Crossroads (Weds) ATV	11.15
4=	Never Mind the Quality, Feel the Width Thames	11.15
6	Crossroads (Thurs) ATV	11.00
7=	Leave it to Charlie Granada	10.40
7=	The Incredible Hulk ITV	10.40
9	Crossroads (Tues) ATV	10.35
10	Coronation Street (Wed) Granada	10.25
11	The Krypton Factor Granada	10.15
12	Crossroads (Fri) ATV	10.10
13	You're Only Young Twice YTV	10.00
14=	3-2-1 YTV	9.95
14=	Backs to the Land Anglia	9.95
16	Master of the Islands BBC	9.85
17=	**Out Thames**	**9.70**
17=	Charlie and Julie YTV	9.70
19=	Survival Anglia	9.30
19=	Don't Ask Me YTV	9.30
19=	Paul Daniels' Blackpool Bonanza Granada	9.30

Episode	tx.	position	figure
2	31/7	*	9.65
3	7/8	*	9.05
4	14/8	11	11.30
5	21/8	15	10.85
6	28/8	*	9.05

Figures produced by AGB for JICTAR.
* Not in Top Twenty.

The Sweeney
Series 4
7/9/78 – 28/12/78 Thurs, 9pm, 52 mins.
Episode 1 tx. 7/9/78

1	On Her Majesty's Secret Service ITV	16.75
2	3-2-1 YTV	16.45

3	The Freddie Starr Experience LWT	16.15
4	Starsky and Hutch BBC	14.05
5	The Rag Trade LWT	13.95
6	The Return of the Saint ATV	13.90
7	**The Sweeney Thames**	**13.85**
8=	George and Mildred Thames	13.50
8=	The Good Life BBC	13.50
10	Seaside Special BBC	13.35

Episode	tx.	position	figure
2	14/9	5	14.10
3	21/9	7	13.65
4	28/9	6	14.25
5	5/10	9	13.75
6	12/10	10	14.20
7	19/10	4	16.45
8	26/10	6	14.85
9	2/11	3	14.95
10	9/11	4	16.60
11†	16/11	*	10.95
12	23/11	10	16.60
13	30/11	3	18.25
14‡	7/12	9	15.85
15	14/12	*	13.40
16§	21/12	8	19.05

Episode 17 tx. 28/12/78

1	The Morecambe and Wise Christmas Show Thames	19.15
2	The Sound of Music BBC	18.50
3	Starsky and Hutch BBC	17.05
4	This Is Your Life Special Thames	16.90
5	George and Mildred Thames	15.85
6	Jim'll Fix It BBC	15.75
7	The Queen BBC	15.55
8	Coronation Street (Weds) Granada	15.35
9	Larry Grayson's Generation Game BBC	15.10
10	The Two Ronnies BBC	14.80
11	Call of the Wild BBC	14.65
12	Diamonds Are Forever ITV	14.35
13	Oliver! BBC	14.15
14	The Muppet Show ATV	14.10
15	The Liver Birds BBC	14.05
16	Carry On Girls BBC	13.70
17	Crossroads (Weds) ATV	13.60
18	The Benny Hill Show Thames	13.30
19	**The Sweeney Thames**	**13.15**
20	Steptoe and Son Ride Again BBC	12.95

Figures produced by AGB for JICTAR.
* Not in Top Twenty
† Repeat of Series 3 Episode 3.

‡ Repeat of Series 3 Episode 4.
§ Repeat of Series 3 Episode 1.

Danger UXB
8/1/79 – 2/4/79 Mon, 9pm, 52 mins. (repeated on Thursdays at 2.25pm)

Episode	tx.	position	figure
1	8/1	*	10.75
2	15/1	*	11.70
3	22/1	*	12.95
4	29/1	*	13.50
5	5/2	5	16.00
6	12/2	*	13.45
7	19/2	*	12.60
8	26/2	*	11.95
9	5/3	20	13.70
10	12/3	*	11.95
11	19/3	*	12.30
12	26/3	19	13.60

Episode 13 tx. 2/4/79

1	This Is Your Life Thames	17.65
2	Coronation Street (Weds) Granada	17.45
3	Chalk and Cheese Thames	16.70
4	Coronation Street (Mon) Granada	16.65
5	**Danger UXB Thames**	**16.05**
6	Crossroads (Tues) ATV	15.50
7	Flambards YTV	15.45
8	Crossroads (Weds) ATV	15.40
9	Blankety Blank BBC	15.30
10	Thomas and Sarah LWT	14.65

Figures produced by AGB for JICTAR.
* Not in Top Twenty

Quatermass
24/10/79 – 14/11/79 Weds, 9.10pm, 52 mins.
Episode 1 tx. 24/10/79

Top Twenty of week ending 28/10/79

1	The Rockford Files BBC	19.95
2	Last of the Summer Wine BBC	19.55
3	It's A Knockout BBC	19.35
4	Angels (Mon) BBC	18.40
5	To The Manor Born BBC	18.25
6=	Nine O'Clock News (Tues) BBC	16.30
6=	Nationwide (Mon) BBC	16.30
6=	Nationwide (Tues) BBC	16.30
9	Blankety Blank BBC	16.25
10	Starsky and Hutch BBC	16.00
11	Larry Grayson's Generation Game BBC	15.90

12	Nine O'Clock News (Mon) BBC	15.85
13	Coronation Street (Weds) Granada	15.10
14	The Two Ronnies BBC	14.80
15	Shoestring BBC	14.15
16=	George and Mildred Thames	13.70
16=	Roots BBC	13.70
18=	Prince Regent BBC	13.65
18=	3-2-1 YTV	13.65
20	Are You Being Served? BBC	13.55

Owing to an industrial dispute ITV was off the air until 17.45 on Wednesday 24 October.

Episode	tx.	figure
1	24/10	12.40
2	31/10	10.80
3	7/11	10.50
4	14/11	11.25

Figures produced by AGB for JICTAR.
Not in Top Twenty.

Minder
Series 1
29/10/79 – 14/1/80 Mon, 9pm, 52 mins.
Episode 1 tx. 29/10/79

Top Twenty of week ending 4/11/79

1	To The Manor Born BBC	21.40
2	Shoestring BBC	17.65
3	Blankety Blank BBC	17.05
4	Larry Grayson's Generation Game BBC	17.00
5	Roots BBC	16.85
6	Citizen Smith BBC	15.65
7	Are You Being Served? BBC	15.40
8	Top Of The Pops BBC	14.95
9	It's A Knockout BBC	14.80
10	Secret Army BBC	14.50
11	Mike Yarwood in Persons BBC	13.95
12	The Two Ronnies BBC	13.80
13	Coronation Street (Weds) Granada	13.75
14	London Night Out Thames	13.40
15	3-2-1 YTV	13.30
16	Dr Who BBC	13.15
17	Last Of The Summer Wine BBC	13.05
18	Coronation Street (Mon) Granada	12.85
19	The Professionals LWT	12.70
20	Only When I Laugh YTV	12.60

Episode	tx.	figure
1	29/10	9.15
2	5/11	8.75
3	12/11	7.45

4	19/11	7.80
5	26/11	8.75
6	3/12	10.65
7	10/12	9.15
8	17/12	12.65
9	1/1	9.55
10	7/1	9.60
11	14/1	13.30

Figures produced by AGB for JICTAR.
Not in Top Twenty.

Charlie Muffin
11/12/79 Tues, 8pm, 105 mins.
Rating: 11.65
Figures produced by AGB for JICTAR.
Not in Top Twenty.

The Knowledge
27/12/79 Thurs, 9pm, 79 mins.
Rating: 8.70
Figures produced by AGB for JICTAR.
Not in Top Twenty.

Stainless Steel and the Star Spies
1/1/80 Thurs, 4.45pm, 52 mins.
Rating: 7.90
Figures produced by AGB for JICTAR.
Not in Top Twenty

Fox
10/3/80 – 2/6/80   Mon, 9pm, 52 mins.
Episode 1 tx. 10/3/80
Top Twenty for week ending 16/3/80

1	All Creatures Great and Small	BBC	17.75
2	Jim'll Fix It	BBC	17.30
3	Dallas	BBC	17.00
4=	This Is Your Life	Thames	16.95
4=	The Little and Large Show	BBC	16.95
6	Coronation Street (Weds)	Granada	16.30
7	Coronation Street (Mon)	Granada	15.85
8	Play Your Cards Right	LWT	15.80
9	Crossroads (Weds)	ATV	15.25
10	Life Begins At Forty	YTV	15.10
11	Armchair Thriller: High Tide (Tues)	Southern	14.15
12=	Crossroads (Thurs)	ATV	14.10
12=	The British Academy Awards	Thames	14.10
14	Crossroads (Tues)	ATV	14.05
15	Crossroads (Mon)	ATV	14.00
16	Armchair Thriller: High Tide (Thurs)	Southern	13.90

17	Potter BBC	13.85
18	Wonder Woman BBC	13.80
19	Hart To Hart ITV	13.70
20	The Kenny Everett Video Show Thames	13.55

Episode	tx.	figure
1	10/3	8.05
2	17/3	8.95
3	24/3	9.40
4	31/3	8.00
5	7/4	7.20
6	14/4	9.35
7	21/4	8.30
8	28/4	9.30
9*	5/5	5.70
10	12/5	7.55
11	19/5	8.10
12	26/5	8.00
13	2/6	8.30

Figures produced by AGB for JICTAR.
* Transmission delayed until 10.40pm (Iranian Embassy Siege coverage). Not in Top Twenty.

Minder
Series 2
11/9/80 – 11/12/80   Thurs, 9pm, 52 mins.
Episode 1 tx. 11/9/80

Top Twenty of week ending 14/9/80

1	The Morecambe and Wise Show Thames	18.00
2	Cowboys Thames	16.05
3	Coronation Street (Weds) Granada	15.70
4	Just Liz Thames	15.20
5	Keep It In The Family Thames	14.60
6	Coronation Street (Mon) Thames	14.35
7	Larry Grayson's Generation Game BBC	14.25
8	The Return of the Pink Panther ITV	14.15
9	Blankety Blank BBC	13.45
10	Crossroads (Tues) ATV	13.40
11	Juliet Bravo BBC	13.35
12	The Paul Daniels Magic Show· BBC	13.00
13	Hammer House of Horror ATV	12.65
14	Crossroads (Weds) ATV	12.35
15	Give Us A Clue Thames	12.30
16	Hart of the Yard (Weds) ITV	12.15
17	Yes Minister BBC	12.05
18	Play Your Cards Right LWT	11.85
19	Arthur C. Clarke's Mysterious World YTV	11.80
20	The Professionals LWT	11.70

Episode	tx.	figure
1	11/9	11.20
2	18/9	10.70
3	25/9	10.00
4*	2/10	8.90
5	9/10	12.30
6	16/10	10.90
7	23/10	12.55
8	30/10	12.15
9	6/11	12.65
10	20/11	14.45
11	27/11	12.80
12	4/12	13.35
13	11/12	12.60

Figures produced by AGB for JICTAR.
* Not in Top Twenty. Shown in London region 18/12/80.

The Sailor's Return
9/12/80 Tues, 8 pm, 112 mins.
Rating: 10.95
Not in Top Twenty

Figures produced by AGB for JICTAR.

The Flame Trees of Thika
1/9/81 – 13/10/81 Thurs, 8.30 pm, 50 mins.
Episode 1 tx 1/9/81

Individual channel Top Tens for the week ending 6 September 1981
BBC-1
1   Mastermind
2   Juggernaut
3   Blood Money
4   Nine O'Clock News (Fri)
5   Jim'll Fix It
6   Larry Grayson's Generation Game
7   Knots Landing
8   Blankety Blank
9   Juliet Bravo
10 It Ain't Half Hot Mum

BBC-2
1   Valdez is Coming
2   Cricket: Sixth Test (Mon)
3   The FBI Story
4   Cricket: Sixth Test (Sat)
5   Gardeners' World
6   Cricket: Sixth Test (Tues)
7   Rhoda
8   Sunday Grandstand

9   The Body in Question
10 Secret Army

ITV
1   Coronation Street (Weds)   Granada
2   Only When I Laugh   YTV
3   The Eagle Has Landed
4   Spider Man
5   The Morecambe and Wise Show   Thames
6   Callan . . . Wet Job   ATV
7   Quincy
8   The Benny Hill Show   Thames
9   The Flame Trees of Thika
10 Coronation Street (Mon)   Granada

Episode	tx.	position*	figure
1	1/9	9	12.30
2	8/9	7	12.70
3	15/9	†	10.50
4	22/9	†	11.00
5	29/9	†	11.40
6	6/10	†	9.90
7	13/10	†	12.10

Figures produced by AGB for BARB.
* i.e. in ITV weekly Top Ten.
† Not in ITV Top Ten.

Minder
Series 3
13/1/82 – 7/4/82 Weds, 9pm, 50 mins.
Episode 1 tx. 13/1/82

ITV Top Ten
1   Coronation Street (Weds)   Granada
2   This Is Your Life   Thames
3   London Night Out   Thames
4   Coronation Street (Mon)   Granada
5   Bruce Forsyth's Play Your Cards Right   LWT
6   Family Fortunes   Central
7   Minder   Thames
8   The Fall Guy   ITV
9   Shine On Harvey Moon   Central
10 Let There Be Love   Thames

Episode	tx.	position*	figure
1	13/1	7	14.80
2	20/1	†	14.80
3	27/1	†	13.75
4	3/2	†	13.55
5	10/2	†	13.60
6	17/2	†	14.05

7	24/2	†	12.80
8	3/3	10	13.90
9	10/3	10	13.20
10	17/3	6	13.75
11	24/3	9	13.20
12	31/3	4	14.95

Episode 13 tx. 7/4/82
ITV Top Ten

1	Coronation Street (Weds) Granada	16.90
2	The Benny Hill Show Thames	16.20
3	Coronation Street (Mon) Granada	15.40
4	**Minder Thames**	**15.00**
5	3-2-1 YTV	13.80
6	Give Us a Clue Thames	13.35
7=	Where There's Life YTV	12.85
7=	Family Fortunes Central	12.85
9	Crossroads (Tues) Central	12.60
10	Crossroads (Weds) Central	12.45

Figures produced by AGB for BARB.
* i.e. in ITV Top Ten.
† Not in ITV Top Ten.

Widows
Series 1
16/3/83 – 20/4/83 Weds, 9pm, 50 mins.
Episode 1 tx. 16/3/83

1	Coronation Street (Mon, Weds) Granada	16.58
2	This Is Your Life Thames	15.10
3	Crossroads (Mon to Fri) Central	14.99
4	Family Fortunes Central	14.93
5	3-2-1 YTV	14.21
6	The Citadel BBC	13.35
7	Murder On Flight 502 ITV	12.54
8	Punchlines LWT	12.40
9	Kenny Everett Television Show BBC	12.28
10	The Benny Hill Show Thames	12.05
11	British Academy Awards Thames	11.62
12	Top of the Pops BBC	11.52
13	The Fall Guy ITV	11.36
14	Pig in the Middle LWT	11.29
15	Holiday BBC	11.24
16	Village Earth Central	11.06
17	Emmerdale Farm (Mon to Thurs) YTV	11.02
18	**Widows Thames**	**11.00**
19	Dallas BBC	10.37
20	Cagney and Lacey BBC	10.27

Episode	tx.	position	figure
2	23/3	17	11.19
3	30/3	18	10.58
4	6/4	19	10.13
5	13/4	5	12.78

Episode 6 tx. 20/4/83

1	Coronation Street (Mon, Weds) Granada		15.67
2	Family Fortunes Central		13.01
3	Crossroads (Mon to Thurs) Central		12.90
4	**Widows Thames**		**12.49**
5	Eurovision Song Contest BBC		12.48
6	Where There's Life YTV		12.19
7	Dallas BBC		12.11
8	Knight Rider (Tue, Thurs, Sat) ITV		11.82
9	Are You Being Served? BBC		11.72
10	The Fall Guy (Fri, Sat) ITV		11.12

N.B. Audiences for programmes appearing more than once a week are averages.

Figures produced by AGB for BARB.

Reilly – Ace of Spies

5/9/83 – 16/11/83 Weds, 9pm, 52 mins. (except Episode 1, tx. Mon, 8.30pm, 75 mins.)

Episodes 1 & 2 tx. 5 & 7/9/83

1	Coronation Street (Mon, Weds) Granada	14.56
2	The Sea Wolves ITV	13.31
3	Winds of War ITV	12.17
4	Morecambe and Wise Show Thames	12.13
5	The Benny Hill Show Thames	12.01
6	Escape From Alcatraz ITV	11.94
7	Crossroads (Mon, Tues, Weds) Central	11.09
8=	Punchlines LWT	10.95
8=	Keep It In The Family Thames	10.95
10	The A-Team ITV	10.94
11	The Krypton Factor Granada	10.91
12	Stunt Challenge '83 Thames	10.89
13	Where There's Life YTV	10.69
14	Game For A Laugh LWT	10.62
15	Give Us A Clue Thames	10.35
16	Winner Takes All YTV	10.23
17	Blankety Blank BBC	9.93
18	Hart to Hart ITV	9.91
19	**Reilly – Ace of Spies (Mon, Weds) Thames**	**9.68**
20	Play Your Cards Right LWT	9.52

N.B. Audiences for programmes appearing more than once a week are averages.

Episode	tx.	position	figure
3	14/9	25	8.58
4	21/9	26	8.34

5	28/9	31	7.45
6	5/10	32	8.00
7	12/10	43	7.34
8	19/10	36	7.30
9	26/10	31	8.80
10	2/11	37	7.77
11	9/11	38	8.09
12	16/11	29	8.82

Figures produced by AGB for BARB.

The Nation's Health
6/10/83 – 27/10/83 Channel Four, Thurs, 9.30pm.

The Nation's Health did not figure in the Top 100. The following figures are taken from Channel Four ratings data only.
Episode 1 tx. 6/10/83 (100 mins)

1	Danger Within	3.70
2	Brookside (Tues)	2.75
3	Brookside (Weds)	2.65
4	The Paul Hogan Show	2.45
5	A Frame with Davis	2.20
6	The Avengers	1.70
7	The Prisoner	1.65
8	**The Nation's Health**	**1.45**
9=	Sports Quiz	1.40
9=	American Football	1.40

Episode	tx.	position*	figure	duration
2	13/10	5	1.70	105 mins.
3	20/10	5	1.80	95 mins.
4	27/10	9	1.30	100 mins.

Figures produced by AGB for BARB.

* i.e. in Channel Four Top Ten.

Minder
Series 4
11/1/84 – 21/3/84 Weds, 9pm, 50 mins.

Episode 1 tx. 11/1/84

1	Coronation Street (Mon, Weds) Granada	16.91
2	This Is Your Life Thames	14.78
3	Wish You Were Here Thames	14.66
4	Bergerac BBC	14.51
5	The Thorn Birds (Mon, Sun) BBC	14.48
6	Name That Tune Thames	14.43
7	The A-Team ITV	14.12
8	Up The Elephant & Round the Castle Thames	13.82
9	3-2-1 YTV	13.59
10	The Two Ronnies BBC	13.55
11	Child's Play LWT	13.36

12	**Minder Thames**			**12.96**
13	A Fine Romance LWT			12.89
14	That's Life BBC			12.61
15	Hi-De-Hi BBC			12.57

Episode	tx.	position	figure
2	18/1	7	13.51
3	25/1	12	11.91
4	1/2	8	13.84
5	8/2	5	14.72
6	15/2	2	15.28
7	22/2	9	14.70
8	29/2	4	13.94
9	7/3	4	15.08
10	14/3	2	16.26

Episode 11 tx. 21/3/84

1	Coronation Street (Mon, Weds) Granada	16.18
2	**Minder Thames**	**15.90**
3	Duty Free YTV	15.65
4	This Is Your Life Thames	15.44
5	T J Hooker ITV	14.03
6	The Price Is Right Central	13.71
7	Fresh Fields Thames	13.64
8	Wish You Were Here Thames	12.69
9	Child's Play LWT	12.39
10	Dallas BBC	11.83

NB. Audiences for programmes appearing more than once a week are average figures.

Figures produced by AGB for BARB.

REPEATS

The Euston Films television productions which ran for more than one series (*Special Branch, Van der Valk, The Sweeney*, and *Minder*) have been repeated several times, but not necessarily in their original series sequence. Repeats are often out of sequence and, in some cases, compilations of several series.

The following table details the repeats of single productions and series.

Title	Day	Time	Repeat Date
Armchair Cinema 'The Prison'	Tues	10.30 pm	11/3/75
Armchair Cinema 'Regan'	Thurs	10.40 pm	8/9/83
When Day Is Done	Weds	2.25 pm	30/3/77
Danger UXB	Thurs	10.30 pm	14/1/82 to 22/4/82
Charlie Muffin	Weds	8.00 pm	31/8/83
The Knowledge	Weds	10.30 pm	29/7/81
Fox (Channel Four)	Sat	10.00 pm	1/10/83 to 31/12/83
The Flame Trees of Thika	Tues	9.00 pm	19/4/83 to 7/6/83
Out	Weds	9.10 pm	18/4/83 to 2/5/83
Out (Channel Four)	Thurs	9.30 pm	4/8/83 to 8/9/83
Quatermass	Weds	10.30 pm	9 & 16/5/84

Appendix 2 Foreign Sales of Euston Productions

Thames Television International earns revenue (not just for drama, of course) from every country with a television service except China, although there is very little business conducted with the USSR and Japan. When researching foreign sales of Euston's productions we discovered that none have been sold to the USSR or India and just two have been sold to Japan (*Special Branch* and *The Sweeney*). With the exception of Argentina (13 programmes), Brazil (8 programmes) and Mexico (1 programme) the countries of Latin America are not individually specified on the sales computer print-outs, presumably because only three programmes have been sold there overall. If one looks at the top ten overseas markets for Thames Television International (listed in Chapter 1 in order of financial importance) it is possible to see that Australia and New Zealand almost automatically take Euston's products, whilst France takes hardly any. For these countries the total of Euston programmes taken are as follows:

USA – 10 programmes; Australia – 21; Canada (French and English) – 12; Italy – 9; West Germany – 9; France – 3; New Zealand – 17; Spain – 7.

Looking at the figures another way, we have drawn up a table of the international sales of Euston's products based on *the number of countries to which each programme or series has been sold*, i.e. not based on size of revenue earned, which would create a different order. We have done this because the ideological implications of the potential size and range of an audience is, in some ways, more interesting than knowing the amount of money the company earns from a particular product. However, we are fully aware that the area of work we are thereby opening up – the relationship between the economic, institutional, political, ideological, social and cultural understood in terms of the international circulation of television fiction – has yet to be researched. Nevertheless, in making this listing some potentially interesting information would seem to be revealed. For example, whereas the most distant English-speaking countries – Australia and New Zealand – take almost all Euston's productions, the closest – Eire – has taken only seven. It is also interesting to note the number of Eastern European countries that have bought Euston's productions and also the occasional purchase by other communist countries; it is also worth noting what they didn't buy. It is for this reason that we have indicated sales to communist countries. Of similar interest are the purchases made by South Africa.

The lists drawn upon were dated 21 February 1984 and obviously one would expect some of the more recent programmes to have sold to less countries given the shorter selling time available.

211

1 *The Sweeney*	–	51 countries including Poland, Rumania, Cuba, Libya, South Africa.
2 *Armchair Cinema* (*The Prison* and *Regan*)	–	47 countries including Bulgaria, Czechoslavakia, East Germany, Yugoslavia, South Africa.
3 *Special Branch*	–	39 countries including Poland.
4 *The Flame Trees of Thika*	–	33 countries. It is interesting to note that this programme only sold to four countries in the non-Arab African continent: Kenya, Swaziland, Zambia and Zimbabwe.
5 *The Sailor's Return*	–	26 counties including Czechoslovakia, Yugoslavia and Albania. Gabon and Swaziland were the only two countries from the non-Arab African continent to buy it.
5 *Minder*	–	26 countries.
7 *Van der Valk*	–	22 countries including East Germany, Poland, Yugoslavia and South Africa.
8 *Danger UXB*	–	20 countries plus the UK satellite.
8 *Charlie Muffin*	–	20 countries including South Africa.
8 *Widows*	–	20 countries
11 *Out*	–	18 countries including Yugoslavia and South Africa.
11 *Reilly – Ace of Spies*	–	18 countries.
13 *The Knowledge*	–	17 countries including Poland.
13 *Fox*	–	17 countries.
15 *Quatermass*	–	14 countries plus the UK satellite.
16 *Sea Song*	–	13 countries plus the UK satellite.
17 *When Day is Done*	–	12 countries plus the UK satellite and including Yugoslavia and South Africa.
18 *Tully*	–	11 countries including South Africa.
19 *In Sickness and in Health*	–	6 countries plus the UK satellite and including Poland.
20 *Stainless Steel and the Star Spies*	–	6 countries.
21 *The Nation's Health*	–	1 country.

Appendix 3 Production Credits

Special Branch (Series 3)
Tx: Weds 9.00pm. 52 mins.
Executive producers: Lloyd Shirley, George Taylor. *Producer*: Geoffrey Gilbert. *Script editor*: Ian Black. *Production manager*: Laurie Greenwood. *Location manager*: Nick Gillott. *Lighting cameramen*: John Keeling, Dusty Miller. *Camera operator*: John Maskall. *Editors*: Chris Burt, John S. Smith. *Art directors*: John Woods, Malcolm Middleton. *Sound mixer*: Tony Dawe. *Boom operator*: Mike Silverlock. *Dubbing editor*: Ian Toynton. *1st assistant director*: Eamonn Duffy. *Casting director*: Dodo Watts.
Cast: George Sewell (*Det. Chief Insp. Craven*), Roger Rowland (*Det. Sgt. North*), Patrick Mower (*Insp. Tom Haggerty*), Sheila Scott-Wilkinson (*Pam Sloane*).

			Writer	Director
1	04/04/73	'A Copper Called Craven'	Roger Marshall	William Brayne
2	11/04/73	'Round The Clock'	Tom Brennand, Roy Bottomley	Mike Vardy
3	18/04/73	'Inquisition'	Trevor Preston	Mike Vardy
4	25/04/73	'Assault'	Tom Brennand, Roy Bottomley	Douglas Camfield
5	02/05/73	'Polonaise'	Allan Scott, Chris Bryant	Mike Vardy
6	09/05/73	'Red Herring'	Peter Hill	Mike Vardy
7	16/05/73	'Death By Drowning'	John Kershaw	Dennis Vance
8	23/05/73	'All The King's Men'	Trevor Preston	Dennis Vance
9	06/06/73	'Threat'	Tom Brennand, Roy Bottomley	William Brayne
10	13/06/73	'The Other Man'	Roger Marshall	Dennis Vance
11	20/06/73	'You Won't Remember Me'	Anthony Skene	John Robbins
12	27/06/73	'Hostage'	John Kershaw	David Wickes
13	04/07/73	'Blueprint For Murder'	Peter Hill, Ian Black	William Brayne

Special Branch (Series 4)
Tx: Thurs 8.30pm. 52 mins.
Executive producers: Lloyd Shirley, George Taylor. *Producer*: Ted Childs. *Script editor*: Ian Black. *Production manager*: Nick Gillott. *Location manager*: Stuart Freeman. *Lighting cameramen*: John Keeling, Dusty Miller. *Camera operator*: John Maskall. *Editors*: Chris Burt, John S Smith. *Art director*: William Alexander. *Sound mixer*: Tony Dawe. *Boom operator*: Mike Silverlock. *Dubbing editor*: Ian Toynton. *Assistant director*: Eamonn Duffy. *Casting director*: Dodo Watts.
Cast: George Sewell (*Det. Chief Insp. Craven*), Patrick Mower (*Det. Chief Insp. Haggerty*), Paul Eddington (*Strand*), Frederick Jaeger (*Cmdr. Fletcher*).

			Writer	Director
1	14/02/74	'Double Exposure'	Michael J Bird	Don Leaver
2	21/02/74	'Catherine The Great'	John Brason	Douglas Camfield
3	28/02/74	'Jailbait'	Michael Chapman	William Brayne
4	07/03/74	'Stand And Deliver'	Michael J Bird	Tom Clegg

5	14/03/74	'Something About A Soldier'	Michael J Bird	William Brayne
6	21/03/74	'Rendezvous'	T Williamson	Terry Green
7	28/03/74	'Sounds Sinister'	David Butler	Terry Green
8	04/04/74	'Entente Cordiale'	John Kershaw	William Brayne
9	11/04/74	'Date Of Birth'	Lewis Griefer	Don Leaver
10	18/04/74	'Intercept'	Ian Kennedy-Martin	William Brayne
11	25/04/74	'Alien'	Ray Jenkins	Douglas Camfield
12	02/05/74	'Diversion'	Peter J Hammond	William Brayne
13	09/05/74	'Downwind Of Angels'	Peter Hill	Tom Clegg

Armchair Cinema : 'The Prison'
Tx: 28 May 1974 Tues 8.30pm 90 mins.
Executive producers: Lloyd Shirley, George Taylor. *Producer*: Geoffrey Gilbert. *Director*: David Wickes. *Script*: Geoffrey Gilbert from the novel by Georges Simenon. *Production manager*: Laurie Greenwood. *Location manager*: John Southwood. *Lighting cameraman*: Dusty Miller. *Camera operator*: Mike Berwick. *Editor*: Bill Blunden. *Art director*: Ken Court. *Sound mixer*: Ivan Sharrock. *Dubbing mixer*: Hugh Strain. *Dubbing editor*: Ian Toynton. *Assistant director*: Ken Baker. *Casting director*: Dodo Watts.
Cast: James Laurenson (*Alain Poitaud*), James Maxwell (*Roland Blanchet*), Ann Curthoys (*Jacqueline Poitaud*), Kenneth Griffith (*Julien Bour*), George Murchell (*Maître Rabut*), André Morell (*André Fage*).

Armchair Cinema : 'Regan'
Tx: 4 June 1974 Tues 8.30pm. 77 mins.
Executive producers: Lloyd Shirley, George Taylor. *Producer*: Ted Childs. *Associate producer*: Mary Morgan. *Director*: Tom Clegg. *Script*: Ian Kennedy-Martin. *Production manager*: Nicholas Gillott. *Lighting cameraman*: John Keeling. *Camera operator*: John Maskall. *Editor*: Chris Burt. *Art director*: Jack Robinson. *Sound mixer*: Tony Dawe. *Dubbing mixer*: Hugh Strain. *Dubbing editor*: Ian Toynton. *Assistant director*: Stuart Freeman. *Casting director*: Lesley de Pettitt.
Cast: John Thaw (*Det. Insp. Jack Regan*), Dennis Waterman (*Det. Sgt. George Carter*), Lee Montague (*Arthur Dale*), Garfield Morgan (*Det. Chief Insp. Haskins*), David Daker (*Tusser*), Janet Key (*Kate*), Maureen Lipman (*Annie*).

Armchair Cinema : 'Sea Song'
Tx: 10 September 1975 Tues 8.30pm. 80 mins.,
Executive producers: Lloyd Shirley, George Taylor. *Producer/director*: Peter Hammond. *Script*: Guy Slater. *Production manager*: Laurie Greenwood. *Lighting cameraman*: Dusty Miller. *Camera operator*: John Boulter. *Editor*: Peter Delfgou. *Art director*: Arnold Chapkis. *Sound mixer*: Ivan Sharrock. *Dubbing mixer*: Hugh Strain. *Assistant director*: Ken Baker. *Casting director*: Dodo Watts.
Cast: Tom Bell (*Ray Carter*), Kika Markham (*Marnie Miller*), Phillipe Leotard (*Jean Jacques Brialy*), June Ritchie (*Susan Carter*), Rachel Thomas (*Lil Carter*).

The Sweeney (Series 1)
Tx: Thurs 9.00pm. 52 mins.
Executive producers: Lloyd Shirley, George Taylor. *Producer*: Ted Childs. *Associate producer*: Mary Morgan. *Series created by:* Ian Kennedy-Martin. *Production manager*: Nick Gillott. *Lighting cameramen*: Norman Langley, Dusty Miller. *Camera operator*: John Maskall. *Editors*: Chris Burt, John S Smith. *Art director*: Jack Robinson. *Sound mixer*: Tony Dawe. *Boom operator*: Mike Silverlock. *Dubbing editor*: Ian Toynton. *Assistant director*: Stuart Freeman.

214

Casting director: Lesley de Pettitt.
Cast: John Thaw (*Det. Insp. Regan*), Dennis Waterman (*Det. Sgt. Carter*), Garfield Morgan (*Det. Chief Insp. Haskins*).

			Writer	Director
1	02/01/75	'Ringer'	Trevor Preston	Terry Green
2	09/01/75	'Jackpot'	Tony Marsh	Tom Clegg
3	16/01/75	'Thin Ice'	Troy Kennedy-Martin	Tom Clegg
4	23/01/75	'Queen's Pawn'	Ranald Graham	Viktors Ritelis
5	30/01/75	'Jigsaw'	Tudor Gates	William Brayne
6	06/02/75	'Night Out'	Troy Kennedy-Martin	David Wickes
7	13/02/75	'The Placer'	Trevor Preston	Ted Childs
8	20/02/75	'Cover Story'	Ranald Graham	Douglas Camfield
9	27/02/75	'Golden Boy'	Martin Hall	Tom Clegg
10	06/03/75	'Stoppo Driver'	Allan Prior	Terry Green
11	13/03/75	'Big Spender'	Allan Prior	Viktors Ritelis
12	20/03/75	'Contact Breaker'	R B Stewart	William Brayne
13	27/03/75	'Abduction'	Trevor Preston	Tom Clegg

Armchair Cinema: 'When Day Is Done'
Tx: 7 January 1975 Tues 8.25pm. 80 mins.
Executive producers: Lloyd Shirley, George Taylor. *Producer/director:* Reginald Collin. *Associate producer:* Laurie Greenwood. *Script:* John Kershaw. *Lighting cameraman:* Norman Langley. *Camera operator:* John Maskall. *Editor:* John S Smith. *Art director:* Malcolm Middleton. *Sound mixer:* Tony Dawe. *Dubbing mixer:* Hugh Strain. *Dubbing Editor:* Ian Toynton. *Assistant director:* Eamonn Duffy. *Casting director:* Lesley de Pettitt.
Cast: Edward Woodward (*Philip Warne*), Rosemary Leach (*Rosemary Warne*), Patricia Maynard (*Sue Flack*), Julia Goodman (*Judy Warne*).

Armchair Cinema: 'In Sickness And In Health'
Tx: 21 May 1975 Weds 8.30pm. (London Region only) 51 mins.
Executive producers:: Lloyd Shirley, George Taylor. *Producer/director:* Reginald Collin. *Associate producer:* Laurie Greenwood. *Script:* John Kershaw. *Lighting cameraman:* Norman Langley. *Camera operator:* Jan Morgan. *Editor:* John S Smith. *Art director:* Malcolm Middleton. *Sound mixer:* Derek Rye. *Dubbing mixer:* Hugh Strain. *Dubbing editor:* Peter Compton. *Assistant director:* Bill Westley. *Casting director:* Lesley de Pettitt.
Cast: Patrick Mower (*Dr Ian Bell*), Prunella Ransome (*Kate Bell*), Michael Goodliffe (*Dr David Murray*), Shelagh Fraser (*Mrs. Heath*).

The Sweeney (Series 2)
Tx: Mon 9.00pm. 52 mins.
Executive producers: Lloyd Shirley, George Taylor. *Producer:* Ted Childs. *Associate producer:* Mary Morgan. *Series created by:* Ian Kennedy-Martin. *Production manager:* Nicholas Gillott. *Location manager:* Laurie Greenwood. *Lighting cameramen:* Norman Langley, Dusty Miller. *Camera operator:* John Maskall. *Editors:* Chris Burt, John S Smith. *Art Director:* William Alexander. *Sound mixer:* Tony Dawe. *Boom operator:* Mike Silverlock. *Dubbing editor:* Ian Toynton. *Assistant director:* Roy Corbett. *Casting director:* Lesley de Pettitt.
Cast: John Thaw (*Det. Insp. Regan*), Dennis Waterman (*Det. Sgt. Carter*), Garfield Morgan (*Det. Chief Insp. Haskins*).

			Writer	Director
1	01/09/75	'Chalk And Cheese'	Trevor Preston	Terry Green
2	08/09/75	'Faces'	Murray Smith	William Brayne
3	15/09/75	'Supersnout'	Ranald Graham	Tom Clegg

215

4	22/09/75	'Big Brother'	Trevor Preston	Tom Clegg
5	29/09/75	'Hit And Run'	Roger Marshall	Mike Vardy
6	06/10/75	'Trap'	Ray Jenkins	Jim Goddard
7	13/10/75	'Golden Fleece'	Roger Marshall	David Wickes
8	20/10/75	'Poppy'	Trevor Preston	Tom Clegg
9	27/10/75	'Stay Lucky, Eh?'	Trevor Preston	Douglas Camfield
10	03/11/75	'Trojan Bus'	Roger Marshall	Ted Childs
11	10/11/75	'I Want The Man'	Ray Jenkins	Tom Clegg
12	17/11/75	'Country Boy'	Andrew Wilson	Jim Goddard
13	24/11/75	'Thou Shalt Not Kill'	Ranald Graham	Douglas Camfield

Armchair Cinema: 'Tully'

Tx: 26 November 1975 Weds 8.30pm. 80 mins.

(An Insignia Production in association with Euston Films, Australian Broadcasting Commission and Deutscher Filmdienst)

Executive producers: Lloyd Shirley, George Taylor. *Producer/director*: James Gatward. *Script*: Ian Stuart Black. *Production manager*: Michael Baynham. *Unit manager*: Michael Collins. *Lighting cameramen*: Brian Probyn, Geoff Burton. *Camera operators*: John Winbolt, John Seale. *Editor*: Ray Alchin. *Art director*: Laurie Johnson. *Sound recordist*: Sid Butterworth. *Sound mixer*: Alan Allen. *Dubbing editor*: Harry Hall. *Assistant director*: Dickie Bamber.

Cast: Anthony Valentine (*Tully*), Ted Eastman (*Henri Szeps*), Kevin Miles (*Brandon*), Jack Thompson (*Vic*), Barbara Nielson (*Silvia*).

The Sweeney (Series 3)

Tx: Mon 9.00pm. 52 mins.

Executive producers: Lloyd Shirley, George Taylor. *Producer*: Ted Childs. *Associate producer*: Mary Morgan. *Series created by*: Ian Kennedy-Martin. *Production manager*: Nicholas Gillott. *Location manager*: Laurie Greenwood. *Lighting cameramen*: Dusty Miller, Mike Davis. *Camera operator*: John Maskall. *Editors*: Chris Burt, John S Smith. *Art director*: William Alexander. *Sound mixer*: Tony Dawe. *Boom operator*: Mike Silverlock. *Dubbing editor*: Ian Toynton. *Assistant director*: David Bracknell. *Casting director*: Lesley de Pettitt.

Cast: John Thaw (*Det. Insp. Regan*), Dennis Waterman (*Det. Sgt. Carter*), Garfield Morgan (*Det. Chief Insp. Haskins*).

			Writer	Director
1	06/09/76	'Selected Target'	Troy Kennedy-Martin	Tom Clegg
2	13/09/76	'In From The Cold'	Tony Hoare	Terry Green
3	20/09/76	'Visiting Fireman'	Troy Kennedy-Martin	Tom Clegg
4	27/09/76	'Tomorrow Man'	Andrew Wilson	David Wickes
5	04/10/76	'Taste Of Fear'	Roger Marshall	David Wickes
6	11/10/76	'Bad Apple'	Roger Marshall	Douglas Camfield
7	19/10/76	Repeat of 'Night Out'	Series 1 Episode 6	
8	25/10/76	'May'	Trevor Preston	Tom Clegg
9	01/11/76	Repeat of 'Jackpot'	Series 1 Episode 2	
10	08/11/76	'Sweet Smell of Succession'	Peter Hill	William Brayne
11	22/11/76	'Down To You Brother'	Richard Harris	Chris Menaul
12	29/11/76	'Payoff'	P J Hammond	Douglas Camfield
13	06/12/76	'Loving Arms'	Robert Wales	Tom Clegg
14	13/12/76	'Lady Luck'	Ranald Graham	Mike Vardy
15	20/12/76	'On The Run'	Roger Marshall	David Wickes

Sweeney! (Feature Film)
Great Britain, 1976. 89 mins.
Executive producers: Lloyd Shirley, George Taylor. *Producer*: Ted Childs. *Director*: David Wickes. *Script*: Ranald Graham. *Production manager*: Laurie Greenwood. *Location manager*: Stephen Pushkin. *Lighting cameraman*: Dusty Miller. *Camera operator*: John Maskall. *Editor*: Chris Burt. *Art director*: Bill Alexander. *Sound mixer*: Tony Dawe. *Boom operator*: Mike Silverlock. *Dubbing mixer*: Hugh Strain. *Assistant Director*: Bill Westley. *Casting director*: Marilyn Johnson.
Cast: John Thaw (*Det. Insp. Regan*), Dennis Waterman (*Det. Sgt. Carter*), Barry Foster (*McQueen*), Ian Bannen (*Baker*), Colin Welland (*Chadwick*), Diane Keen (*Bianca*), Michael Coles (*Johnson*), Joe Melia (*Brent*), Brian Glover (*Mac*), Lynda Bellingham (*Janice*).

Van Der Valk (Series 3)
Tx: Mon 9.00pm. 52 mins.
Executive producers: Lloyd Shirley, George Taylor. *Producer*: Geoffrey Gilbert. *Associate producers*: Chris Burt, Mary Morgan. *Originally created by*: Nicholas Freeling. *Production manager*: Laurie Greenwood. *Lighting cameraman*: Dusty Miller. *Camera operator*: John Maskall. *Editor*: John S Smith. *Art directors*: William Alexander, Terry Parr. *Sound mixer*: Tony Dawe. *Boom operator*: Mike Silverlock. *Dubbing editor*: Geoff R Brown. *Assistant director*: Michael Murray. *Casting director*: Marilyn Johnson.
Cast: Barry Foster (*Van Der Valk*), Joanna Dunham (*Arlette*), Nigel Stock (*Samson*).

			Writer	Director
1	05/09/77	'Enemy'	Paul Wheeler	Mike Vardy
2	12/09/77	'Accidental'	Ted Childs	Tom Clegg
3	19/09/77	'The Runt'	Leslie Sands	Mike Vardy
4	26/09/77	'Wolf'	Philip Broadley	Mike Vardy
5	03/10/77	'Man Of Iron'	Michael Chapman	William Brayne
6	10/10/77	'Everbody Does It'	Philip Broadley	Ben Bolt
7	17/10/77	'Face Value'	Robert Wales	Mike Vardy
8	24/10/77	'Dead On Arrival'	Patrick O'Brien	Ted Childs
9	31/10/77	'The Professor'	Roger Marshall	Ted Childs
10	07/11/77	'In Hazard'	Paul Wheeler	William Brayne
11	14/11/77	'Gold Plated Delinquents'	Roger Marshall	Tom Clegg
12	21/11/77	'Diane'	Philip Broadley	Mike Vardy

Out
Tx: Mon 9.00pm 52 mins.
Executive in charge of production: Johnny Goodman. *Producer*: Barry Hanson. *Associate producer/ story consultant*: Linda Agran. *Director*: Jim Goddard. *Script*: Trevor Preston. *Production supervisor*: Peter Manley. *Location manager*: Peter Cotton. *Lighting cameraman*: Phil Meheux. *Camera operator*: John Maskall. *Editor*: Ralph Sheldon. *Assistant editor*: Michael Crowley. *Art director*: Frank White. *Sound mixer*: Dudley Plummer. *Boom operator*: Chris Gurney. *1st assistant director*: Bill Westley. *Casting director*: Ann Fielden.
Cast: Tom Bell (*Frank Ross*), Brian Croucher (*Chris Cottle*), Lynn Farleigh (*Ann*), Pam Fairbrother (*Eve Ross*), Andrew Paul (*Paul Ross*), John Junkin (*Ralph Veneker*), Bryan Marshall (*Hallam*), Brian Cox (*McGrath*), Derrick O'Connor (*John Pavey*), Norman Rodway (*Bryce*), Robert Walker (*Rimmer*), Katherine Schofield (*Cimmie Vincent*).

1	24/07/78	'It Must Be The Suit'
2	31/07/78	'Not Just Pennies'
3	07/08/78	'Maybe He'll Bring Back A Geisha'
4	14/08/78	'A Little Heart To Heart With Miss Bangor'
5	21/08/78	'The Moment He Opened His Envelope'
6	28/08/78	'I Wouldn't Take Your Hand If I Was Drowning'

Sweeney 2 (Feature Film)
Great Britain, 1978. 108 mins
Executive producers: Lloyd Shirley, George Taylor. *Producer*: Ted Childs. *Director*: Tom Clegg.
Script: Troy Kennedy-Martin. *Production manager*: Laurie Greenwood. *Location manager*:
Stephen Pushkin. *Lighting cameraman*: Dusty Miller. *Editor*: Chris Burt. *Art director*: William
Alexander. *Sound mixer*: Derek Rye. *Dubbing mixer*: Hugh Strain. *Dubbing editor*: Ian Toynton. *Assistant director*: Bill Westley.
Cast: John Thaw (*Det. Insp. Regan*), Dennis Waterman (*Det. Sgt. Carter*), Barry Stanton (*Big John*), John Flanagan (*Willard*), David Casey (*Goodyear*), Derrick O'Connor (*Llewellyn*),
John Alkin (*Daniels*), James Warrior (*Jellyneck*).

The Sweeney (Series 4)
Tx: Thurs 9.00pm. 52 mins.
Executive producers: Lloyd Shirley, George Taylor. *Producer*: Ted Childs. *Associate producer*:
Mary Morgan. *Series created by*: Ian Kennedy-Martin. *Production manager*: Laurie Greenwood. *Location manager*: Stephen Pushkin. *Lighting cameramen*: Norman Langley, Roy Pointer. *Camera operator*: Mike Proudfoot. *Editors*: John S Smith, Ian Toynton. *Art director*:
William Alexander. *Sound mixer*: Derek Rye. *Boom operator*: Mike Silverlock. *Dubbing editor*:
Michael Murr. *1st assistant director*: Michael Murray. *Casting director*: Marilyn Johnson.
Cast: John Thaw (*Det. Insp. Regan*), Dennis Waterman (*Det. Sgt. Carter*), Garfield Morgan
(*Det. Chief Insp. Haskins*).

			Writer	Director
1	07/09/78	'Messenger Of The Gods'	Trevor Preston	Terry Green
2	14/09/78	'Hard Men'	Troy Kennedy-Martin	Graham Baker
3	21/09/78	'Drag Act'	Ted Childs	Tom Clegg
4	28/09/78	'Trust Red'	Richard Harris	Douglas Camfield
5	05/10/78	'Nightmare'	Ranald Graham	David Wickes
6	12/10/78	'Money, Money, Money'	Trevor Preston	Sid Roberson
7	19/10/78	'Bait'	Trevor Preston	Sid Roberson
8	26/10/78	'The Bigger They Are'	Tony Hoare	Mike Vardy
9	02/11/78	'Feet Of Clay'	Roger Marshall	Chris Burt
10	09/11/78	'One Of Your Own'	Tony Hoare	Chris Menaul
11	16/11/78	repeat of 'Visiting Fireman'	Series 3 Episode 3	
12	23/11/78	'Hearts And Minds'	Donald Churchill, Ted Childs	Mike Vardy
13	30/11/78	'Latin Lady'	Ted Childs	Peter Smith
14	07/12/78	repeat of 'Tomorrow Man'	Series 3 Episode 4	
15	14/12/78	'Victims'	Roger Marshall	Ben Bolt
16	21/12/78	repeat of 'Selected Target'	Series 3 Episode 1	
17	28/12/78	'Jack Or Knave'	Ted Childs	Tom Clegg

Danger U.X.B.
Tx: Mon 9.00 pm 52 mins.
Executive in charge of production: Johnny Goodman. *Producer*: John Hawkesworth. *Associate producer*: Christopher Neame. *Production manager*: Ron Jackson. *Location manager*: Patrick
Cassavetti. *Lighting cameraman*: Norman Langley. *Camera operator*: Peter Sinclair. *Editors*:
John Trumper, Ralph Sheldon. *Art director*: James Weatherup. *Special effects*: Bill Warrington. *Sound mixer*: Paul Lemare. *1st assistant director*: Peter Cotton. *Casting director*: Weston
Drury Jnr.
Cast: Anthony Andrews (*Brian Ash*), Judy Geeson (*Susan*), Iain Cuthbertson (*Dr. Gillespie*),
Deborah Watling (*Norma Baker*), Ken Kitson (*Corporal Horrocks*), Jeremy Sinden (*Lt.

218

Rodgers), George Innes (*Sapper Wilkins*), Maurice Roëves (*Sgt. James*), Kenneth Cranham (*Sapper Salt*), Robert Pugh (*Sapper Powell*).

			Writer	Director
1	08/01/79	'Dead Man's Shoes'	John Hawkesworth	Ferdinand Fairfax
2	15/01/79	'Unsung Heroes'	John Hawkesworth	Ferdinand Fairfax
3	22/01/79	'Just Like A Woman'	Jeremy Paul	Roy Ward Baker
4	29/01/79	'Cast Iron Killer'	Don Shaw	Jeremy Summers
5	05/02/79	'The Silver Lining'	John Hawkesworth	Henry Herbert
6	12/02/79	'The Quiet Weekend'	Jeremy Paul	
7	19/02/79	'Digging Out'	Paul Wheeler	Ferdinand Fairfax
8	26/02/79	'Bad Company'	Don Shaw	Ferdinand Fairfax
9	05/03/79	'Seventeen Seconds to Glory'	John Hawkesworth	Douglas Camfield
10	12/03/79	'Butterfly Winter'	Jeremy Paul	Roy Ward Baker
11	19/03/79	'Dead Letter'	Kenneth Clark	Simon Langton
12	26/03/79	'The Pier'	Don Shaw	Douglas Camfield
13	02/04/79	'With Love From Adolf'	John Hawkesworth	Henry Herbert

Quatermass

Tx: Wed 9.10pm 52 mins.

Executive producer: Verity Lambert. *Executive in charge of production*: Johnny Goodman. *Producer*: Ted Childs. *Associate producer*: Norton Knatchbull. *Director*: Piers Haggard. *Script*: Nigel Kneale. *Story editor*: Linda Agran. *Production manager*: Laurie Greenwood. *Location manager*: Stephen Pushkin. *Director of photography*: Ian Wilson. *Camera operator*: Neil Binney. *Sound mixer*: Dudley Plummer. *Boom operator*: Chris Gurney. *Editor*: Keith Palmer. *Dubbing editors*: Ian Toynton, Roger Wilson. *Production designer*: Arnold Chapkis. *Assistant director*: Bill Westley.

Cast: John Mills (*Quatermass*), Simon MacCorkindale (*Kapp*), Barbara Kellerman (*Clare Kapp*), Margaret Tyzack (*Annie Morgan*), Brewster Mason (*Gurov*), Ralph Arliss (*Kick-along*).

1	24/10/79	'Huffity, Puffity, Ringstone Round'
2	31/10/79	'Lovely Lightening'
3	07/11/79	'What Lies Beneath'
4	14/11/79	'An Endangered Species'

Charlie Muffin

Tx: 11 December 1979, Tues 8.00pm. 105 mins.

Executive producer: Verity Lambert. *Executive in charge of production*: Johnny Goodman. *Producers*: Ted Childs, Norton Knatchbull. *Director*: Jack Gold. *Script*: Keith Waterhouse (from the novel by Brian Freemantle). *Story executive*: Linda Agran. *Production manager*: Laurie Greenwood. *Location manager*: Alex Gohar. *Director of photography*: Ousama Rawi. *Camera operator*: Peter Macdonald. *Editor*: Keith Palmer. *Art director*: Michael Bailey. *Sound mixer*: Sandy Macrae. *Boom operator*: Pat Heigham. *1st assistant director*: Bill Westley. *Casting director*: Joyce Gallie.

Cast: David Hemmings (*Charlie Muffin*), Sam Wanamaker (*Ruttgers*), Jennie Linden (*Edith*), Pinkas Braun (*Kalenin*), Ian Richardson (*Cuthbertson*), Sir Ralph Richardson (*Sir Archibald Willoughby*), Shane Rimmer (*Braley*), Donald Churchill (*Wilberforce*), Rohan McCullough (*Janet*).

The Knowledge

Tx: 27 December 1979. Thurs 9.00pm. 79 mins.

Executive producer: Verity Lambert. *Executive in charge of production*: Johnny Goodman. *Producer*: Christopher Neame. *Director*: Bob Brooks. *Script executive*: Linda Agran. *Script*: Jack

Rosenthal. *Production manager:* Jake Wright *Location manager:* Patrick Cassavetti. *Director of photography:* David MacDonald. *Camera operator:* Jerry Dunkley. *Editor:* Ben Rayner. *Art director:* Brian Morris. *Sound mixer:* Clive Winter. *Boom operator:* Ken Weston. *1st assistant director:* Simon Hinkly. *Casting director:* Maggie Cartier.

Cast: Nigel Hawthorne (*Mr. Burgess*), Mick Ford (*Chris Mathews*), Kim Taylforth (*Janet*), Jonathan Lynn (*Ted Margolies*), David Ryall (*Titanic Walters*), Michael Elphick (*Gordon Weller*), Maureen Lipman (*Brenda Weller*), Lesley Joseph (*Val Margolies*).

Minder (Series 1)
Tx: Mon 9.00pm. 52 mins.

Executive producer: Verity Lambert. *Executive in charge of production:* Johnny Goodman. *Producers:* Lloyd Shirley, George Taylor. *Associate producer:* Ian Toynton. *Series devised by:* Leon Griffiths. *Script executive:* Linda Agran. *Production supervisor:* Nicholas Gillott. *Location manager:* Michael John Knatchbull. *Lighting cameraman:* Roy Pointer. *Camera operator:* Brian Elvin. *Editors:* Roger Wilson, Sue Collins. *Dubbing editor:* Mike Murr. *Art director:* James Weatherup. *Sound recordist:* Derek Rye. *Boom operator:* John Samworth. *Assistant directors:* Dusty Symonds, John O'Conner. *Casting director:* Weston Drury Jnr.

Cast: George Cole (*Arthur Daley*), Dennis Waterman (*Terry McCann*), Glynn Edwards (*Dave*).

			Writer	Director
1	29/10/79	'Gunfight At The OK Laundrette'	Leon Griffiths	Peter Sasdy
2	05/11/79	'Bury My Half At Waltham Green'	Paul Wheeler	Chris King
3	12/11/79	'The Smaller They Are'	Leon Griffiths	Roy Ward Baker
4	19/11/79	'A Tethered Goat'	Murray Smith	James Gatward
5	26/11/79	'The Bounty Hunter'	Bernie Cooper	Peter Sasdy
6	03/12/79	'Aces High And Sometimes Very Low'	Leon Griffiths	Roy Ward Baker
7	10/12/79	'The Bengal Tiger'	Leon Griffiths	Peter Sasdy
8	17/12/79	'Come In T-64 Your Time Is Slowly Ticking Away'	Tony Hoare	Francis Megahy
9	01/01/79	'Monday Night Fever'	Leon Griffiths	Mike Vardy
10	07/01/80	'The Dessert Song'	Andrew Payne	Roy Ward Baker
11	14/01/80	'You Gotta Have Friends'	Leon Griffiths	Ian Toynton

Stainless Steel and the Star Spies
Tx: 1 January 1980 Thurs 4.45pm 52 mins.

Executive producer: Verity Lambert. *Executive in charge of production:* Johnny Goodman. *Producer:* Roy Corbett. *Director:* Anthony Simmons. *Script:* Ray Jolliffe. *Script executive:* Linda Agran. *Production designer:* Peter Richardson. *Director of photography:* Freddie Young. *Editor:* Peter Boyle.

Cast: Deryck Guyler (*Vicar*), Anna Karen (*Mum*), Debbie Farrington (*Young Girl*), Charles Pemberton (*Dad*), Fabia Drake (*Miss Ruby*), with the voices of Ed Bishop, Bill McAllister, Graham Stark, Paddie O'Neil, Bob Hoskins and Richard Hope as the 'Metaliens'.

Fox
Tx: Mon 9.00pm. 52 mins.

Executive producer: Verity Lambert. *Executive in charge of production:* Johnny Goodman. *Producer:* Graham Benson. *Director:* Jim Goddard. *Script executive:* Linda Agran. *Script:* Trevor Preston. *Unit manager:* Jean Walter. *Location managers:* Barry Beckett, Bill Lang. *Director of photography:* Ernest Vincze. *Camera operator:* Nicholas Beeks-Sanders. *Supervising editor:* Ralph Sheldon. *Editor:* Andrew Nelson. *Art director:* Michael Porter. *Sound mixer:*

Andrew Boulton. *Dubbing editor*: Alfie Cox. *1st assistant director*: Gino Marotta. *Casting director*: Ann Fielden.
Cast: Peter Vaughan (*Billy Fox*), Elizabeth Spriggs (*Connie Fox*), Bernard Hill (*Vin Fox*), Derrick O'Connor (*Ray Fox*), Larry Lamb (*Joey Fox*), Eamon Boland (*Phil Fox*), Ray Winstone (*Kenny Fox*), Rosemary Martin (*Renie Fox*), Richard Weinbaum (*Andy Fox*), Yvette Dotrice (*Anna Pegram*), Cindy O'Callaghan (*Nan*).

1	10/03/80	'King Billy'
2	17/03/80	'Arched Fingers For Bach, Flat Fingers For Love'
3	24/03/80	'Pugilism Not Vandalism'
4	31/03/80	'It's All Them Pschia-Whatever-You-Call-It Books He Reads'
5	07/04/80	'Shim-Me-Sha-Wabble'
6	14/04/80	'Stick Or Twist'
7	21/04/80	'The Perfect Scapegoat Syndrome'
8	28/04/80	'If It's Good Enough For New Orleans It's Good Enough For Clapham'
9	05/05/80	'Fox Big "F" – Family'
10	12/05/80	'Just An Iron Monkey'
11	19/05/80	'Just Another Villain In A Cheap Suit'
12	26/05/80	'Oh Dear, Oh Dear, Oh Dear!'
13	02/06/80	'The Family . . . And The Future'

The Sailor's Return
(An Ariel Production for Euston Films / National Film Finance Corporation)
Tx: 9 September 1980. Tues 8.00pm. 112 mins.
Executive producer: Verity Lambert. *Executive in charge of production*: Johnny Goodman. *Producer*: Otto Plaschkes. *Director*: Jack Gold. *Script*: James Saunders from the novel by David Garnett. *Production manager*: Clive Reed. *Location manager*: Chris Kenny. *Lighting cameraman*: Brian Tufano. *Editor*: Michael Taylor. *Art director*: Carmen Dillon. *Music composed by*: Carl Davis. *Sound mixer*: Ivan Sharrock. *1st assistant director*: Vincent Winter. *Casting director*: Patsy Pollock.
Cast: Tom Bell (*William Targett*), Shope Shodeinde (*Tulip*), Elton Charles (*Olu/Billy*), Mick Ford (*Tom Madquick*), Clive Swift (*Rev Pottock*), George Costigan (*Harry*), Paola Dionisotti (*Lucy Sturmey*).

Minder (Series 2)
Tx: Thurs 9.00pm. 52 mins.
Executive producer: Verity Lambert. *Executive in charge of production*: Johnny Goodman. *Producers*: Lloyd Shirley, George Taylor. *Associate producer*: Ian Toynton. *Series devised by*: Leon Griffiths. *Production supervisor*: Nicholas Gillott. *Location manager*: David Shanks. *Lighting cameramen*: Roy Pointer, Mike Davis. *Camera operator*: John Maskall. *Editor*: Roger Wilson. *Art director*: William Alexander. *Sound recordist*: Paul Le Mare. *Boom operator*: Tony Bell. *Dubbing editor*: Mike Murr. *Assistant director*: John O'Connor. *Casting director*: Weston Drury Jnr.
Cast: George Cole (*Arthur Daley*), Dennis Waterman (*Terry McCann*), Glynn Edwards (*Dave*).

			Writer	Director
1	11/09/80	'National Pelmet'	Willis Hall	Martin Campbell
2	18/09/80	'Whose Wife Is It Anyway'	Tony Hoare	Roy Ward Baker
3	25/09/80	'You Lose Some, You Lose Some'	Jeremy Burnham	James Gatward
4	09/10/80	'Don't Tell Them Willie Boy Was Here'	Paul Wheeler	Dennis Abey
5	16/10/80	'Not A Bad Lad, Dad'	Tony Hoare	Ian Toynton
6	23/10/80	'The Beer Hunter'	Willis Hall	Tom Clegg

7	30/10/80	'A Nice Little Wine'	Stanley Price	Chris Menaul
8	06/11/80	'All Mod Cons'	Andrew Payne	Ian Sharp
9	20/11/80	'Diamonds Are A		
		Girl's Worst Enemy'	Paul Wheeler	Chris King
10	27/11/80	'The Old School Tie'	Jeremy Burnham	James Gatward
11	04/12/80	'All About Scoring, Innit?'	Willis Hall	Martin Campbell
12	11/12/80	'Caught In The Act, Fact'	Tony Hoare	Terry Green
13	18/12/80	'A Lot Of Bull And		
		A Pat On The Back'	Tony Hoare	Terry Green

The Flame Trees of Thika

Tx: Thurs 8.30pm. 52 mins.

Executive producer: Verity Lambert. *Executive in charge of production*: Johnny Goodman. *Producers*: John Hawkesworth, Christopher Neame. *Director*: Roy Ward Baker. *Script:* John Hawkesworth from the novel by Elspeth Huxley. *Script executive*: Linda Agran. *Production co-ordinator*: Malcolm R Burgess. *Production manager*: Clifton Brandon. *Lighting cameraman*: Ian Wilson. *Camera operator*: Peter Sinclair. *Editor*: Ann Chegwidden. *Assistant editor*: Maysoor Pachachi. *Art director*: Roy Stannard. *Sound mixer*: John Mitchell. *Boom operator*: Keith Pamplin. *1st assistant director*: Michael Hamlyn. *Casting director*: Weston Drury Jnr. *Cast:* Hayley Mills (*Tilly Grant*), David Robb (*Robin Grant*), Holly Aird (*Elspeth Grant*), Sharon Mughan (*Lettice Palmer*), Nicholas Jones (*Hereward Palmer*), Morgan Sheppard (*Mr. Roos*), Carol Macready (*Mrs. Nimmo*), Ben Cross (*Ian Crawford*), Dai Bradley (*Alec Wilson*), John Nettleton (*Major*), Tony Osoba (*Ahmed*), Steve Mwenesi (*Sammy*), Mick Chege (*Njombo*), M'zee Pembe (*Chief Kupanya*), Paul Ohsongo (*Juma*).

1	01/09/81	'The Promised Land'
2	08/09/81	'Hyenas Will Eat Anything'
3	15/09/81	'Happy New Year'
4	22/09/81	'Friends In High Places'
5	29/09/81	'A Real Sportsman'
6	06/10/81	'Safari'
7	13/10/81	'The Drums Of War'

Minder (Series 3)

Tx: Weds 9.00pm. 52 mins.

Executive producer: Verity Lambert. *Executive in charge of production*: Johnny Goodman. *Producers*: Lloyd Shirley, George Taylor. *Script executive*: Linda Agran. *Story editor*: Frances Heasman. *Series devised by*: Leon Griffiths. *Production manager*: John O'Connor. *Location manager*: Peter Carter. *Lighting cameramen*: Roy Pointer, Dusty Miller. *Camera operator*: John Maskall. *Supervising editor*: Peter Delfgou. *Editor*: Roger Wilson. *Art director*: William Alexander. *Sound mixer*: Tony Dawe. *Boom operator*: Colin Dandridge. *Dubbing editor*: Brian Blamey. *Assistant directors*: Derek Whitehurst, Ray Stevens. *Casting director*: Weston Drury Jnr. *Cast:* George Cole (*Arthur Daley*), Dennis Waterman (*Terry McCann*), Glynn Edwards (*Dave*).

			Writer	Director
1	13/01/82	'Dead Men Do Tell Tales'	Tony Hoare	Robert Young
2	20/01/82	'You Need Hands'	Andrew Payne	Ian Sharp
3	27/01/82	'Rembrandt Doesn't Live		
		Here Anymore'	Dave Humphries	Tom Clegg
4	03/02/82	'Looking for Mickey'	Tony Hoare	Tom Clegg
5	10/02/82	'Dream House'	Andrew Payne	Tom Clegg
6	17/02/82	'Another Bride, Another		
		Groom'	Willis Hall	Mike Vardy

7	24/02/82	'The Birdman of Wormwood Scrubs'	Leon Griffiths	Ian Toynton
8	03/03/82	'The Son Also Rises'	Paul Wheeler	Francis Megahy
9	10/03/82	'Why Pay Tax?'	Leon Griffiths	Roy Ward Baker
10	17/03/82	'Broken Arrow'	George Day	Roy Ward Baker
11	24/03/82	'Poetic Justice – Innit?'	Tony Hoare	Terry Green
12	31/03/82	'Back In Good Old England'	Andrew Payne	Francis Megahy
13	07/04/82	'In'	Leon Griffiths	Ian Toynton

Widows

Tx: Weds 9.00pm. 52 mins.

Executive producer: Verity Lambert. *Executive in charge of production*: Johnny Goodman. *Producer*: Linda Agran. *Director*: Ian Toynton. *Script*: Lynda La Plante. *Production manager*: Stephen Pushkin. *Location manager*: Ray Freeborn. *Director of photography*: Ray Parslow. *Camera operator*: Mike Proudfoot. *Supervising editor*: Roger Wilson. *Assistant editor*: Colin Chapman. *Art director*: Christopher Burke. *Sound mixer*: Derek Rye. *Boom operator*: David Pearson. *1st assistant director*: Ted Morley. *Casting director*: Marilyn Johnson.

Cast: Ann Mitchell (*Dolly Rawlins*), Maureen O'Farrell (*Linda Perelli*), Fiona Hendley (*Shirley Miller*), Eva Mottley (*Bella O'Reilly*), David Calder (*Det. Insp. George Resnick*), Paul Jesson (*Det. Sgt. Alec Fuller*), Maurice O'Connell (*Harry Rawlins*), Stanley Meadows (*Eddie Rawlins*).

16/03/83	Episode One
23/03/83	Episode Two
30/03/83	Episode Three
06/04/83	Episode Four
13/04/83	Episode Five
20/04/83	Episode Six

Reilly – Ace of Spies

Tx: Weds 9.00pm. 52 mins (Episode One 75 mins)

Executive producer: Verity Lambert. *Executive in charge of production*: Johnny Goodman. *Producer*: Chris Burt. *Directors*: Martin Campbell, Jim Goddard. *Script executive*: Linda Agran. *Script*: Troy Kennedy-Martin. *Music*: Harry Rabinowitz. *Production supervisor*: Ray Frift. *Location managers*: David Barron, Claude Gresset. *Director of photography*: Peter Jessop. *Camera operator*: John Maskall. *Editors*: Ralph Sheldon, Edward Marnier. *Assistant editors*: Mike Feinberg, Mark Newson. *Production designer*: Roger Hall. *Sound mixer*: Sandy Macrae. *Boom operators*: Dushko Indjic, Don Smith. *Assistant directors*: Paddy Carpenter, Gino Marotta. *Casting director*: Ann Fielden.

Cast: Sam Neill (*Reilly*), Leo McKern (*Zaharov*), Norman Rodway (*Cummings*), Peter Egan (*Fothergill*), Jeananne Crowley (*Margaret*), John Rhys-Davies (*Tanyatos*), David Hayman (*Von Jaegar*), Bill Nighy (*Goschen*), Diana Hardcastle (*Anna*), Brian Protheroe (*Grammaticoff*), Celia Gregory (*Nadia Massino*), John Castle (*Count Massino*), Tom Bell (*Dzerzhinsky*), Michael Aldridge (*Orlov*), Kenneth Cranham (*Lenin*), Hugh Fraser (*Hill*), Ian Charleson (*Lockhart*), Clive Merrison (*Savinkov*), Laura Davenport (*Pepita*), David Burke (*Stalin*), Anthony Higgins (*Trilisser*).

			Director
1	05/09/83	'An Affair With a Married Woman'	Jim Goddard
2	07/09/83	'Prelude to War'	Jim Goddard
3	14/09/83	'The Visiting Fireman'	Martin Campbell
4	21/09/83	'Anna'	Martin Campbell
5	28/09/83	'Dreadnoughts and Crosses'	Jim Goddard
6	05/10/83	'Dreadnoughts and Double Crosses'	Jim Goddard
7	12/10/83	'Gambit'	Jim Goddard

223

8	19/10/83	'Endgame'	Jim Goddard
9	26/10/83	'After Moscow'	Martin Campbell
10	02/11/83	'The Trust'	Martin Campbell
11	09/11/83	'The Last Journey'	Jim Goddard
12	16/11/83	'Shut Down'	Martin Campbell

The Nation's Health

Tx: Thurs 9.00pm. (Channel 4) Each episode 100 mins. approx.

Executive producer: Verity Lambert. *Executive in charge of production:* Johnny Goodman. *Producer:* Irving Teitelbaum. *Associate producer:* Raymond Day. *Director:* Les Blair. *Script:* G. F. Newman. *Production manager:* Selwyn Roberts. *Location manager:* Alex Gohar. *Director of photography:* Charles Stewart. *Editor:* John Gregory. *Assistant editor:* Sue Baker. *Art director:* Evan Hercules. *Sound mixer:* Malcolm Hirst. *Boom operator:* Don Banks. *1st assistant director:* Chris Rose. *Casting director:* Sheila Trezise.

Cast: Vivienne Ritchie (*Dr. Jessie Marvill*), Sebastian Shaw (*Dr. Percy Thurson*), Angela Warren (*Chloe Shallcross*), Paddy Ryan (*Henry Staples*), Oona Kirsh (*Bernice Attwood*), Max Stafford-Clark (*Dr. Clive Hendrix*).

1	06/10/83	'Acute'
2	13/10/83	'Decline'
3	20/10/83	'Chronic'
4	27/10/83	'Collapse'

Minder (Series 4)

Tx: Weds 9.00pm. 52 mins.

Executive producers: Verity Lambert, Lloyd Shirley. *Executive in charge of production:* Johnny Goodman. *Producer:* George Taylor. *Associate producer:* Ian Toynton. *Script executive:* Linda Agran. *Series devised by:* Leon Griffiths. *Story editor:* Frances Heasman. *Production supervisor:* Ron Purdie. *Location manager:* Rufus Andrews. *Lighting cameramen:* Roy Pointer, Dusty Miller. *Camera operator:* John Maskall. *Supervising editor:* Roger Wilson. *Editor:* Maysoor Pachachi. *Art director:* William Alexander. *Sound mixer:* Tony Dawe. *Boom operator:* John Samworth. *Dubbing editor:* Mike Murr. *Assistant directors:* Simon Channing-Williams, Ian Elsey. *Casting director:* Weston Drury Jnr.

Cast: George Cole (*Arthur Daley*), Dennis Waterman (*Terry McCann*), Glynn Edwards (*Dave*).

			Writer	Director
1	11/01/84	'Rocky Eight And A Half'	Leon Griffiths	Ian Toynton
2	18/01/84	'Senior Citizen Caine'	Andrew Payne	Robert Young
3	25/01/84	'High Drains Pilferer'	Dave Humphries	Robert Young
4	01/02/84	'Sorry Pal, Wrong Number'	Leon Griffiths	Terry Green
5	08/02/84	'The Car Lot Baggers'	Trevor Preston	Francis Megahy
6	15/02/84	'If Money Be the Food Of Love, Play On'	Tony Hoare	Terry Green
7	22/02/84	'A Star Is Gorn'	Tony Hoare	Ian Toynton
8	29/02/84	'Willesden Suite'	Andrew Payne	Francis Megahy
9	07/03/84	'Windows'	Geoff Case	Robert Young
10	14/03/84	'Get Daley!'	Andrew Payne	Ian Toynton
11	21/03/84	'A Well-Fashioned Fit Up'	Barry Purchese	Jim Hill

Appendix 4 Another View of Thames Television

The following two-part article was written by William Phillips. We reprint it for its trenchant and independent overview of Thames' operations and for the valuable financial and other data which it assembles. The views expressed are of course Phillips' own.

PART I: THAMES TV'S SHOTGUN LEGACY

In 1979 the Independent Broadcasting Authority commissioned a study of viewers' attitudes to ITV. It found that only 44 per cent of the London audience knew that Thames Television was their local station.

That statistic sums up the anonymity of Thames, the biggest ITV company in terms of employment and output and sometimes called the richest – though this, as we shall see, is doubtful. Thames shares with other very large features of the landscape the peculiar property of being too big to be noticed. But now that ITV is marching (or being dragged) into an epoch of multilateral competition for the audience's attention, Thames cannot go on keeping its head down. It will have to choose what part, if any, it wishes to play in diversifying into new forms of programme distribution, and in influencing the ITV system's adaptation to them.

If Thames wished, it might become in fact what it has always had the right to be: ITV's leader and spokesman. But that would take a dramatic change of corporate style.

Set up in 1967, Thames was a shotgun marriage. The ITA, as it then was, thought that Rediffusion – the station which had pioneered ITV with the London weekday contract – was efficient, but complacent and stale; it also thought that ABC Television, part of the Associated British cinema empire, was bright, brash and deserved a richer pasture than the North/Midlands weekend franchise. Together they made Thames. Each side kicked in £3 million of assets; but ABC contributed all the top management.

Below the executive-suite level, Thames's employees tended for years afterwards to think of themselves as ABC or Rediffusion people. This was fostered by physical *apartheid*. Current affairs and documentary input came from Rediffusion's old HQ at Kingsway, which moved *en bloc* to Euston in 1969. Down by the riverside at Teddington, 15 miles away, ABC's studios became Thames's entertainment and drama factory.

Drawing a Steady Income
Here was a recipe for factionalism, accentuated by Thames's ITA-dictated voting control structure. At first ABC held a bare majority of votes, but its takeover by EMI upset the delicate balance. For nearly three years the ITA dithered and dickered, until it solved the 'problem' by letting Sir Charles Forte and an obscure property developer, along with a few executive directors, acquire three-fifths of EMI's voting power. This separation of ownership from control helped Thames's

225

management feel, correctly, that they were safer from proprietorial interference; but it also made the emasculated owners less able to do anything with Thames except draw a steady income from it.

The temptation was stronger because each needed Thames's profits. In the Seventies, Rediffusion and its conglomerate parent, BET, were stagnant and drifting. Meanwhile EMI, an entertainment melange incapable of extending a Sixties success founded on the Beatles, flirted at first successfully but in time disastrously with medical electronics. Neither group in the early Seventies saw TV as an area for investment – it took Thorn, which bought the ailing EMI in 1979, to perceive the possibilities of screen entertainment.

Fifteen Years and Few Reserves
In Thames's early years (1968-72) it had to cope with the merger's birth-pangs, the financial strain of 'colorisation' and the move to Euston, and a cyclical advertising slump, made worse by the fact that the Exchequer Levy was then subtracted from sales, not profits. As soon as the station emerged from all this into an ad boom, Rediffusion and EMI began to milk it. Southern Television's three conglomerate owners were often criticised for taking too much out; but Thames has been the biggest milch cow. Until 1980 the owners' policy was to extract its entire after-tax earnings, every year: in 10¾ years to March 1983, Thames distributed all but £1.78 million of its £27.68 million ordinary shareholders' profits.

After 15 years holding Europe's most valuable commercial-TV concession Thames still has virtually no revenue reserves: asset backing for its recently enlarged equity capital of £11.57 million consists almost wholly of revaluation surpluses. The station was not starved of funds: in lean times, when internal cash generation was not enough, it could borrow from its parents, albeit on a pretty short string. Between June 1979 and March 1981, their short-term loans to Thames rose from £6.8 million to £14.25 million, though they were all repaid the next year. From late 1975 until March 1983, the owners also provided £2 million of debenture loan capital. But these debts have cost Thames full commercial interest rates.

In 1980 Thames applied for a new contract, which it won in the absence of serious opposition. It disclosed that its owners had benevolently agreed to be paid only two-thirds of its earnings in future: a reflection of the coming cost of Channel Four. But Thames's balance sheet still looks etiolated. Last March, shareholders' funds of £13.87 million stood against deferred tax and creditors of £14.09 million and net debts of £12.70 million, up by two-thirds in a year. Not the sort of ratio to set investors' pulses racing. And thereby hangs another tale.

When the IBA announced that Thames could keep its franchise, it made some vague noises about letting the public buy shares in the company.

Thames had already volunteered to let employees hold up to five per cent of its equity. Both moves would broaden ownership and bolster Thames's management's autonomy, giving them accountabilities other than to Thorn and Rediffusion. But the real IBA warning shot came in a few bland words: it said it wished to ensure that 'in the developing conditions of the franchise, the interests of the parent companies do not conflict with those of the television company and the audience which it is serving.'

Translated from Bromptonese, the hint to the proprietors was plain: don't cream off ITV profits to bankroll your own pet new-media ventures; let Thames make its own choices with its own earnings. From the start of the new contract period in 1982, Thames was to be encouraged, even expected, to be its own master in medium-term planning, as well as in its day-to-day operations. How has it responded to the IBA's invitation? We shall soon see next month.

PART II: IS THERE MEDIA LIFE AFTER BENNY HILL?

In 1972-73, Thames Television's overseas programme sales were sundry income: they totalled only £500,000, against advertising revenue of £21 million. Ten years later, in the year to March 1982, exports had risen thirty-fold to £11.8 million, against advertising worth £107.7 million. And in the following year, 1982-83, exports of £17.8 million, up 51 per cent, compared with a gain of only 6.9 per cent in advertising to £115 million.

In a year when Thames's group profit was £8.86 million after levy, programme exports saved its face. The growing importance of these was underlined by the fact that for the last ten months of 1982-83, Thames's programme director was J. A. Muir Sutherland. He had come from such obscurity to the top production job in ITV that a London newspaper deriding his appointment had referred to him throughout as 'Mr Henderson'. Where had Mr Sutherland been? Not making programmes, but flogging them. He had been the chief salesman at Thames Television International, the company's overseas arm, throughout that decade of dramatic growth.

Furnished in 1980 with a new tenure of London's weekdays, Thames is now at the point where paths fork. One path points towards the dazzling, hard-to-see horizon, where satellites fly through the sky and cables snake through the grass. The other path is for dutiful little ITV executives who keep their eyes firmly fixed on the well-beaten track – which might just be taking them round and round in ever-decreasing circles.

Thames's business so far has been the London ITV franchise pure and simple, and the performance of Mr Sutherland's salesmen, admirable though it has been, has to some extent been a triumph over adversity, for the station's production policy has been far from determinedly commercial-minded. If this seems a harsh judgement, I should explain at once that I take the acid test of commercial success in TV exporting to be the sale to the USA (not Canada or Bulgaria) of series (not specials) for transmission in peak time (not fringe hours) on commercial broadcast networks or network-sized rosters of independent commercial stations – not, repeat not, sales for prestige and peanuts to the Public Broadcasting Service or obscure cable channels.

The Re-packaged Freak
By this stern test, Thames is only just in the hunt. It has syndicated one strip, the half-hour version of the *Benny Hill Show,* with remarkable success. But he is a bit of a freak hit: a repackaging job rather than an American-targeted concept. And he has been Thames's only sizeable and consistent earner Stateside.

Thames failed to develop the line laid down by its Teddington ancestor, ABC, with *The Avengers:* a slick but terribly British modification of the action-adventure genre. Instead, Thames emphasised its other ABC inheritance – a naturalistic drama, *à la Armchair Theatre* – and gave it a strong London lowlife flavour. British viewers were regaled with a stream of serials and series, from *Special Branch* and *The Sweeney,* via *Fox* and *Out,* to *Minder* and *Widows.* They were

227

shot on location and on film by Euston Films, a separate unit, and were technically suitable for US network screening; but their dialogue and dialect disqualified them. An American audience would have needed subtitles.

During these years, Thames also produced a good deal of lavish period drama, from *Napoleon in Love* and *Jennie* down to *Edward and Mrs Simpson*. But this, perversely, was done on tape – and US networks just don't like tape for drama. So most of Thames's costume productions wound up on *ad hoc* station line-ups such as Mobil's, relegated to the 'Masterpiece Theatre' slot.

Until 1982 Thames's programme chiefs – Jeremy Isaacs, then Nigel Ryan – were men whose background was current affairs, not entertainment fiction. From its other ancestor, Rediffusion, Thames drew a taste for large-canvas documentaries such as *Mountbatten*. Isaacs initiated *The World at War*, *Destination America* and *Hollywood*, but not even the last subject could have expected to command US network prime time: it was PBS material.

Since Isaacs, signs of a more hard-nosed approach to overseas markets have appeared. The last and most luxurious of the cul-de-sac period videotapes, *Clemmie* (Churchill's wife) died on the drawing-board. Instead, we have lately seen two handsome filmed series. *The Flame Trees of Thika* and, costliest yet, *Reilly – Ace of Spies*. These look more squarely aimed at the United States big time; *Thika* was a co-production with John Hawkesworth, one of Britain's most seasoned campaigners there.

A Comic Syndication Situation

Sutherland has done more than any other British broadcast salesman, including the BBC's, to push format deals. Situation comedy notoriously does not travel the Atlantic, but this is one way to give parochial product a foreign after-market: Thames's US retreads (whose fans barely realise their Limey origins) include one network smash, *Three's Company*, derived from the series *Man about the House*, and several milder successes. In 1982-83, Thames's income from format revamps rose from £849,000 to £2.23 million. Its US agent is even syndicating 'The Thames Originals' on the back of their imitators' popularity.

Now that Sutherland is in the programme driving seat, he can bring his knowledge of overseas buyers' requirements and preferences in to play when Thames's production slate is being assembled. With managing director Bryan Cowgill, 57 and nearing retirement, Sutherland may have a freer hand than his predecessors.

In other ways, Thames is still back-tracking about the future. Sales director Jim Shaw, a cable and satellite enthusiast, left in mid-career last spring. His successor, Tony Logie, fresh from the 'old technology' of commercial radio, has expressed considerable scepticism about new competitive forms of TV, calling cable a 'non-starter' and claiming that video has stolen a decisive march on it. Whether this reflects the corporate appraisal remains to be tested, but Thames's balance sheet is innocent of investments in innovation.

If Thames sees itself concentrating on production, without worrying too much about which method of distribution lays its wares before the consumer, it has a programme director with the right pedigree to keep its output attuned to the demands of ancillary markets. Perhaps for the leading ITV contractor, that is the most politically and financially prudent.

(Reprinted with permission from *Televisual*, December 1983, January 1984.)

228